Composers of North America

Series Editors: Sam Dennison, William C. Loring, Margery Lowens

NORMAND LOCKWOOD

His Life and Music

by
Kay Norton

Composers of North America, No. 11

The Scarecrow Press, Inc.
Metuchen, N.J., & London
1993

This work is based on Kay Norton, "Normand Lockwood, 1930-1980: Fifty Years in American Composition." Boulder: University of Colorado doctoral dissertation, 1990.

British Library Cataloguing-in-Publication data available

Library of Congress Cataloging-in-Publication Data

Norton, Kay.
    Normand Lockwood : his life and music / by Kay Norton.
        p.   cm. -- (Composers of North America ; no. 11)
    Includes catalog of music, bibliographical references, and index.
    ISBN 0-8108-2683-6 (alk. paper)
    1. Lockwood, Normand, 1906- . I. Title. II. Series.
ML410.L795N67 1993
780'.92--dc20
    [B]   93-16889

TABLE OF CONTENTS

FOREWORD

This Series on Composers of North America is designed to focus attention on the development of art music and folk music from colonial times to the present. Few of our composers of art music before 1975 had their works performed frequently during their lifetime. Many suffered undeserved neglect.

Each volume includes a substantial essay about a composer and a complete catalog of his or her compositions, published and unpublished. Part I deals with a composer's life and works in the context of the artistic thought and the musical world of his or her time. In Part II the goals of a composer and the critical comments by contemporaries and by later reviewers are included, as are illustrations and musical examples. Some works which merit performance today are singled out for analysis and discussion. In Part III the catalog of a composer's output has full publication details, and locations of unpublished works. We hope that this Series will make readers conscious and appreciative of our North American musical heritage to date.

The books are also intended to help performers and teachers seeking works to use. For them we designed the Part III Catalog of a composer's music to allow a quick search for works the author finds of historic or current interest that may be considered for readings and hearings.

Series Editors:
Sam Dennison, William C. Loring, Jr., Margery M. Lowens, Ezra Schabas, Martha Furman Schleifer.

PREFACE AND ACKNOWLEDGEMENTS

In supporting this study of a living American composer, Scarecrow Press reflects the spirit of contemporary American musical studies in two ways. First, Normand Lockwood's successful compositional and academic careers, his impressive body of works, and his enduring commitment to composition as a way of life are pertinent reminders that American music is as much a thing of the present and future as it is one of the past. Second, because Lockwood's music is less well-known than that of some of his peers, Scarecrow Press has supported the view that American studies addresses any good music— even if it has not yet received as much attention as it deserves. I share with the editors the hope that their Composers of North America series will engender renewed interest in the works of our finest native composers.

In each of the five biographical chapters of Part I, I have tried to present Lockwood in the context of the fascinating story of American twentieth-century composition. His academic career from 1932 to 1974 serves as the organizing factor, flanked at the beginning by a discussion of his uncommonly musical ancestry and European training, and at the end by commentary on his role as I see it in the American music of our age and his own words about his music and the discipline of composition.

Although Lockwood's music has been published by nearly forty different establishments, the published works alone are inadequate to represent the many facets of his music in all genres. Consequently, I have included 129 musical examples in the six chapters of Part II, 121 of which represent unpublished compositions. In preparing these illustrations, I have avoided editing the original manuscripts except in cases of obvious copying errors or inconsistencies. The typeset examples are, in essence, literal transcriptions of Lockwood's originals. For the high level of musicianship and professionalism they brought to the task of typesetting my musical examples, I wish to thank Leslie DeGrassi and Larry Worster of The Full Measure, Boulder, Colorado.

I received permission to reproduce excerpts of Lockwood's published music from the American Composers Alliance, Broude Brothers Limited, Hal Leonard Publishing Corporation, G. Schirmer, Inc., Shawnee Press, Inc., and Westminster Choir College.

Many works included in Lockwood's present total of 447 compositions may be purchased in facsimile edition from the American Composers' Alliance. For perusal and wider study, however, the Normand Lockwood Archive (NLA) at the Music Library, University of Colorado, Boulder, houses the only comprehensive collection of Lockwood's music. My profound gratitude is extended to William K. Kearns, past director of the American Music Research Center at the University of Colorado, and Karl Kroeger, Head of the Music Library, for facilitating my continuing access to the Lockwood Archive. I offer my special thanks to Leah Riddick of the Music Library for acting as my extra set of hands during the years since 1990. I could not have completed this study, and particularly the Catalog, without her continuing help.

The Catalog of Music comprising Part III originated with an inventory of the NLA appended to my dissertation (University of Colorado, Boulder, 1990). I am grateful for the Music Library grant that enabled me to begin that initial list in the summer of 1988. Since May of 1990, I have received valuable help in completing the present Catalog of Lockwood's works. I wish to thank Susan L. Porter, author of the *New Grove American* article on Lockwood, for allowing me access to her earlier research and list of compositions. Rosalie Calabrese and Deborah Long have provided valuable resources from the archives of the American Composers Alliance. Most importantly, I wish to thank Normand and Vona Lockwood for allowing me to draw upon the astounding completeness of their memories, and for their countless letters written and phone calls made on my behalf.

I would also like to thank Lockwood's many former students and associates whose words appear throughout this monograph. Although they are too numerous to mention here, I have cited their contributions at various places in this study.

To William C. Loring, Jr., my editor for this project, I extend my thanks for his meticulous reading, suggestions, and kind encouragement.

Many of my professional colleagues at the Conservatory of Music, University of Missouri-Kansas City, have generously read and commented upon portions of the text, including Joanne Baker, Jane M. Carl, Gary W. Hill, Charles Robinson, and Ann Launey, who also enlisted the operatic expertise of Eugene Cline in New York. Dean David L. Kuehn and my department chair, H. Lee Riggins, have supported this project in ways that range from teaching load adjustments to technical and financial help. I would also like to thank my research assistants, Christina McElroy and Susanna Reichling, the latter especially for her meticulous attention to the tedious final stages of indexing and page proofing.

For introducing me to the music of Normand Lockwood, for his guidance of my dissertation, and for his excellent critique of the biographical portion of this monograph, I wish to thank William K. Kearns, Professor Emeritus at the University of Colorado, Boulder. His definitive study of Horatio Parker, Number Six in the present series, has never left my desk during the final stages of my work. University of Colorado faculty members Steven Bruns, John Galm, Richard Knaub, and Karl Kroeger also read and improved the earlier form of this study.

Finally, I wish to thank my husband and most supportive colleague, Gary W. Hill, for sharing the wealth of his professional expertise and for the countless hours he has contributed to the editing, proofing, and production of this book.

Kay Norton
Kansas City, Missouri
November, 1992

LIST OF PHOTOGRAPHS

PART I
THE LIFE OF NORMAND LOCKWOOD

Chapter One

Ancestry and Pre-European Years

Ancestry (c. 1840-1906)

Normand Lockwood was born to Angelina Normand Smith Lockwood and Samuel Pierson Lockwood on March 19, 1906, at their apartment on 106th Street and Riverside Drive, in New York City.[1] Although he would become a composer of music that is substantially American, Lockwood's family history has a strong European cast; Rome, Leipzig, Vienna, and Davos, Switzerland provide highlights in an international family genealogy. Many members of the two generations preceding the birth of the composer traveled extensively abroad. Others lived and worked there, showing a mobility available only to the advantaged segments of nineteenth-century society in the United States. Of the many family anecdotes recalled by the composer, some of the most cherished ones take place in Europe.

Lockwood shares his given name with his maternal grandfather, Normand Smith. After graduating from Yale University in 1858, this native of Hartford, Connecticut received his M. D. Degree from Columbia University in 1861.[2]

He then traveled to Rome to absorb the culture and to practice medicine for a time. Upon arrival in that city, his search for lodging led him to the Piazza di Spagna, where he saw an advertisement for a room. As fate would have it, the young physician applied at the wrong house, the home of his future wife, Elena Imhof.[3]

In previous centuries, the Imhof ancestors had fled their native Russia for political reasons. Later they had lived in and left Zurich, Switzerland, and by the time of Elena's encounter with Normand Smith in the 1860s, they had settled in Rome. Elena was so taken with the young man that she persuaded her mother to offer him a room, even though they had not advertised for a renter. The couple began their married life in Hartford, and both maintained a pattern of frequent, trans-Atlantic travel. Upon the death of Normand Smith in 1896, Elena moved, first, to Germany, and eventually to Zurich, where she lived until her death in the second decade of this century.

Normand Smith made abundant artistic and literary contributions to Normand Lockwood's ancestry. The physician was eclectic in his interests, having studied sculpture in Rome, and pursued Wagnerian opera as far as Bayreuth, often with family in tow in later years. Grandson Normand remembers that his mother Angelina, one of the five Normand Smith children, was quite well versed in both Wagnerian plots and leitmotifs. The collection of books in Normand Smith's Connecticut home was also quite impressive, so much so that their neighbor, writer/humorist Samuel Clemens (Mark Twain), often treated it as a lending library.[4]

The five children of Elena and Normand Smith, three girls and two boys, spent the majority of their childhood years between Yonkers, New York and Dresden, Germany. Three of them later engaged in musical pursuits, including Thomas Max Smith, whose music degree at Yale was completed in 1898. Although he completed a law degree from Columbia

University in 1901, Max Smith maintained his absorption in music by writing criticism for the *New York Press* from 1903 to 1916, and *The New York American* from 1916 to 1923. Smith was an advocate of the grand Germanic tradition in music; consequently, he was unsympathetic to the fellow Easterner he encountered at Yale, Charles Ives. Ives's writings contain several comments about Max Smith.

> Dave [David Stanley Smith] and Max Smith were old friends of mine, and real friends at that, men I respected and got along with, except when it came to music. Max Smith and [his wife] Mary spent one Sunday with us in May 1912 or 1913 at the Whitman House in Hartsdale. I played over the Third Symphony and Max asked how I had got so modern. [Max said] "It's even worse than ten years ago!"[5]

On another occasion, Ives remembered,

> I played the whole [Concord] sonata to Max Smith last year (1912)—the Hartsdale piano didn't help!—through the last [movement], "Thoreau," in the middle section, I played partly from the sketch and with a few improvisations in a few places, as it was not all written out fully completed . . . Max said the Alcott movement was by far the best—by "best" Maxie meant (but didn't know it) the easiest to listen to—that is, for his nice ears. But his ears were so tired when it came to "Thoreau"—he just changed the subject. And it was the same . . . with the "Hawthorne" and the "Emerson"—he didn't try to get it, made him half sore, half cuckoo, etc. Max did get the Drum Corps chords, and smiled at the Rollo's moaning question, which I had to play twice and take off—the "What's all this?"[6]

Normand Lockwood now considers it unfortunate that his Uncle Max was in the position to give Ives critical support when he needed it, and yet apparently refused to do so.

Max's sister, Gertrude Normand Smith, was another professionally trained musician, eventually developing a compositional style in her lieder akin to that of Richard Strauss. Yet, while Max and Gertrude undeniably contributed to Normand Lockwood's musical heritage, the composer's mother Angelina was most influential. During her childhood, which took place primarily in Dresden, she studied violin privately with a tutor hired for the children by Normand Smith. She remained into adulthood a gifted, amateur violinist, playing for several years both in the violin section of her husband's orchestra at the University of Michigan, and in the faculty string quartet.[7] Her daughter Albertine remembers, "My father's violin playing was much more scholarly than Mother's, but Mother had a sweeter tone, and I enjoyed hearing her better."[8] Additionally, Mrs. Lockwood made the household musical by singing American songs and German lieder to her children, and her son remembers that her sense of pitch was keen.[9]

Normand Lockwood's maternal grandfather fostered another legacy besides a musical family. Before his death in 1896, he accumulated approximately 3000 acres of land in Keene Valley, in the Adirondacks near Lake Placid, New York. Normand Smith initiated the family practice of retreating to this property, and for over a century, his descendants have considered Keene Valley a point of reference. For Normand Lockwood in particular, it has provided a place of family identity that has remained constant throughout a life of frequent change. He attributes the balanced, well-rounded nature of his childhood to his family's summer excursions on the property, stating, "We went up there instead of pursuing culture, and I can't say I'm sorry."[10] Trout fishing, hiking, and climbing were favorite activities of the would-be composer, and he has maintained the love of nature these activities engendered.

Normand Lockwood's paternal grandfather, Charles Nichols Lockwood (1820-1913), was a native of Troy, New

York. The composer's grandmother, Albertine Lewis, was his second wife, and her ancestry can be traced to England and Holland. Together Charles and Albertine had three children: Albert Lewis, George, who died of tuberculosis in his teens, and Samuel Pierson, the father of the composer. Samuel, the youngest, was born in Troy in 1879.

In 1886 the family moved to Leipzig, following the path of Albert's early training as a concert pianist at the Leipzig Conservatorium. The family subsequently relocated in Davos, Switzerland, where Samuel completed boys' school.[11] Samuel's studies at Columbia University in New York prompted the entire family to return to the States, this time to a home they called Ardmore, in Yonkers. At Columbia, Samuel completed an AB degree in 1902 and an AM (Master's) degree in 1903.[12] His thesis, somewhat in conflict with his eventual musical specialization, was entitled "Victor Hugo as Dramatist."[13] Samuel soon distinguished himself as a violinist and orchestral conductor, enough so to be hired on the faculty of the University of Michigan in 1907, holding the position until 1930. In that decade, he was divorced from Angelina Lockwood, and later married a second time. Samuel Pierson Lockwood died in 1948 in Lake Tahoe, Nevada.

Albert Lockwood (b. 1871), preceded his sibling to the Michigan faculty in 1900. So great was his reputation as a concert pianist during his thirty-three-year tenure there that local critic W. S. B. Matthews eulogized him in 1933 as "one of the three outstanding American pianists of all time."[14] Albert graduated from the Leipzig Conservatorium in 1891, studying further in Florence, and finally becoming a student in the studio of the famed Theodor Leschetizky in Vienna. His orchestral debut came in 1898 with the New York Symphony Orchestra, under the direction of Anton Seidl. Although he continued to perform on the Ann Arbor campus, he curtailed his international concert career when he was hired by the School of Music at the University of Michigan.[15] There he remained active until his death in 1933. His annotated catalog of piano literature, *Notes on the Literature of the Piano*, was completed by Samuel and published in 1940 by the University of Michigan Press.

During the early decades of this century the Lockwood brothers exerted a sizable influence on the School of Music at the University of Michigan. In addition to teaching musical criticism, Samuel served as head of the Violin and Orchestral Departments and Conductor of the University Symphony Orchestra from 1908 until 1930. Numbered among his students were Bertrand Bronson, editor and collector of *The Traditional Tunes of the Child Ballads (1959-72)*, and conductor Thor Johnson, who would later interpret several of Normand's major choral works in performance.

Orchestral repertoire during the first decade of Samuel's Michigan tenure reflects a strong bias toward German Romanticism, which must surely have affected the teen-aged Normand, a member of the percussion section. A preference for the masterworks of the German symphonists was typical of the period prior to World War I in this country, but Samuel Lockwood's admiration of the Germanic culture went beyond an artistic one. According to his son, Samuel was so zealous in his German propensity that he insisted on a bilingual home environment for his children, although the Lockwood ancestry contains "not one drop of German blood."[16] At the outbreak of activities that led to World War I, Samuel Lockwood was sympathetic with the Prussian cause, but as soon as the United States became involved in the war, he immediately erected a flagpole and the flag of his native country in front of his family's Ann Arbor residence.[17]

Samuel Lockwood's active interest in orchestration is evident in the University Symphony's repertoire list; included are his *Valse de Concert*, as well as his rescorings of two of Brahms's Hungarian dances for string orchestra.[18] He also wrote a handbook entitled *Elementary Orchestration*, published in 1923 by the University of Michigan. Lockwood's monograph was dedicated to Frederick Stock, conductor of the Chicago Symphony from 1905 to 1942, and whom Lockwood had encountered through the Chicago orchestra's participation in the Ann Arbor May Festivals.[19] Samuel showed his admiration for this German-born champion of American music by referring to him as "Supreme Master of the Orchestra" in his dedication.[20] Stock would, in 1924, figure prominently in the early career of Samuel's composer son, Normand, by facilitating his study with Ottorino Respighi.

Albert Lockwood's contribution to the Michigan campus was also outstanding, and may have been more widespread than that of his brother, since he served as Acting Director of the School of Music beginning in 1923. His Historical Lecture Recitals, given from 1902 to 1913, are highlighted in Richard Crawford's history of the University School of Music.[21] The pianist's concert repertoire was extensive, including 232 titles; he regularly gave twenty-eight to thirty recitals from memory in a single season.[22] His repertoire list included several Debussy works, the Edward MacDowell sonata, and three Scriabin pieces, in addition to more standard, European Romantic works. Albert Lockwood might therefore have been more a representative of modern music than his brother, not only to his students, but also to his nephew, Normand.

Childhood and Youth (1906-24)

Normand Lockwood's parents were initially drawn together by their mutual interest in the violin. According to their son's best guess, they met in the studio of Edward Hermann, a New York violin teacher. Angelina had been living for some time in New York with her composer sister, Gertrude, and Samuel was a student at Columbia University. They were married early in the first decade of this century.[23]

In 1908 the Lockwood family moved to 800 Oxford Road in Ann Arbor, and the next year, 1909, Albertine was born. In 1910, Charles Nichols Lockwood and his wife joined the new community in Ann Arbor, building a home neighboring that of their son on Oxford Road.

Normand's sister Albertine played piano in her youth, but did not pursue it as a career. As a young adult, she remembers accompanying her mother's violin playing for fun at her home on the Mediterranean island of Capri. Albertine eventually married Charles Ransom Reynolds on December 17, 1938, and had two sons, one named for her brother and one named for her husband. She was living in Keene Valley at the time of this biography.

With a conductor and violinist as father, violinist and singer as mother, and an uncle who was a concert pianist, Normand Lockwood's early interest in making music is far from remarkable. As early as 1912, student recital programs from the University of Michigan's preparatory piano department include the name of Normand Lockwood. His recital appearances are documented through March 30, 1924, when Lockwood performed six of his own compositions: *Sonata in F Minor* (first movement), *Prelude in F-Sharp Major, Etude in G Major, Prelude in F Minor, Valse-Prelude in G Major,* and *Etude in F Minor.*[24]

Performance, however, was never a primary attraction for Lockwood. On the contrary, one of his most painful memories occurred on stage. Drafted at the last minute as a recital page turner in his early teens, he became confused during a repeat and the performance halted as a result. The natural mortification of the shy teenager was, perhaps, amplified by the importance of the performers within his family. The singer was Clara Clemens, Mark Twain's daughter, and she was accompanied by her husband Ossip Gabrilowitsch, who was not only one of the finest pianists of the day, but was also the conductor of the Detroit Symphony Orchestra.[25] Either as a result of this painful experience or claiming it as evidence, Normand abhorred public performance in his youth, seeing himself as lacking the desire and control to appear on stage.[26] At that time, the measure of a great performer was a virtuoso such as his uncle Albert or family friend Josef Lhévinne. Perhaps instinctively, Normand knew it would be difficult or impossible to make his mark as a performer. However, if his early models caused him to seek success elsewhere, they also instilled in him a taste for the best in musical tone and technique.

In contrast to his aversion for performing, his interest in composition appeared quite early, beginning in 1912 with an "Improvisation" and a piece called *Russisches Schlummerlied*, both notated by his father. The German title indicates the curiously bilingual home environment in which he was reared. Eighteen other manuscripts exist from the period before 1924, including twelve works for piano, one of which, *Eight Dances* (1921), was orchestrated by Samuel. His mother contributed the text for one of his two songs, *Mein Haus* (1922). Other works include one movement for string quartet (1922), a transcription of Brahms's *The Little Dustman* for piano (1922), and one whimsical work—with skull and crossbones drawn in place of a title—for piano, bells, dish pan, voice (no words), egg beater, and triangle.[27] These youthful forays into composition not only document his lifelong passion for creating music, they also indicate the sense of humor that has continued to be evident.

Samuel Lockwood must have presented a formidable presence to his aspiring son. Normand remembers his father as a stern disciplinarian; yet, he never directly discouraged his son from composition. In one remembered scenario, Samuel asked the teen-aged Normand why he wanted to compose, "when Beethoven had already said it all?"[28] Seventy years of experience now prompt the composer to answer simply, "composing is an obsession," but at age fifteen, his inability to answer his father's challenge must have inspired him all the more.[29]

Musical influences outside the family included the rehearsals of the Flonzaley String Quartet and other groups which took place at their home. Albertine Lockwood Reynolds added,

> It seemed to me for a long time—quartet, trio, or quintet practices went on in the evenings at 800 Oxford Road. . . . My room was over the living room, so I heard it all and some of it wore off on me, because I love chamber music.[30]

Although the composer cannot remember specific works he heard, the Flonzaley, active from 1902 to 1928, was noted for playing recent French and Russian works.[31]   In fact, Stravinsky wrote his *Concertino* (1920) specifically for the group. Lockwood's one memory from this time was a general response to the music, as he related in 1988, "Some music would terrify me and some would make me cry."[32]

Two years of private school provided the first formal education for the composer, after which he transferred to Tappan (Public) Elementary School. His first piano teacher was Esta Ella Mewmaw at the University of Michigan's School of Music. His second piano teacher, Otto Jacob Stahl, exerted more influence on the young composer; piano lessons eventually disintegrated into composition lessons, as Stahl utilized studio time to help the boy with his new compositions. On one youthful composition, *Three-Voice Invention* (1923), Stahl's pencilled comments are legible. After commenting on various technical aspects of the assignment, Stahl wrote, "Very musical—a fitting ending to a year of good work. It has real originality."[33]   Although music lessons were consistently provided in his youth, Lockwood insists that none of his early piano teachers helped him to clarify the direction his musical interests should take.   Music fascinated him, but this fascination had no successful application.

Lockwood characterizes himself as an extremely shy, often secretive child, whom nothing interested in grade school.[34] If anything, geography and world history held some interest for him, but games and sports did not. Perhaps it was this boredom which precipitated his early departure from Ann Arbor High School in 1924. He had attended the University of Michigan unofficially since 1921, studying ear training with Beryl Fox Bacher and form and analysis with Earl Vincent Moore. He hated theory, and could see no sense in studying it; "I was so disinterested that nothing made much of an impact."[35] However, a few pieces made a lasting imprint on the composer, as he related in 1979:

> I never had any inclination toward choral music until I heard in Ann Arbor, when I was fourteen or fifteen years old, the *Dirge for Two Veterans* of Gustav Holst. That made a great impression on me—also *Sea Drift* of Delius and [a work by] Frederick Stock. I don't know why, but they did. Classical things, Beethoven and Bach, left me cold.[36]

Lockwood first met Holst in Ann Arbor when the British composer stayed at the home of Albert Lockwood during a visit to the University of Michigan campus. Normand later visited the British composer in London in 1924, and saw him several times during his stay at the American Academy from 1929 to 1932.[37] Lockwood would later create his own settings of the Walt Whitman texts used by Holst and Delius; in fact, these early experiences may account for his lifelong fascination with Whitman's poetry.

The mature composer later regretted his lack of a formal college education, missing the rigorous training he would have received in his early twenties. The much-appreciated discipline

Normand Lockwood, aged 15. Photo courtesy of Heidi Lockwood.

he gained through his later study with Nadia Boulanger he characterizes as being of a different sort, that of self-discipline, which did not substitute for the advantages of institutional discipline. Furthermore, his missed undergraduate education left him with a poor understanding of world history, a deficit he felt sorely as an eighteen-year-old in Rome.[38]

Chapter Two

European Years

Rome (1924-25)

In the summer of 1924 Normand and Albert Lockwood departed for a tour of England, France, Austria, and Switzerland. Of his travels with his uncle Normand remembers, "He was a great help: a very cultivated man. He knew a great deal about art."[1] At the end of the summer the teenager remained in Italy.

> I stayed there . . . in a terrible part of Rome; I just loved it. You know, no central heat, no bathroom in the building, and I just loved it over there.[2]

With the entree provided by Frederick Stock's letter of recommendation, Lockwood began the school year in the studio of Ottorino Respighi.

Lockwood's limited formal training had its effect on his early compositional experiences. He admits, "It was ridiculous—I wasn't ready. [Respighi] wasn't the kind of teacher

who could [help] an inexperienced novice. He was probably
very good, though, I'm sure of it."[3] As he remembers,

> Respighi was a gentle, dear man, but I was then too
> unschooled to learn all that he could teach me. We com-
> municated in German. If there were any influences from him,
> they were on a symphony I wrote in the late twenties which I
> later withdrew from circulation.[4]

As a result of the extensive musical experiences provided by his
family and his innate preoccupation with composition, Lockwood's desire to express himself musically had outdistanced his
ability to do so. His only formal composition lessons had
taken place in the piano studio, and he had been bored by form
and analysis at the University of Michigan. Small wonder that
his sudden arrival in the salon of a master composer would
have proven less than productive.

Lockwood accepts the entire responsibility for the
unprofitable period in Rome, when the fault might more
accurately be divided between student and teacher. The
remarks of Respighi's wife, Elsa, suggest that her husband was
not altogether committed to his teaching position at the Ac-
cademia di Santa Cecilia.

> At the beginning of 1924 Respighi was appointed director of
> the Academy, a post he filled reluctantly for only two years. It
> is easy to see how ill-suited Ottorino's temperament was to a
> bureaucratic position, and the many commitments which often
> kept him away from Rome only aggravated his relations with
> the Ministry. Respighi also wanted to give up his professorship
> of composition, but to prevent his resignation, the Minister
> introduced an advanced course of composition for him at the
> Academy. This course involved only forty lectures which he
> was allowed to give whenever convenient.[5]

This brief capsule of the 1924-25 year at the Academy reveals a composer forced not only into teaching, but into an administrative position. His wife states plainly that both capacities were incongruent with his personality and interests. The decade of the 1920s was an incredibly fruitful one for Respighi; the demands of composition and subsequent performance would have created a busy calendar without the added distraction of teaching and administration. Even if Normand Lockwood had been in the advanced composition course she mentions, one that apparently met at Respighi's convenience, he would not have been exposed to a highly structured compositional approach he feels he needed at the time. That need would be addressed in the fall of 1925, in the studio of Nadia Boulanger.

The student compositions surviving from Lockwood's first Roman period add little to a study of his compositional growth. The musical environment of the city, on the other hand, offered experiences that were highly memorable for the composer. On one occasion, he heard a performance of Respighi's *The Pines of Rome* conducted by Bernardino Molinari, and as Lockwood remembers,

> When the time came for the prerecorded nightingale song [in the second movement], the uninhibited Italian crowd gave a rousing boo. There was a long interval before they could begin again.[6]

Elsa Respighi's account of the famous performance concurs with Lockwood's: "At the end of the first part there were protests in the form of booing and hissing which subsided with the sudden pianissimo of the second section."[7] The young Lockwood could scarcely have been untouched by such an event.

Influences on Lockwood's compositional style springing from this apprentice period are difficult to trace. Although he maintains that his time with Respighi did not make a lasting impact, Lockwood's early interest in bichordal writing and the melodic use of the tritone might have been engendered by the Italian composer's music. These devices are especially evident in the overture to the opera *Belfagor* (1922), a performance of which Lockwood witnessed in Rome.

Also in Rome, Lockwood first manifested his interest in writing for the voice. In that respect he was further influenced by the Roman Catholic services he attended. He remarked in 1979,

> When I went to Rome, I had a sort of romantic fascination for Gregorian chant as I would hear it sung around churches. That was also the first time I had ever heard works of Palestrina. So I probably got something out of being in Rome—Respighi or no Respighi.[8]

The pure, homogeneously blended vocal sounds of the Roman Catholic liturgy found an appreciative audience in Lockwood, and throughout his career, he often incorporated this "ideal" sound in his choral compositions.

Paris (1925-28)

For many United States' composers in the 1920s, Paris exuded an almost irresistible appeal. Like several of his compatriots, Normand Lockwood made his way to the city, moving directly from Rome in 1925. In retrospect, the previous year appears to have been a light-hearted, extended holiday; he had absorbed the libraries, art, and architecture of Rome, and had taken frequent side trips to Naples and Florence, while studying privately with Respighi. His Parisian experience proved to be very different for several reasons, one of which was his immediate affinity with the sophisticated French musical public. In an indirect comparison of the two cities, Lockwood stated,

> Paris was a wonderful place to hear new music. The French
> are so nonchalant and insouciant about music. They are able
> to reject what they don't like without any fuss. It was not a
> case of immediate shifts in their feeling for new works.[9]

His mention of a "fuss" calls to mind the Respighi performance which caused a stir in the audience. Certainly, the Parisian public did not hesitate to show their disdain at the premiere of an earlier work of Stravinsky's, *Le Sacre du Printemps*. Nevertheless, Lockwood believes that the 1920s Parisian audience was less constrained by conventional expectations than its Roman counterpart.[10]

Lockwood was introduced to the color and light of Paris through its memorable music. Clearly the experience of living in Paris for three years was at least as valuable as studying with any teacher. For the first time he heard Ernst Krenek's *Jonny spielt Auf*, Honegger's *Le Roi David*, Schoenberg's *Pierrot Lunaire*, Debussy's *Pelléas et Mélisande*, Mussorgsky's *Boris Godonov*, Hindemith's *Das Marienleben*, and works by Ravel, Milhaud, Florent Schmitt, and Roy Harris. Although Stravinsky's works were prominent in the Boulanger studio, Lockwood remembers that they were "not to be imitated beyond what simply seeped into the veins. And why not that? As far as I know, Beethoven never made any apologies over Haydn."[11] Lockwood's absorption of Stravinsky's style is understandably evident in his early works. The impressionable young composition student had finally begun to express his creative urge, and the works of one of the giants of twentieth-century composition helped to supply the materials.

Paris was, indeed, an education in itself for the nineteen-year-old son of a conservative orchestra conductor. Still, Nadia Boulanger supplied the missing ingredient that gave these musical experiences meaning for Lockwood. The master pedagogue guided him through a strict and disciplined study of the classics such as the cantatas of Bach and the Beethoven string quartets, as well as various contemporary composers. Her biographer, Léonie Rosenstiel, provided a comprehensive list of composers studied in a typical class that includes Wagner, Schmitt, Dupré, Prokofieff, Bartók, Bloch, Dukas, Debussy, Auric, Poulenc, Honegger, Ravel, and Fauré.[12]

Lockwood has often reflected upon Boulanger's pedagogical gifts.

> Boulanger was a teacher if there ever was one. . . . She had what I'd call perspective. She could spot what was unique in a student; she was the first person to give me a point of view on myself and my own work. When the breakthrough to my own language finally came, it was with a little piece. I took a poem by Whitman and set it for tenor, flute, and alto flute.[13]

This "little piece" was soon performed for the International Society for Contemporary Music in Paris. Probably a testament to his youth and no stronger conviction, the score bears the signature of Charles Caxton, Lockwood's erstwhile pseudonym.[14] Entitled *When Lilacs Last in the Dooryard Bloom'd*, its harmonic simplicity belied its importance in Lockwood's later career. Not only is this version of "Memories of President Lincoln" Lockwood's first setting of Whitman's poetry, the compositional language Lockwood mentions is one he consistently employed in subsequent choral and vocal settings of the poet's work. Consisting of a specific, close-position configuration of conventional harmonies, this pattern, dubbed the "Paumanok pattern," is discussed more specifically in the choral chapter of this book.

Lockwood's private composition lessons took place every week, at the cost of about ten dollars per hour. Rosenstiel elaborated on the finances of several Boulanger students at the time, including Lockwood.

> Americans who went to Paris to study with Nadia generally expected to stay for about three years. That was how long Virgil Thomson, Aaron Copland, and Melville Smith remained with her, and most students who could manage to scrape together the money tried to maintain themselves in Paris for that long. Claire Leonard, a young M. A. from Harvard, was able to stay for almost four years on a Paine Traveling Fellowship. But Normand Lockwood was on his own, as was Illinois-born organist Barrett Spach who, fortunately, could look to his family for help.[15]

Boulanger saw a great many students at that time, teaching both privately and in classes at the American Conservatory in Fontainebleau, the Ecole Normale, her Paris apartment, and her summer home in Gargenville. Lockwood was involved in her Ecole Normale class on the Beethoven quartets, but because his childhood shyness remained with him, Lockwood did not make any close friends. He does, however, remember a few composers in particular from the studio.

> Susanne Bloch I remember quite well, and an English composer, full of mischief, Lenox Berkeley. Roy Harris showed up there, and Robert Russell Bennett. . . . Barrett Spach of Chicago and Bernard Rogers from Eastman in Rochester were people I enjoyed in particular.[16]

In composition lessons, Boulanger often criticized student works quite sharply. She involved herself very closely with the music itself, and "she wouldn't palaver about it . . . she could see what was extraneous and what was essential. She would say, 'This is not right,' and prove it with some structural reason."[17]

Nadia Boulanger and Normand Lockwood, Oberlin, OH, January
1937. Photo courtesy of Normand Lockwood.

Regarding his own self-discipline, Lockwood related,

> She gave me "the works" and I studied hard. I owe her one
> of the most important things. She taught me discipline, not just
> from the outside, doing what you're told, but also from the
> inside, selecting what you are going to do and doing it.[18]

Boulanger's distinctive contribution to music education was her
desire to allow students the experience of self-discovery, instead
of revealing their styles to them. She has described her own
teaching style on several occasions, as in this interview with
Bruno Monsaingeon.

> I have a student who is very nice, but frightened. He wants
> to please me, he wants me to like his harmony. He plays and
> then turns toward me, desperately anxious: "Is that how it
> should be?" I say, "But I've no idea, I don't know what you
> want. As long as I don't know what you want, musically you
> don't exist for me."[19]

As a result of his study with this exacting individual, the lack
of focus that was so present in Lockwood's youth soon disap-
peared. With regard to internal discipline, he must have
learned her lessons well. Beginning with his appointment at
Oberlin, Lockwood has not taken a significant hiatus from
composition during his entire musical career, including one
lengthy period when he was without the external demands of an
academic position, and the eighteen years since his retirement
from the University of Denver.

Lockwood adopted the role of student twice more with
Boulanger when she came to the United States in the 1930s.
One meeting is commemorated by a photograph of the two.
Still displayed in Lockwood's studio, it documents the change
in their relationship from student and teacher to peers. By
1932, he was a member of the Oberlin Conservatory faculty,

and in those later sessions with Boulanger, he realized he had learned all he could from her: "She had begun to repeat herself a bit."[20] From the time of his appointment to the Oberlin faculty, he relied on his own hard-won sense of discipline to achieve professional success.

Lockwood made a memorable impression on Boulanger, as evident in her letters to him and in a story concerning one of Lockwood's Denver composition students.[21] In 1925, the very young Lockwood had been embarrassed to tell his composition teacher his correct age, and had added four years to the total. As the story goes, the next year he forgot what he had said the previous year, and told her, again, that he was twenty-three. Whether or not he compounded the exaggeration by stating the same age the third year is unknown, but when John Ryan gave Lockwood's greeting to Boulanger nearly five decades later, she quipped, "Oh, is Lockwood still twenty-three?"[22]

Lockwood's Paris period marks another milestone in his life. On September 21, 1926, he was married to his first wife, Chicago-born Dorothy S. (Dolly) Sanders (1903-77). A well-bred, petite woman with a Victorian sensibility and a strong sense of propriety, she was the daughter of Milton Sears Sanders, a shipping executive in Traverse City, Michigan, and Hedwig Schager Sanders. Having completed an AB degree and a certificate in journalism from the University of Michigan in 1925, Dorothy studied in the Parisian theater school of stage designer Ladislas Medgyés during the early years of her marriage. She would eventually become a free-lance writer during their decade in New York, assisting her husband Normand in the libretto preparation of his opera, *The Scarecrow*. The Lockwoods had three daughters: Deborah (1928-89), Angeline Rose (1935-80), and Hedwig Marie (Heidi, b. 1939).

Although their public image suggested a harmonious relationship, their marriage was apparently always a turbulent one. Life in New York underscored the differences between the passionate composer who considered social events a trial, and the refined, cultivated writer who was at home in any social situation. If Normand was not actively seeking refuge from New York life or his strained marriage when he accepted a position at Trinity University in San Antonio, he nonetheless embarked on an alternate path when he moved there in 1953. Geographically extended across half a continent, the relationship strained at the seams for a year before the final rift took place. Although they never lived together again after 1954, their divorce was not finalized until 1976. Soon afterwards, Dorothy died, but not before she and her first husband had each found and married new partners.

Interim: Traverse City (1928-29)

After spending three academic years in Paris with Boulanger, the Lockwoods moved to the home of Dorothy's parents in Traverse City, Michigan, and awaited the birth of their first child. Lockwood busied himself with the composition of his first large work, the orchestral suite *Odysseus*, which secured his fellowship at the American Academy in Rome. Lockwood said of his attempts to win the Rome prize, "I tried, I think, three times for that three consecutive . . . years, and I finally won it. By Jove, I got it!"[23] The work was performed by the Chicago Symphony Orchestra in March of 1929, under the direction of Frederick Stock. The score was subsequently withdrawn from circulation and lost. Before departing from Traverse City, Lockwood also began his *Symphony in E*, which he finished in Rome in 1929.

Rome (1929-32)

In 1929 the Rome prize, or fellowship to the American Academy in Rome, included a stipend that enabled the recipient to pursue study in Rome for three years. Lockwood's particular endowment was called the Horatio Parker Award, named after America's foremost turn-of-the-century choral composer and educator. Since Lockwood completed only a few compositions during the three-year fellowship period, the return to Rome seems to signify a return to his less-disciplined manner of working. While there, he completed his *Symphony in E*, a conservative, three-movement work that lacks the continuity he would achieve a few years later in his large-scale works. Although it has never been performed by an orchestra, Lockwood and another composer in Rome at the time, Alex Steinert, performed the symphony in a two-piano version at the Academy.

Another work from the period is a pontifical ensemble piece that bears the lengthy title, *Brass Music for Their Majesties' Entry: At the Opening of the May Exhibition of the American Academy in Rome*. The title reveals the only historical information available, except that it was written in 1929 or 1930. Finally, as a testament to Lockwood's interest in vocal writing, which was first awakened in Rome, he composed a motet for four-voice choir. Unfortunately, the score for this initial work for choir has been lost.

Even if he was not a prolific composer during the second Rome stay, the experience made a significant impact. Lockwood's most vivid concert memory is of Stravinsky's *Symphony of Psalms* (1930), a piece that incorporates one of Lockwood's fascinations, liturgical chant, with neoclassical structures and a powerfully expressive musical language. While in Rome, Lockwood purchased a score of the piano reduction that remained in his library throughout his career. The ominous opening of Stravinsky's work may have provided a model for the young composer; as late as the 1950s, his large-scale, sacred choral works are built of a similarly ancient-sounding tonal language.

Along with those of Stravinsky, Lockwood was also exposed to the works of his compatriot Roger Sessions, another fellow at the Academy. Lockwood remembers his peer as a person with "a prodigious brain," but for whom composition was a long and agonizing process.[24] Like Sessions, Lockwood would not incorporate advances of the other prominent European of the time, Arnold Schoenberg, in his works until mid-career. Long before that time, both made their fascination with Stravinsky's works evident in their own compositions.

Chapter Three

The Early Professional Years

Oberlin, Ohio (1932-43)

Lockwood's peripatetic apprenticeship in the world of composition was modified abruptly in 1932, when the twenty-six-year-old was hired as Assistant Professor of Music by Oberlin College. There, for the first time since 1924, he was exposed to the rigors of institutional discipline. Teaching the most architectonic of musical topics—theory, harmony, and counterpoint—gave him the opportunity to develop his own musical discipline in a forum of students close to his own age. He was thus a guide among peers, as he learned along with his students. In his words, "I acquired ways of teaching as I went. My discipline began immediately when I went to Oberlin."[1] He was apparently successful at meeting the challenges of his position, being promoted to the rank of Associate Professor in 1937.

At Oberlin, Lockwood replaced retiring theory professor Friedrich J. Lehmann, in a department chaired by Arthur E. Heacox, a member of the faculty since 1893. Referring to the year of Heacox's retirement, Oberlin historian Willard Warch wrote,

> The theory course of 1936 seems from the catalogue description to have been little changed from that of 1916. But Mr. Heacox, who was a strong teacher and department head, had just retired, and the old Leipzig-style approach to theory teaching was about to give way to the integrated teaching of sight-singing, ear-training, keyboard work, analysis, and written work. The composition teacher, Mr. Normand Lockwood, an ardent disciple of Nadia Boulanger, was upsetting some of the older faculty conservatives by writing in the then-modern Stravinsky-Hindemith vein of neo-classicism, and was prodding individuals and organizations into performing works of this style.[2]

According to Warch, thirteen students were working toward Master of Music or Master of School Music degrees at Oberlin in 1936.[3]   Emphasis areas in the Master of Music degree included performance, composition, theory, and history of music.   Among these Master's students, Lockwood would encounter several memorable individuals.   Perhaps his best known composition student from this period was Peter Mennin, who eventually became president of the Juilliard School in New York.

Approximately four decades after Lockwood's initial appointment at Oberlin, many of his former associates were asked to contribute to an album of letters commemorating two events: his retirement from the University of Denver in 1971, and his receipt of an honorary doctorate from that institution in 1977.[4]   In his 1971 letter, Mennin wrote of his former teacher:

He richly deserves that honor [the honorary doctorate] for the many contributions he has made in music as a truly fine teacher and highly gifted and sensitive composer whose works cover virtually every possible medium. . . . He opened up many areas of music for me, for which I shall always be grateful.[5]

Another prominent student was Paul Christiansen, heir to a strong family tradition in choral music fostered by his father, F. Melius Christiansen. From his position as director of the Concordia (Minnesota) College Choir, Paul wrote in 1971,

I shall always be deeply grateful to you for many things. I shall always value your personal friendship and interest, even from my student days at Oberlin, when you as a faculty member invited me to your home. Your help in getting some of my music performed will also be appreciated always. Mostly I want to thank you for opening new doors for me at a time when I needed this experience very much. When I was nineteen, you did what I think any true educator should—you helped me see new possibilities for music, and new ways to technically carry out some of these possibilities in composition. I feel it is impossible to overestimate the value to me of knowing you as an artist, and being privileged to study with you, and be stimulated by your imagination.[6]

Evidently Lockwood's European study made him somewhat of a champion of new music at Oberlin.

Lockwood's affinity with his students was due, in part, to closeness in age. In addition, he was a working composer himself, experimenting with the same new musical languages that characterized early twentieth-century music. He was, therefore, a "first among equals" in his studio, creating a learning situation that was doubtless very dynamic.

Christiansen mentions the degree of personal interest Lockwood maintained in his students, a characteristic many at

Lockwood family portrait (c. 1941): Angie, Dorothy, Heidi, Normand, and Debby. Photo courtesy of Heidi Lockwood.

Oberlin and elsewhere would experience. Composition lessons, reflecting those of his European models, often took place in the Lockwood home. Former student William Hoskins recalled,

> Although we students were relatively frequent visitors to the Lockwood's home, it was usually for musical, rather than purely social, occasions. We saw relatively little of his family, and that little was mostly confined to his first (and very decorative) wife, Dolly. The house had been the manse for a small church, and somehow an ecclesiastical atmosphere still clung to it. Everything was always very, very correct and spruced-up.[7]

Hoskins also commented on Lockwood's concern for the students' musical experiences outside of the Oberlin environment. As he remembered,

> Lockwood liked to see to it that his student composers were exposed to unusual, good music. He took several of us to Cleveland on one occasion to hear Hindemith give a recital of his own viola works.[8]

Helen Strassburger, a soprano Lockwood knew first as a student at Oberlin, has remained a favorite associate; no fewer than six vocal works are dedicated to her and have been performed by her on numerous occasions.[9] Later she would marry Ives scholar Howard Boatwright, who remarked on another connection between the young Helen and Lockwood.

> Time telescopes in memory straight back to Oberlin where you, more than anyone else, set Helen on her lifetime pursuit of the American art song by introducing her to Ives, and not less important, yourself. To Howard, musical jack-of-all-trades, your singular devotion to composition and your almost in-

comprehensible fertility (Could you possibly produce a list of your works?) have always been an unattainable model.[10]

Unlike some other students of Nadia Boulanger such as Aaron Copland and Virgil Thomson, Lockwood was less interested in creating music which signified a national identity than creating music which expressed his own musical ideas. He acknowledged this tendency in 1974, illuminating his particular orientation toward German models.

> I never felt myself to be a prophet of "American Music," as I guess some composers did. I was never passionate to the degree of some composers. I am told there are a great many Americanisms in my music, but there is also a strong Germanic influence. My father had spent time in Leipzig with his family, while my Mother had stayed for a time in Dresden. My parents loved German culture, so this Germanic influence lasted from my early childhood into my teens. I never did feel it was anything to disown, although during World War I, I was very much aware of the national hatred for Germans and things Germanic.[11]

Lockwood's directing Helen Boatwright to American song illustrated his belief in the individual works he considered to be exemplary. For the young soprano, his guidance also engendered an interest in the broader topic of American art song. Such a procedure, while not self-consciously "Americanistic," achieved the same purpose. Lockwood's students were acquainted with native composers through his genuine, nonpartisan interest in the music of Ives and others of his compatriots.

Lugwig Lenel, a composer now retired from Muhlenberg College in Allentown, Pennsylvania, was another of Lockwood's composition students at Oberlin. He came to the

College in 1939, where he found Lockwood to be very helpful in his pursuit of composition.

> One outstanding trait was Normand's ability to rather quickly seize upon a student's compositional talent and his potentialities of growth. He tried to develop compositional skills which were as yet undeveloped, but within reach of the student—without ever imposing his personal style. He very quickly saw weak passages and suggested how to improve them. . . . All this was accompanied by an ever-present positive attitude (although he could be quite outspoken at times, but never hurtful), by pushing a student forward at his own pace.[12]

Evidently, Lockwood had adopted many of the characteristics he had admired in Nadia Boulanger, especially the belief that a composition teacher should attempt to reveal a student's own unique gifts, instead of imposing upon them a particular style, or composing vicariously through them.

Composer Fred Steiner graduated from Oberlin in 1943, after which he became involved in composing scores for radio, television, and motion pictures, eventually earning a doctorate in composition from the University of Southern California. In a touching letter dated July 6, 1943, Steiner gives evidence of yet another role played by Lockwood.

> Today I got my greeting from F. D. R., and I'm reporting on the 16th. The only thing I'm really sorry about is that I don't think I'll get a chance to finish something I was working on for violin and piano.
> . . . [Shirley] and I are very much in love, have been for well over a year now, and . . . we want to get married some day. I'd like you to sort of take care of her for me if you can. . . . I know that you and Mrs. Lockwood are darn good "fixer-uppers," the best in that little one-horse town. You both made me feel wonderfully at home when ever I came to see you, even at the

odd hours of the night when I used to drop in with my problems. And you never let me down once.[13]

Steiner took advantage of ample opportunities to repay the Lockwoods' kindnesses after their move to New York. In Lockwood's words, "When I first went to New York and [during] those early years there, Fred was responsible for having gotten almost every job in radio that I had."[14]

Faculty associates at Oberlin included choral director Olaf C. Christiansen, another of F. Melius's sons, to whom Lockwood dedicated several works. The conductor's choir fueled Lockwood's interest in the medium, as he remembered,

> I was fascinated with Olaf Christiansen's choir I heard there, and I think that set me off on that track . . . where I was able to accomplish something positive.[15]

In discussing Lockwood's *Stabat Mater (Mary, Who Stood in Sorrow,* 1950), his compositional debut at the college, Christiansen indicates that the inspiration was mutual.

> It was about the first contemporary piece within my experience that required no more than the natural resources of the human voice. The linear lyricism and adherence to verbal rhythm also aroused my interest in your music and you. Each year thereafter you contributed a piece for the choir program. You will recall *David Mourneth for Absalom, Three Psalms, Christmas Lullaby, Inscriptions from the Catacombs,* and *Monotone.* All of these helped me to understand the contemporary idiom. I am most grateful to you Normand, for this opening of vistas and giving me the broader view when I had much to learn. . . . Temporary as the world seems at times, you can be assured that what you have done and continue to do will benefit the world both in art and education.[16]

In the pieces mentioned by Christiansen, Lockwood's compositional idiom included modality, asymmetrical meters, bichords, and polychords—not new in the greater musical world, but fairly fresh in the realm of American choral composition in the 1930s.

During Lockwood's tenure at Oberlin, former Boulanger student Melville Smith was a faculty member at Flora Stone Mather College at Western Reserve University in nearby Cleveland, Ohio. Written after her husband's death, Martha (Mrs. Melville) Smith's letter recounts a cherished memory involving Lockwood's mother, who was living in Europe in the 1930s.

> It seems like yesterday that we all had such good times together in Cleveland and Oberlin. A high point in our lives was your introduction of us to your mother in Capri in 1938. Her beautiful villa there and her hospitality made our stay there most memorable. I see by my diary that Melville and Albertine [Lockwood's sister] played duets and then Melville played Chopin and Bach for your mother one evening, which pleased your mother very much.[17]

Angelina Lockwood had purchased a small villa in Capri in the late 1920s and moved there after her divorce from Samuel Pierson Lockwood in the early 1930s. The composer's mother then divided her time between Capri in Europe and Florida in the United States until World War II restricted her travel. From then until her death in 1955, Angelina Lockwood remained in the United States.

During the Oberlin years Lockwood became friends with Walter Blodgett, curator of the Cleveland Museum of Art. Several performances of Lockwood's music took place at the museum and were reviewed by fellow composer Herbert Elwell, music critic for *The Cleveland Plain Dealer*. Lockwood had earlier met Elwell in the company of Randall Thompson, when all three were apprentice composers in Rome.[18] Although the chance encounter in 1925 had been an enjoyable one, Lockwood did not see either of them again in Italy. The Oberlin position created the opportunity for Lockwood to renew his acquaintance with Elwell.

Other affiliations with the Cleveland Museum of Art include Oberlin faculty member Arthur Dann's performance of Lockwood's *Sonatina* for piano in 1939. The choral piece *How Far Is It to Bethlehem?* (early 1940s) was commissioned and performed by the Cleveland Museum of Art Chorus. As late as 1973, when Walter Blodgett commissioned Lockwood's *Concerto for Organ and Chamber Orchestra*, the museum served the important function of presenting Lockwood's compositions in public performance.

Oberlin, Compositions

Perhaps the greatest evidence that Lockwood had found his internal discipline at Oberlin rests in the number of instrumental works composed during his residence there. Piano works occupied some of his creative attention, while eleven of his fifteen extant string quartet works were completed during the period. With regard to compositional style, these genres exhibit Stravinskian octatonicism, modality, and quartal writing, as well as major-against-minor chords. In addition, several important solo songs come from the Oberlin period, including his first version of the Stephen Vincent Benet text, *Prelude to Western Star* (1942) for soprano and piano. Genres such as choral and orchestral works are represented equally well in the period from 1932 to 1943.

During this first segment of his academic career, Lockwood was affirmed in the instrumental area by several commissions and awards. His *Symphony: A Year's Chronicle* (1934) won the Chicago Symphony's Gustavus F. Swift Prize, for which he

competed with 115 other applicants.[19] According to an unsigned *Cleveland Plain Dealer* article, Lockwood's "three-
movement symphony received the unanimous vote of the
judges, Sir Hamilton Harty, John Alden Carpenter and
Howard Hanson."[20] The work was performed by Frederick
Stock and the Chicago Symphony on April 4, 1935. Critic Carl
Engel of *Modern Music* offered a mixed review of Lockwood's
programmatic, cyclic look at the events of one year in the
artist's life.

> The symphony, *A Year's Chronicle*, by Normand Lock-
> wood of Oberlin, Ohio, was advertised as the "pièce de résis-
> tance." Swift and Company awarded their thousand dollar
> prize in this case to a work of sporadic enthusiasm and spas-
> modic workmanship, but one which gives promise of interesting
> future accomplishments, if Mr. Lockwood can learn to think in
> longer periods, can overcome his inability to handle more than
> one rhythmic pattern at a time, and can stop letting the
> deliberate ugliness of his harmonic idiom trip him up.[21]

Engel's description of Lockwood's "harmonic idiom" may
have reflected the conservative tastes of mid-depression
America; however, when viewed in the context of the first half
of the twentieth century, Lockwood's harmony in this work
seems rather unadventurous. Written for typical orchestra, in
three conventional movements, the work encompasses a miscel-
lany of jazz motives and chords, impressionistic seventh
sonorities, and a fugue on a quartal subject.

In 1936 another orchestral work, *Erie*, now withdrawn, was
premiered by Artur Rodzinsky and the Cleveland Symphony
Orchestra. Herbert Elwell reviewed the work in *Modern Music*
of that year.

> Another atmospheric piece recently performed by Rodzinski
> is *Erie* by Normand Lockwood. Naive and tentative in struc-

ture, but original in its sonorities, this piece is excellent tone-painting and more, an evidence of something intimately personal that achieves unsuspected significance by a curious sort of understatement. This music offers imaginative adventure with simple means and without effort.[22]

Elwell complimented Lockwood's freshness and inventiveness, while his more critical remarks suggest that the work was structurally unsubstantial. Lockwood's subsequent withdrawal of the work may indicate his agreement with Elwell. Even in this mixed review, however, Elwell remarked on an essential Lockwood trait that persists and develops throughout his career—the ability to present his innermost musical convictions through the use of understatement.

In response to the strong choral tradition at Oberlin, Lockwood composed many works, including two settings of Whitman texts, *Dirge for Two Veterans* (1935) and *Out of the Cradle Endlessly Rocking* (1938). Unlike his procedure for the instrumental works, Lockwood wrote in a consonant, largely homophonic choral style—one that was also favored by contemporary composers such as Randall Thompson. Perhaps this choral idiom reflects the very nature of choral singing in the 1930s. As opposed to the professional nature of the symphony orchestra, choruses nationwide were comprised largely of volunteers whose experiences and abilities with new music were limited. In contrast to his more experimental orchestra works, his more reliable, consonant choral idiom brought him widespread success with conductors and publishers.

The houses of Witmark and G. Schirmer published the two Whitman works in 1937 and 1939, respectively. Providing a strong link with Lockwood's childhood, these pieces recall his early fascination with the Holst setting of *Dirge for Two Veterans* and Delius' *Sea Drift*, the latter being the longer Whitman poem from which Lockwood's text for *Out of the Cradle Endlessly Rocking* was excerpted. For this work,

Lockwood received the G. Schirmer World's Fair Prize in 1938.
    Nearly twenty years after the composition of *Dirge for Two Veterans*, composer/critic Peggy Glanville-Hicks reviewed it for the *New York Herald Tribune*.

> Lockwood's *Dirge* is a beautiful and moving little work: the bitonal subtlety of the total effect is arrived at by a simplicity in the individual parts that insures spontaneity in performance. The whole is consonant, yet unexpected: a clear-cut prosodic technique and a mood powerfully set and deeply held add up to a gem among modern choir pieces.[23]

The review not only confirms the success of Lockwood's more intimate choral idiom with critics, it also documents the fact that this 1930s work was not considered "old," even as late as 1954.
    Out of the Cradle Endlessly Rocking also deserves special mention because of its many documented performances.[24] Another early example of Lockwood's sensitive, understated "Whitman" style, the work was performed widely after G. Schirmer's publication of it in 1939, appearing on programs by the Harvard/Radcliffe Choral Society, Westminster Choir College Choir, and the George Lynn Singers of Denver. Jean Riegger, sister of the composer Wallingford Riegger and former secretary to Lockwood's uncle, Max Smith, was a choir member in a 1940 performance at Northwestern University. She wrote to Lockwood, thanking him for the piece and reporting of the positive progress of the rehearsals.

> I met you several years ago, when I was your uncle Max's secretary. . . . Every once in a while I see your name in the papers, but now it will be everywhere with your fair song. I sing in the "Schola Cantorum," have, for several years, and I was delighted the other night when [Hugh] Ross [conductor of the group] told us we were to learn this song of yours. In

speaking of it he said, "considering the vocal limitations imposed, Mr. Lockwood has written an extremely interesting
work; in fact, he has managed to write something very difficult.
However, this is one of the finest pieces of American choral
writing I have ever seen."

I thought it might please you to have "expert opinion" on the
subject. Last Wednesday, we were given the song to read over,
and if you haven't heard it yet, you have something in store for
you. At first sight, it appears to be rather easy, but I think it
will take considerable effort to work it out properly and artis-
tically. . . . We aim to show how it really should be done! How
proud Max would have been![25]

Indeed, the conservative Max Smith would certainly have
approved of his nephew's choral works at this time.

Another choral composer, Mabel Daniels, heard one of the
Harvard/Radcliffe concerts on March 12, 1942 and wrote an
equally complimentary letter to Lockwood.

May I tell you how much I enjoyed your very beautiful *Out
of the Cradle Endlessly Rocking*. . . . In these days one is ab-
solutely surfeited with the brittle, the dissonant, the restlessness
in music. Your piece was a joy to hear—beautiful in feeling,
modern in harmony, interesting throughout. Awfully hard
words to set effectively. I once considered them so I know![26]

The ten-minute work still deserves repeated performance,
although accessibility is a problem. G. Schirmer's 1939 edition
is out of print at the time of this writing.

Other Lockwood choral works were performed even further
outside Oberlin's periphery. The collection, *Psalms 117, 63,
and 134*, also called *Three Psalms*, was sung at the second
American Festival of Modern Music, at the First Congregational Church of Los Angeles. Published in 1938 by Neil A.
Kjos, the *Psalms* were dedicated to Olaf Christiansen and his

wife, Ellen. Conductor Arthur Leslie Jacobs of the Los Angeles church also included a Lockwood piece, *Passion after the Seven Last Words of Christ* (1941), in the same festival two years later, and the work was dedicated to Jacobs. Lockwood was quite successful at securing performances of his works throughout his career, and often, as in the case of the *Passion*, locations were far removed from Lockwood's academic position.

Oberlin, Organizations and Affiliations

The Oberlin years saw Lockwood's earliest involvement in organizations that advanced contemporary American music. His first affiliation was with Yaddo, an artist's colony established in 1924. The first Yaddo-sponsored concert took place in 1932, when Aaron Copland and Hubert Linscott introduced seven of Charles Ives's *114 Songs*. Enduring until the present time, Yaddo has served not only as a performance outlet, but also a forum on American Music for native composers. Lockwood was initially drawn into the group by two friends and fellow composers: Richard Donovan, then on the faculty of Smith College; and Quincy Porter, who held the position of dean at the New England Conservatory of Music. By 1940, Lockwood was serving on the program committee for a Yaddo series called Concerts of Contemporary American Music, with Donovan (the chair), Henry Cowell, Paul Creston, David Diamond, Roy Harris, Otto Luening, Porter, and Elizabeth Ames, Executive Director of the Festivals from 1924 to 1969. Lockwood's *Piano Quintet* (1939) was performed there in September of 1940, featuring pianist Johana (Mrs. Roy) Harris and the Galimir String Quartet. Reviewer Harold Taubman of the *New York Times* called it a work "of merit," and continued, "The Lockwood quintet is in a lush, romantic vein. Its ideas are coherent and impassioned, especially in several slow movements."[27]

About the festival, he wrote,

> The sixth Yaddo music period, which came to an end here today, justified its existence. It . . . gave a hearing to works of thirty-six composers, all but one of whom is alive. . . . The general impression left by the thirty-eight compositions heard in four programs was of less tentativeness and cerebration than one is accustomed to note in such a cross-section of contemporary writing.[28]

Taubman's remarks suggest that Yaddo was one of the more successful of several similar ventures active at the time.

Apart from having his works performed there, Lockwood's presence was known through opinions and preferences he expressed as a member of the program committee. Because works submitted for performance required committee approval, the Yaddo composers could control the programs at the Yaddo Festivals. Consequently, in their screening for this purpose, these composers shaped a portion, however small, of the American musical scene in the 1930s.

According to the Oberlin College Archives, Lockwood was granted a second-semester leave of absence in 1940 to study with Stravinsky at Harvard University.[29] While the younger composer met unofficially with Stravinsky that year, the plans he made to remain for the semester did not materialize.[30] Still, Lockwood must have been known to this great composer of the twentieth century. According to Robert Craft,

> On May 18, 1945, answering a request from the music section of the Office of War Information, 224 West 57th Street, Stravinsky sent a list of ten composers of "the younger generation" whose music he recommended: [Aaron] Copland, [Harold] Shapero, [David] Diamond, [William] Schuman,

[Walter] Piston, Roy Harris, [Alexei] Haieff, Theodore Chanler, Robert Delaney, and [Normand] Lockwood.[31]

Lockwood's fourteen-year affiliation with Oberlin officially came to a close in 1945, although the first of two consecutive Guggenheim awards prompted him to move to New York earlier, in 1943. That fall, Oberlin granted him a leave of absence with half salary, and the subsequent year, he was granted another leave, this time with no remuneration. Although he did not officially resign from Oberlin until August of 1945, he taught there for the last time in the spring of 1943.

New York, Compositions (1943-53)

A second fruitful period in Lockwood's career began when a fellowship from the John Simon Guggenheim Memorial Foundation precipitated his return to the city of his birth, where he remained until 1953. Only partially supported by the Guggenheim award, another remunerative activity drew his attention upon arrival: composing and arranging for radio. Lockwood credits former Oberlin student Fred Steiner with introducing him to the world of radio composition.[32] Soon a Yaddo performance brought together the several strands of his professional experience in 1946. On September 13-15 of that year, his new work, *Mary, Who Stood in Sorrow*, was performed in a concert of music by members of the American Society of Music Arrangers.[33] Helen Strassburger Boatwright was the featured soloist, and, while the reviewer inaccurately characterized Lockwood as a "formerly" serious composer, he showed his admiration for the piece.

Normand Lockwood, who was a serious composer before he identified himself with the brotherhood of arrangers, contributed a composition that had a good deal more genuine

atmosphere and invention than most of the music of the concert.[34]

Columbia Broadcasting System was a prominent employer
in the New York compositional scene, and Lockwood supplied
original works for their "Columbia Workshop," "Studio One,"
and "The Squibb Show."[35] With regard to this activity Lockwood wrote, "There was an insistence on following certain
formats, and if its composer didn't follow them, he wouldn't
have had the job."[36] In addition to functioning within a strict
format, Lockwood experienced another constraint, one that
was not specifically limited to radio. The economy of means
felt throughout the country during the second world war was
manifested in the small chamber orchestra he encountered at
CBS. This frugality resulted in a sound that appealed to him
and later became evident in his musical preferences, even after
World War II and its resultant lean period were long past.[37]

Arranging resulted in two Columbia recordings from the
1940s, the first being a set of songs performed by the illustrious
baritone, Paul Robeson. For that project, Lockwood arranged
orchestral accompaniments for "Ah Still Suits Me," "Ol' Man
River," and "It Ain't Necessarily So" by George Gershwin. To
complete the recording, Lockwood prepared an arrangement of
the Schubert art song, "An Sylvia." The second recording,
issued in 1948, features Lockwood's arrangements of Irish
songs such as "When Irish Eyes Are Smiling" and "Ballynure
Ballad." The performer was tenor Christopher Lynch, and the
accompaniment was scored for flute, cello, and harp. These
and the Robeson arrangements are cast in the sentimental
popular style that would insure their success; certainly none of
Lockwood's growing independence as a composer is evident.[38]

As had been the case in Oberlin, his many major original
works from the New York period are highlighted by the
various awards bestowed upon him during his residence. The
earliest was in 1945, when he received a commission from the

Alice M. Ditson Fund of Columbia University, given for the "funding of performances, recordings, and publications of works by younger American composers and those older American composers who are not widely known."[39] The resultant work was his first opera, *The Scarecrow*, based on Percy MacKaye's play of the same name. At first, the composer undertook the preparation of the libretto himself, but later was aided by his wife Dorothy, who had majored in journalism at the University of Michigan.

The 1945 advisory committee of the Ditson fund included, among others, Otto Luening, Douglas Moore, and Quincy Porter. Luening remembers,

> At our initial Ditson Committee meeting, Moore and I proposed that we schedule the first Annual Festival of Contemporary American Music at Columbia University for May 1945, devoted to the performance of significant chamber and orchestral compositions by contemporary American composers, and an opera premiere. . . . The programs would be selected by a committee consisting of the advisory committee of the Alice M. Ditson Fund, Pulitzer Prize winners in New York, and the Department of Music of Columbia University.[40]

Others who had received the same honor as Lockwood in previous years included Walter Piston, Leo Sowerby, and Bernard Wagenaar (1942); Randall Thompson and Roger Sessions (1943); and Paul Creston and Gian-Carlo Menotti (1944).[41] Lockwood's inclusion on the Diston/Columbia list of honorees places him among the most successful young composers of the time.

Since 1944, Otto Luening had been director of opera productions at Columbia University, and he directed Lockwood's first work in the genre. Luening remembers, "I was happy when Lockwood told me that I was carrying the torch and keeping the flame burning for American opera, that

I responded to what composers were driving at, and that I understood their music."[42]

The Scarecrow was premiered in May of 1945 at Columbia and received mixed reviews. As evidence of the war's continuing impact on the arts, the male performers who were available for the production were less convincing than the females. Additionally, the Lockwoods' collaboration on the libretto was not wholly successful; MacKaye's voluminous text was only sparingly edited, and often rather awkwardly rhymed. Consequently, the unwieldy libretto overbalanced the music in the final product.

Musically, however, Lockwood's adventurous operatic style foreshadowed his more mature compositions, representing a distinct change from his contemporaneous, less progressive works for choir. *The Scarecrow* is an eclectic, expressive patchwork of octatonicism and bichords; quartal, quintal, and chromatic writing; and sensitive, lyrical melodies. He also exhibited a "good/evil, diatonic/chromatic dichotomy," a technique developed by Rimsky-Korsakov, and perhaps passed on to Boulanger's students via Stravinsky's music.[43] While Lockwood had progressed significantly since his impressionable Paris period, he would take many years to completely digest its strongest influences, especially those of Stravinsky.

Luening supplies further details of *The Scarecrow's* premiere:

> The general reaction was that Lockwood's first operatic venture showed technical mastery, dramatic feeling, and sensitivity for the text that underlined the drama—and that he wrote beautiful melodies. The staging, which projected the fantastic, eerie quality of the work, was a credit to Milton Smith. *The New Yorker* spoke of the work as having "clarity, movement, and sense." My conducting was described as being "highly commendable," "expert," "effective," and "competent."

The now defunct *New York Sun* wrote that it was "prophetic and encouraging to promote the performance of a work based on an American scene, historic event, and folklore." This success made my Columbia teaching job much easier.[44]

New York, Union Theological Seminary and Columbia University

The year 1945 saw Lockwood's appointment to the graduate composition faculty of Columbia University, Columbia College School of General Studies, where he maintained a continuing liaison until 1953. One of a faculty of nine full-time members and twenty-one lecturers, he taught harmony, composition, and orchestration.[45] At Columbia, Lockwood became close friends with department chair and fellow opera composer, Douglas Moore. Many years later, Emily (Mrs. Douglas) Moore characterized Lockwood's contributions to the department in a 1971 letter, written two years after her husband's death.

> I wish I could do Normand Lockwood justice! As a teacher and a composer his personality added luster to his work at Columbia. His own brilliant music was a reflection of his personality. My husband felt this very deeply.[46]

In addition to the part-time position at Columbia, Lockwood was a lecturer in Composition in the School of Sacred Music at Union Theological Seminary from 1946 to 1955. During that period, the student body at Union comprised about 500 students; roughly one-fifth of that number were enrolled in the School of Sacred Music.[47] Lockwood taught only one course per semester, open only to doctoral students, entitled "Sacred Music: Composition and Instrumentation." Typically, about ten students enrolled for the course, all of whom were candidates for the degree Doctor of Sacred Music.[48]

At least two of Lockwood's students at Union Theological Seminary went on to build distinguished careers as musicians. The first, Marilyn Mason, later became chair of the Organ Department at the University of Michigan's School of Music. Mason, a gifted performer and eventually champion of American organ music, is the featured performer in Lockwood's only professionally recorded music for that instrument. The work, *Concerto for Organ and Brasses* (1951), was commissioned by Columbia Broadcasting in 1951 to commemorate ten years of continuous broadcasts by E. Power Biggs. The Ditson Fund sponsored Biggs's initial radio performance of the work on April 27, 1952, part of a series called "Contemporary American Festival of the Air." For this event, Arthur Fiedler conducted the Lockwood concerto.[49]

Mason recorded the work in St. Paul's Chapel on the Columbia University campus in 1953. Subsequently issued on the Remington label, this recording of the concerto accounts, in part, for its popularity with organists.[50] Critics give the work and the recording consistent praise, as seen in these two separate reviews of 1954:

> The Lockwood concerto is boldly dissonant, rough, energetic music in the opening movement, with a serene middle section and a vigorous conclusion. The combination of pipe organ, trumpets, and trombones is surprisingly effective.[51]

> [Both the Lockwood concerto and one by Ulysses Kay on the same recording] are revealed to be well-made, attractive compositions. Of the two the Lockwood . . . seems to be the one of more lasting value. Both performances are first-rate.[52]

Performance programs featuring the first *Concerto* in the Normand Lockwood Archive span the years 1953 to 1984.[53]

Twenty-six years after the composition of the first *Concerto*, Mason commissioned Lockwood to write another work with the same scoring. Their musical collaborations, which began at Union Theological Seminary, thus continued to affect both careers in positive ways.

Austin C. Lovelace was another Lockwood student at Union, one who has since published some 650 works. His recollections include a specific event:

> On the first day [of class] I was the only one who had started any project. So Normand spent the hour mulling over the sixteen pages I had written, humming and sucking on his pipe—with no comments along the way. When he got through, he said, "I think there are a couple of measures which hold promise." Naturally I was crestfallen, for I was sure I had done some great music. Then he talked about studying word rhythms (I ended up with 5/4 [meter] for the opening song . . . as a result), inflections that would indicate rise and fall in the melody, and coloring the harmony to match the moods of the story. It gave me a new insight into letting the words determine the composition—which I continue to do today. . . . Normand didn't require writing in any particular style, but insisted that styles not be mixed in a single work. He gave a lot of freedom, and his comments were always on target. I found him a great teacher.[54]

Lockwood and Lovelace would encounter each other again in Denver, where they continue to share compositional ideas. The former student conducted the premiere of Lockwood's *Acclamations of the Mass* in 1967, and Lockwood wrote his *Canonic Toccata for Two Organs* in 1980 for Lovelace.

New York: Awards and Highlights after *The Scarecrow*

Following the Ditson award for *The Scarecrow*, Lockwood's tenures at Columbia and Union are regularly punctuated by the receipt of several prestigious awards, beginning with the Publication Award of the Society for the Publication of American Music in 1946. The recognized work was his *Third String Quartet* (1938), which was dedicated to the Walden String Quartet of the University of Illinois. That year he also received a Music Award from the National Institute of Arts and Letters. As a result of the NIA&L Award, Lockwood's *Weekend Prelude* (1944) for orchestra was performed at a concert of award recipients' music, in cooperation with the National Orchestral Association. Appearing on the same award-winning program were John Alden Carpenter's *Gitanjali*, Alexei Haieff's *Divertimento*, Ulysses Kay's suite from the ballet *Danse Calinda*, and Arnold Schoenberg's *Theme and Variations, Opus 43B*.[55] Also in 1947 Lockwood received the Ernest Bloch award for his *The Birth of Moses*, written for SSA chorus and piano. The award was bestowed by the United Temple Chorus in New York, and the work was subsequently published by Merrymount Music. Another notable performance took place at the National Gallery of Art in Washington, D. C. For that event, the Gordon Quartet of the Eastman School of Music played Lockwood's *String Quartet Number 6* (1947) along with a work by Randall Thompson. Although the financial climate was uncertain for the arts in the 1940s, Lockwood was consistently reinforced in every area of compositional achievement. Awards usually assured performances, and such distinguished performances often led to publications.

New York: Organizations, Affiliations, and Activities

Lockwood's lasting relationship with the American Composers Alliance (ACA), his primary affiliation, began in the 1940s. Owned and operated by composers, ACA was founded in 1938 by Copland, Thomson, Riegger, and others to promote the interests of American composers. Lockwood served on the Board of Governors, various committees, and was Vice-President from 1947 to 1951. The Alliance not only provided valuable contact with peer composers, but has also served as the repository and rental agency for many of his works.

In 1948 Lockwood was also first Vice-President of the National Association for American Composers and Conductors. Founded by conductor Henry Hadley in 1933, NAACC was re-organized in 1975 and is now known as the National Association of Composers-USA. The goal of the organization was and is to facilitate performances of works by native composers and to promote cooperation between composers and conductors. Like Yaddo, ACA and NAACC provided supportive forums for composers of contemporary music in the United States, perhaps modeled after groups such as the Société Nationale de Musique Française in late nineteenth-century Paris.

Lockwood's report of the Committee on Programs (1948) states the aims of ACA succinctly:

> From each this participation was an expression of faith in, and acceptance of, American music, and a labor of love in its behalf.
>
> It has been the practice of this and former Committees to invite any and all born or naturalized American composers to submit published and unpublished works for their consideration, and to select for public performance music of non-members as well as that of members of the Association. It is hoped that another series of concerts such as these may take

place beginning next Autumn, and that the representation both
of composer-members and of non-members will be wide geographically, and varied from the standpoint of musical style
and type of work.[56]

Although Lockwood often denies having been a "prophet of
American music,"[57] his involvement in ACA and NAACC
attests to his interest in the art of his native country.

Musicologist and critic Oliver Daniel provides further
evidence of Lockwood's interest in ACA in a 1979 letter:

> I'm sure you realize it was you and Otto [Luening] who
> made one of the most profound changes in my life. The time
> when the two of you sounded me out about ACA really altered
> everything. And for that I am eternally grateful.
>
> If I were in charge of things, I would not only give you a
> Doctorate but I would give you a Pulitzer Prize and a Nobel
> one to boot. You deserve them both.[58]

Lockwood's friendship with Daniel began through CBS (Columbia) radio. Daniel was director of educational radio at the
network and directed several of the shows for which Lockwood
composed music. Daniel's longstanding interest in American
music may have been significantly influenced by the 1940s visit
from Lockwood and Luening. Lockwood recalls working
"very hard to convince him to accept a leadership position in
ACA."[59]

In 1955 Daniel assessed his friend's music in the *American
Composers Alliance Bulletin.*

> Few composers today can turn out a song or chorus with the
> artistry of Normand Lockwood. Some are like vintage wines;
> but choruses and songs are not the only works in which Lock-
> wood has exhibited mastery. His *Concerto for Organ and
> Brasses* is one of the most successful works in this medium, and

he achieves at moments the shining quality which one finds in the best works of Gabrieli. Listen to a work by Gabrieli and one by Lockwood and you will know what I mean. Fluent, rhythmical, free-flowing melodies spill out in an abundance that can be found only where natural talent is similarly abundant. With such capacity Lockwood is highly endowed.[60]

Lockwood's quick wit, sophistication, and warm sensitivity made him a valued friend of many New York musicians. Beveridge Webster, who joined the piano faculty of the Juilliard School in 1946, played his *Sonata* (1935) at a concert of the Columbia University Composer's Forum in 1947. Years later, Webster congratulated Lockwood on his honorary doctorate in a delightfully abstract, tongue-in-cheek letter. Webster, who held several honorary degrees himself, also provided a glimpse of the friendship which began in New York.

Heard rumor floating, flowing, flying, fleeting—belated Doctorate award to be Honorably conferred upon the still undoctored N. Lockwood. If rumor substantiated, will his Doctor-rate [sic] soon thereafter elevate to truly inflationary standard. Again hopefully, may this rumor be liable to reliability, and may we greet you NOT as Doctor-to-be-or-not-to-be, but welcome you, O worthy fellow sufferer to the very Elite of the Academe.... That music (and even other alleged Arts) may yet ever die by Degrees, nor yet ever die, due to (even 2) too many Doctors![61]

Commuting Years: Princeton, New York, and New Haven (1948-53)

A September 16, 1948 press release in Lockwood's personnel file at Oberlin College announced that he had recently been appointed head of the Composition and Theory Departments of Westminster Choir College.[62]   At that time, WCC was a thriving school, with a student body of over four hundred. A prestigious choir school, the Westminster group appeared in the 1930s and 1940s in concerts and recordings with great conductors such as Leopold Stokowski, John Barbirolli, Arturo Toscannini, Sergei Rachmaninoff, Bruno Walter, Artur Rodzinsky, Eugene Ormandy, and Charles Munch.[63] As head of the Theory and Composition Departments, Lockwood indirectly succeeded Roy Harris, who held the position from 1934 to 1938. During Lockwood's two years there, the Choir College graduated 161 with a baccalaureate degree, and forty with a Master of Music degree. The reputation of Westminster Choir College was near its zenith.

Lockwood lived in Princeton from 1948 until the spring of 1950, and as he remembers, he made a great many trips to New York, continuing his part-time responsibilities at Columbia University and Union Seminary.

> Once . . . I had driven from Princeton to New York for my composition teaching at Columbia, and, thinking the next day that I'd taken the train, I returned by train to Princeton, reporting to the police that my car had been stolen from the Princeton station parking lot. The next day I got to thinking, and, sure enough, I'd driven to New York the day before. When I apologized to the police they said, "Oh, that's all right, it happens all the time." I felt more crushed than exonerated.[64]

Once moved back to New York in 1950, he also taught for one semester at Queens College in New York. For the school year 1952-53 he traveled to New Haven, Connecticut, for an adjunct teaching position at Yale University. There he held the position of Visiting Lecturer in the Theory of Music, filling Quincy Porter's position during a sabbatical. At that time, Yale's School of Music consisted of 105 undergraduates and twenty-four students in the master's program. During his year

there, Lockwood taught counterpoint and fugue in the class-
room, and composition in the studio. Perhaps more important
than the teaching position were the early professional alliances
he developed at Yale. Members of the Theory Department
that year included Richard Donovan, Quincy Porter, and
Howard Boatwright.[65] Paul Hindemith was also listed on the
theory faculty, and although he was not in residence in 1952-53,
Lockwood met him on one occasion.[66]

In 1971, Lockwood's former graduate assistant in counterpoint at Yale, Robert MacKinnon, wrote Lockwood from his
faculty position at Stanford University in California:

> To recite the many ways you have influenced my musical life
> would take pages. Suffice it to say that you were, and still are,
> a guide-line kind of "presence" that is always hanging around to
> pester me whenever I write or arrange music. All I have to do
> is think how delighted you would be or how disgusted you
> would be, and I automatically leave it in or tear it all up and
> start over. If it is the latter, I curse you up and down for being
> such a fuss-pot. Then later I fall in love with the finished prod-
> uct, and of course forgive you with great magnanimity.[67]

As busy as these transitional years seem to have been, Lockwood still composed noteworthy music, including *Closing
Doxology* (1950) for SATB choir and concert band, later
published by Broude Bros.; *Elegy for a Hero* (1951), for SAT-
BarB divisi choir and based on another Whitman text; and
Prairie (1952), a setting of Carl Sandburg's long narrative poem
for SATB choir and orchestra. The latter two, utilizing texts by
famous American poets, are among the most successful works
from Lockwood's early career.

Elegy for a Hero was commissioned by Dr. Wilfred C. Bain
for the Indiana University Singers in 1951, and subsequently
published in 1962 by Shawnee Press. The twenty-minute work
was originally entitled *Memories of President Lincoln*, after the

Walt Whitman original. Fearing negative repercussions in the South as a result of the title, the management of Shawnee Press suggested the name change and Lockwood consented. Whether or not the country's civil rights issues would have affected its acceptance is not known; certainly, the new name did not negatively affect the success of the work. Under the direction of Lara Hoggard, the Fred Waring Glee Club toured the work in the South in 1962 without mishap.[68]

Whitman's poetry has motivated Lockwood to compose his finest secular works, and this piece is among the best the combination has yielded. Lockwood was more active in the choral genre in the 1950s than in any other decade, honing his skills to best express his musical intent. The focus on choral music resulted in a distinctive choral style, one that is well-suited to the simplicity and immediacy of Whitman's poetry. The style is characterized by rich, consonant harmonies, close-position voicing, and largely homophonic textures. Additionally, words are set with natural word-stress rhythms, that is, with accents and rhythms as close to the spoken word as possible.

Elegy is distinctive because the harmonic framework is spiced with occasional dissonant harmony and bichords to enhance the more pervasive consonant writing. Further departing from his more predictable style, Lockwood wrote a fugal chorus in the final section of the work. For the composer, the words were equal to the music in importance, and elaborate polyphony throughout the cantata would have interfered with the presentation of the text. His use of polyphonic writing in most choral works of the period is similarly restricted.

Lockwood's best-known, large-scale, secular choral work is *Prairie* (1952), commissioned by the University of Michigan Musical Society. Lasting about thirty minutes in performance, it is written in eleven continuous sections. In *Prairie*, the chorus serves as the solo vocal instrument, an arrangement that distinguishes the work from the later oratorios of the 1950s, in which solo vocalists are featured. Based on the Carl Sandburg poem of the same name, *Prairie* features mostly consonant harmonies, in keeping with the homespun quality of the text.

A 1971 letter from Charles A. Sink, President Emeritus of the commissioning organization, recalls that the premiere at the University's May Festival took place before an audience of five thousand.[69] The event, conducted by Thor Johnson, generated considerable enthusiasm among reviewers.

> The choral lines are beautifully written, and were given splendid voice by the Choral Union. . . . The music is, in the main, descriptive of the poem, with outright imitative effects at times. Notable among these was the railroad sequence, filled with the excitement of soaring voices over a steady, rhythmic beat.[70]

Another critic made a prediction for the future of *Prairie*.

> This work will inevitably find favor with choruses. Lockwood has—because of the nature of the poem—written in a style which suggests American folk music in many of its passages. But he hasn't run this Americana into the ground.
>
> There is enough individuality to make it interesting, appealing, and quite exciting. The orchestration is extremely ingenious and contains a short section of the most convincing musical imitation of a railroad train we've ever heard.[71]

Many noteworthy musicians, including Yehudi Menuhin, attended the reception following *Prairie's* premiere. Menuhin was a favorite associate of Nadia Boulanger at this time, and had undoubtedly heard of Lockwood's music through her. Lockwood's daughter Heidi recalls her own excitement at the reception, and especially Menuhin's presence. Apparently, the famous violinist took the time to engage the precocious fourteen-year-old in an extended artistic conversation. Heidi Lockwood considers that discourse a significant influence in her eventual career as a painter. She also remembers that this event was one of many that brought her in contact with the most notable musicians in the country.[72]

Despite its high quality and critical success at the premiere, *Prairie* has not been published, and consequently, its performances have been limited to the initial one, and another a few years later at Miami University of Oxford, Ohio.[73] Perhaps this unfortunate circumstance stems from the fact that publishers were unwilling to make commitments to large-scale works in the 1950s; Lockwood's success with published octavos supports this hypothesis.

While in Princeton, Lockwood also composed the work so inextricably linked with Marilyn Mason, the *Concerto for Organ and Brasses*. His reputation must have been strong, indeed, for Columbia Broadcasting Service to seek him for the commission. Because the *Concerto* was his first work for the organ, CBS necessarily relied upon his expertise in other genres in making their decision. In contrast to *Prairie*, the publication of the *Concerto* has made it accessible, and therefore, has assured many performances.

Departure from the Northeast and Interim (1953-59)

After five years in which his teaching was divided among several schools, the prospect of chairing the small Music Department at San Antonio's Trinity University must have been attractive to Lockwood. Twenty-one years had passed since Lockwood had acquired his first teaching position at Oberlin, and in those years he had found fulfillment in many areas: teaching positions, friends, commissions, performances, and offices and memberships in Yaddo, ACA, and NAACC. A move to San Antonio must have seemed the next logical step in establishing a national reputation. However, he would find the special blend of activities he was leaving behind—especially in the hub of professional composition, New York—hard to duplicate elsewhere. His departure from the East Coast in 1953 began an eight-year, nomadic period in which he continued to move frequently from job to job.

Lockwood also underwent significant changes in his personal life beginning in 1953. By then, his relationship with his wife had begun to show obvious signs of disintegration. In fact, the San Antonio period signals the close of Lockwood's life with Dorothy Sanders Lockwood, although they would remain legally married until 1976. Yet another crisis in the composer's life was the 1954 death of his lifelong mentor, Raymond Edmonds. Edmonds had been the caretaker of the family property in Keene Valley, New York, for the entire span of Lockwood's life. This old woodsman, part American Indian, had been a treasured friend during Normand Lockwood's childhood, providing an essential counterpart to the stern paternal figure of Samuel Lockwood. Heidi Lockwood remembers that Edmonds's death affected her father deeply, and she still remembers the significance with which Lockwood spoke the words, "Something has ended."[74] Indeed, Lockwood was at a crossroads in his life. With his move to San Antonio, Lockwood had effectively isolated himself from his place of birth, his family, and his lifelong friends. As a result, he focused his energy almost solely on his professional life.

Although the administrative duties at Trinity must have kept him busier in the work place than he had been previously, Lockwood continued to produce new music, relying especially on his skills as a choral composer. From 1953 to 1956, many octavo-sized sacred works augmented his published repertoire. Southern Music Company and Shawnee Press published the greatest number, totaling four and three, respectively. American Music Publishers printed a solo song and a set of Christmas carols, while Theodore Presser and Rongwen Music brought out one publication each. These works not only serve the purpose of documenting Lockwood's continued productivity in the vocal genres, they also indicate the preferences of the publishing industry for small-scale compositions. While Lockwood had clearly advanced beyond his prevalent choral style in *Elegy for a Hero*, these shorter works dating from the Texas period reflect his earlier choral language.

Probably his best known choral work from the Texas period is a setting of Whitman's *I Hear America Singing*, a colorful, evocative list of things American. Premiered at the Southwestern Symposium of Contemporary American Music in April of 1954, it is one of Lockwood's personal favorites. The musical language is again that of his earlier, tonal idiom, and its structure is episodic, following the form of Whitman's descriptive, catalog approach the American way of life. Lockwood's penchant for subtle text painting found perfect application in this text which calls forth images that range from motherhood to the splendors of nature.

Also in San Antonio, Lockwood not only composed, but conducted the premiere of his *Magnificat* for soprano, orchestra and chorus on December 5, 1954.[75] In addition, he continued to teach composition students, one of whom was Robert Washburn, now Dean Emeritus and Professor of Music at Potsdam College of the State University of New York, who remembers,

> I was most impressed by his professionalism, his concern for even the tiniest detail in the compositional process (quite likely a Boulanger carry-over) and, even though he could be thoroughly and honestly "academic" it was never the principal impact of his teaching. I believe he has a unique combination of stressing the importance of discipline and at the same time letting the creative imagination be the most important factor.
>
> . . . I think he has had a personal commitment to being a helpful and formative influence in his students' development.[76]

Washburn's sentiment is shared by the many former students who contributed to Lockwood's commemorative album at the University of Denver.

Chapter Four

Mid-Career

Wyoming (1955-57)

When his tenure at Trinity University was completed in 1955, Normand Lockwood moved to Laramie, Wyoming, with the express intent of obtaining a divorce from his wife of nearly thirty years.[1] Negotiations took place between Laramie and New York, and parental and financial issues arose that made it impossible for Dorothy and Normand Lockwood to reach a mutually agreeable settlement. On the advice of his attorney, Lockwood turned to other pursuits. For a divorce, he would have to wait for Dorothy Lockwood's initiation, which did not occur until 1976.

Commissions, royalties, and an inheritance from his late mother's estate enabled Lockwood to live in Laramie without the financial support of a teaching position. This absence of academic responsibilities provided him with the opportunity to further focus and re-organize the elements of his life and career. He composed almost without interruption, as steady publication of his sacred choral works kept Lockwood's name and music before the public, and fueled his own personal momentum.

Very early in this two-year hiatus from teaching, Lockwood was contacted by the National Council of Churches and Berea College of Kentucky, and the wheels were set in motion for his first oratorio. Completed in 1956, the work commemorated the centennial of the college, with particular attention to its motto: "God Hath Made of One Blood All Nations of Men." The following year, *Children of God*, as the oratorio was called, was aptly described as his "magnum opus to date."[2] The oratorio is doubly important for its scope and for the fact that it marks the final adoption of Lockwood's mature choral style. Choral works were no longer insulated from his most modern language; instead, the oratorio combines tone rows with the more familiar octatonicism, bichords, and modality that he inherited from Stravinsky—elements that had been standard in the instrumental works before 1956.

The Biblical text for this ninety-minute work was compiled by Clara Chassel Cooper, then Professor of Psychology at Berea College. In a letter of 1971, she characterized her participation as "probably the most personally satisfying creative effort of my life," and went on to say,

> The Biblical text was compiled from the Revised Standard Version and utilizes more than two hundred verses from the Old and New Testaments. The work consists of two parts: "Am I My Brother's Keeper?" based on selections from the Old Testament; Part Two is entitled "Who Is My Neighbor?" based on selections from the New Testament.
>
> Our Berea College Oratorio Choir was thrilled to have Mr. Lockwood present in Cincinnati in February, 1957, for the initial performance of Part One with the Cincinnati Symphony Orchestra under the direction of Thor Johnson; and likewise to have him present in Berea the following May for their par-

ticipation in the premiere of the entire work with members of
the Louisville Orchestra under the direction of Rolf E. Hovey.

. . . As our Berea College Dean Louis Smith once remarked,
"The message of the oratorio is not only timely; it is also
timeless."[3]

Children of God, with its relatively progressive use of harmonic and melodic tritones, octatonic and whole-tone scales,
and Phrygian mode, provided quite a performance challenge
for the choir of this small liberal arts college in Kentucky.
Nevertheless, Rolf E. Hovey, the group's conductor and chair
of the Music Department, saw great artistry in the oratorio.
He later became an unofficial champion of *Children of God*,
arranging subsequent performances at a 1967 college presiden-
tial inauguration, and at graduation ceremonies in 1972 and
1974.

By the time of the initial performance of the oratorio, Thor
Johnson was an important name in the field of American
music. One of the first native conductors to direct a major
American orchestra, Johnson made a commitment to large-
scale and little-known works during his stay in Cincinnati from
1947 to 1958. Johnson's continuing interest in Lockwood's
music reflected his overriding concern for high-quality presentations of native compositions.[4] He conducted other Lockwood works such as *Prairie* at the Ann Arbor May Festival
during his more than twenty years as conductor of the University of Michigan Choral Union. On these occasions the
Michigan group was regularly joined by the Philadelphia
Orchestra.[5]

In *Children of God*, Lockwood structured a wide array of
materials in an episodic format, and the result is a dramatically
engaging work. This opus, integrating his old and new languages, was somewhat of an uncertainty for the composer. In
the 1950s, few choirs programmed and performed "new" music

Featured artists following the Cincinnati premiere of Lockwood's *Children of God* on February 1, 1957: (L to R) Thor Johnson, Normand Lockwood, pianist Gina Bachauer (appearing separately on the same Cincinnati Symphony Orchestra Program), Clara Chassell Cooper (librettist, *Children of God*), and Rolf E. Hovey (Director of the Berea College Department of Music). Photo courtesy Vona Lockwood.

regularly, especially in the less urban areas of the country. A measure of the aesthetic climate in mid-1950s is suggested by the choruses excerpted from *Children of God* that were published in octavo form by Choral Services, Inc.[6] While all six choruses are beautiful, none feature Lockwood's newer language; in fact, four of them are prime examples of his most consonant 1930s style. *Children of God* marks a watershed in Lockwood's career—in spite of unenthusiastic critical response and conservative publishers, the composer would rarely, if ever, return to the more conservative style that had ensured his popular success for two decades. Beginning in 1956, he consistently blended all elements of his artistic repertoire in the choral works; consequently, his oeuvre as a whole became more unified in style.

The next year, 1957, gave him a second opportunity to refine his new choral language. His second oratorio, *Light Out of Darkness*, was commissioned by Robert I. Millonzi, the president of the board of the Buffalo, New York, Philharmonic Society. Directed by Josef Krips, the premiere took place on February 18, 1958, at Kleinhans Music Hall in Buffalo. The composer found all aspects of Krips's conducting, and especially his tempo choices, to be appropriate and accurate.[7] Krips was also happy with the work and the recording, as his self-effacing letter of November 26, 1958 indicates:

> Well, the recording of your great work is inadequate as nearly all recordings of "live performances" are. But our performance—I had the feeling—was good. We put our souls into it and we all—chorus, orchestra, the soloist, and I myself—felt the *Light Out of Darkness* is a great, a truly great work. 'Per aspera ad astra.' [Through striving, to the heavens.]
>
> What have you done beside that, Mr. Lockwood? You know, I think you could set in music the greatest words in this country ever spoken: Lincoln's Gettysburg address for Chorus and Baryton Solo and Orchestra.[8]

Lockwood eventually took up Krips's suggestion and produced a version of Lincoln's famous speech in 1982. *Thought of Him I Love* is scored for children's choir, narrator/baritone, and chamber orchestra. The composer chose "Memories of President Lincoln" by Walt Whitman, another Lincoln advocate, as supplemental texts.[9]

In contrast to *Children of God*, Lockwood had sole responsibility for the choice and usage of text in his second oratorio. Consequently, words and music are more gracefully united in *Light Out of Darkness*. Another contributing factor to the success of *Light Out of Darkness* was the performance of the Chinese baritone, Yi-Kwei Sze, who, Lockwood felt, gave an especially inspiring performance in the central role.[10]

The second year he was in Laramie, a volume of the *American Composers Alliance Bulletin* was dedicated to Lockwood's music. Choral conductor and composer George Lynn, a friend from Lockwood's Westminster Choir College days, wrote an article entitled "Normand Lockwood and Choral Music," and John McDowell, the editor of the *Bulletin*, contributed another with the title "A Note on Some Facets of Normand Lockwood's Music." Also included in the volume was a list of his principal works, including three orchestral works, nine oratorios or large choral works, one opera, twenty-six choral works, fourteen chamber works, twelve vocal works, and four works for children. At that point, the composer's works had been published by twenty establishments.[11] Lockwood may have been more isolated from ACA than he had been in New York, but his music was still considered to be of great consequence in the organization.

While in Laramie, Lockwood met the woman who would eventually become his second wife, Vona K. Swedell. A native of Chester, Nebraska, Swedell had pursued a colorful career in several departments of the United States government before meeting Lockwood. After working at the Pentagon and in the office of an Air Force Chief of Staff, Swedell accepted a position as executive secretary for a U. S. senior official to NATO in London, where she resided until 1956. In that year she began her job as executive secretary to the Executive Director of the Alumni Association at the University of Wyoming in Laramie, where she first met Normand Lockwood. In spite of the limits imposed by his unresolved first marriage, Swedell and Lockwood formed a liaison that endured the nearly twenty years between their first meeting and their eventual marriage in 1976. She would become Lockwood's strongest advocate in the years preceding and subsequent to their marriage.

The University of Oregon (1957-58)

Normand Lockwood returned to higher education in 1957, when he spent one academic year as visiting professor in theory and composition at the University of Oregon. Only two works are extant from the period, the first being *Triptych to the Memory of W. R. B. Willcox* (1958). Willcox had been head of the Architecture Department at the University of Oregon prior to Lockwood's short tenure there. Commissioned by the School of Architecture, the work was subsequently withdrawn from the files of the American Composers Alliance, but because it represents Lockwood's only orchestral work from the 1950s, *Triptych* is historically important.

Large-scale choral works stemming from the Oregon period include *The Holy Birth, Jesus the King,* and *Old Hundredth Cantata* for SATB choir, children's choir, and orchestra. Jointly commissioned by several Presbyterian Churches in Des Moines, Iowa, *Old Hundredth Cantata* was initiated by choral director John Dexter.[12] By the time of his letter to Lockwood in 1971, Dexter was director of choral ensembles at the Eastman School of Music. He typified Lockwood's method of friendship with great warmth and eloquence.

Aside from the fact that you introduced me to Heyward pipe tobacco, that you write music that always comes off effectively (your conductors bless you), and that you can be cornered into copying parts by commission-poor organists, your happy facility to make one feel at ease in roughly five minutes would set you apart from other professionals I have known, old friend. It's quite unconscious, I suspect. It stems from a sureness about yourself as a person, as an artist, on the one hand, and from an uncommon concern for another's questions about themselves, about art, about life in general on the other. A rare combination this—artistic integrity wedded to a humanity that instantly attracts. It indelibly impresses Normand into one's heart and mind. And a more welcome impression I can't imagine.[13]

Dexter's words are a commentary on Lockwood's sincere interest in the concerns of others, even if the association is brief.

Now on the faculty of the University of New Mexico, former Oregon student William Wood recalls that Lockwood's 1950s teaching method was still based on the principle of self-discovery.

My work with Normand that school year was in private composition lessons and sixteenth-century counterpoint. I wrote a number of chamber music pieces and a master's thesis—a *Passacaglia for Band.* Normand and I spent a lot of time together outside of school talking about music, art and life in general. He even took me to meet his old friend Roy Harris, who was lecturing at Lewis and Clark College.

Normand's teaching style was quite simple; while you were with him in the studio you weren't aware that he was "teaching." He would suggest several ways with which to solve a particular compositional problem—leaving the final choices to you. You began to "see" what you were doing and to hear the page. He made sure that you were sure of the results . . . that it was exactly what you wanted. You gradually realized that you were writing your own music— not what someone else tells you to put down . . . You find out what composing is about with this kind of guidance.[14]

Although years of experience must surely have modified Lockwood's teaching style over his career, his approach to students seemed always to revolve around a sincere respect for their innate compositional impulses. Wood's letter indicates that Lockwood's style of problem solving, one in which the students became accountable for their own musical choices, helped him to find and believe in his own distinctive artistic language.

Return to Wyoming (1958-60)

After his year in Eugene, Oregon, the composer returned to Laramie in 1958, where he soon made his first contact with the University of Denver (DU), his longest institutional affiliate. In his words,

My first contact with DU occurred in 1959 when I was asked if I would be interested in composing a large work for the University's presentation before the Methodist Quadrennial Conference held in Denver. *Land of Promise* is a hybrid of oratorio and opera. I was living in Wyoming at the time where, during its composition, I could confer frequently, as I did, with Dr. [Russell] Porter and Dr. Roger Dexter Fee who coordinated the musical forces and who conducted the performances at Denver City Auditorium Theater, April 30 and May 2, 1960.[15]

This work would mark the beginning of a long and fruitful collaboration, not only with the University of Denver, but also

with librettist Russell Porter of the University's Drama
Department. Another prominent work from his second
Laramie period is *Darest Thou Now, O Soul*(1959), a massive
work for three choirs on a text by Whitman, which was per-
formed in May by the George Lynn Singers, the Colorado
State University Choir, and the University of Denver Choir.
The performance was conducted by Saul Caston, then maestro
of the Denver Symphony Orchestra.

During those early Denver years, before Lockwood moved
his residence from Laramie, many friendships were initiated.
One such contact was Daniel Moe, who began his tenure as
choral director at the University of Denver in 1953. Moe
prepared the University of Denver choir for the performance of
Darest Thou Now, O Soul, and remembered another interac-
tion with Lockwood.

> I was still wet behind the ears when I met Normand Lock-
> wood at the home of George Lynn in Denver. In the course of
> the evening, one of us suggested that the three of us should get
> together to talk about our compositions on a somewhat regular
> basis, to which we all agreed. We subsequently met in George
> Lynn's studio, and on one occasion I brought a new work of
> mine, *Hosanna to the Son of David*. Normand suggested a
> rhythmic change of one tiny note, adding a syncopation on the
> word "the" in measure seven. Without it, the work might have
> been a very boring piece, but as it is, it has sold over 200,000
> copies.
>
> That's the essence of what I gained from knowing Normand
> Lockwood. As a young composer, I thought that when I wrote
> a double bar, the piece was finished. Normand showed me the
> value of continuous revision.[16]

Lockwood's friendship with Moe illustrates one of the many
symmetries evident in the elder composer's life. At the time of
this writing, Daniel Moe was in his nineteenth year as choral

conductor of the Oberlin College Conservatory of Music, the location of Normand Lockwood's first academic position.

In 1959, the year *Darest Thou Now, O Soul* was composed, Lockwood's *Clarinet Quintet* was commissioned by the Cleveland Chamber Music Society. The quintet was premiered in 1960 by clarinetist George Silfies of the Cleveland Orchestra and the Oberlin Quartet at the Cleveland May Festival of Contemporary Music. Critic Frank Hruby was effusive in his praise.

> This is a splendid work, decidedly contemplative in nature and yet quite intense. There is admirable writing for clarinet in it, seemingly as totally integrated with the strings as a clarinet can be. The work was commissioned for the festival by the Cleveland Museum's very eager and active Chamber Music Society.[17]

During his second stay in Laramie, Lockwood's compositional opportunities were quite diverse, allowing him to maintain his eclectic tastes and at the same time forge new links with Denver, his imminent new home.

The University of Hawaii (1960-61)

In the summer of 1960 Lockwood was appointed a visiting faculty member at the University of Denver, but before anchoring finally in that city, one last adjunct teaching position caused him to cross the Pacific Ocean, to the University of Hawaii. Disliking the inherent isolation of this place, he was occupied by little other than teaching and composing during that year. In fact, he never left the island of Oahu.

In an unsigned article for the Honolulu *Star-Bulletin,* a reporter indicated the extent of Lockwood's national reputation in 1960.

The University of Hawaii's Music Department . . . has received news of further prestige with the announcement that one of the nation's better known composers will join the departmental staff for the 1960-61 academic year.

Action on Thursday by the Board of Regents confirmed the appointment of Normand Lockwood as visiting professor in composition and counterpoint.[18]

His compositional efforts were focused on a second collaboration with Russell Porter for the University of Denver, namely the opera *Early Dawn*. In 1957 Porter had written and presented a concert reading by the same name which represented twenty years of his own research and reflection. Yet, despite its favorable reception at the University of Denver, the playwright "kept hearing the music."[19] In 1960 the composer read *Early Dawn* for the first time. In characteristic response to a new compositional challenge, Lockwood said, "I agreed with him that it had a great potential for opera. I jumped at the chance to write the music for it."[20]

The collaborative effort of creating *Early Dawn* is documented in frequent letters between Lockwood, then in Honolulu, and Porter in Denver.[21] Porter considered the composer to be the expert on opera and clearly deferred to the latter's skills, as seen in an undated letter: "As always, of course, feed me your reactions and fear not making me face the whole bloody business all over again if you think this is wrong."[22] Lockwood, as always, seems to have been guided by his innate sense of propriety in music, as Porter's letter from January of 1961 indicates.

I gladly yield to your manipulation of the lines to fit the music and think you have done a great job of preserving the feel of the material. . . .

The only place where I bleed a little is in the omission of the final aria by Jeffry. There thrives within me probably a corny braggadocio which makes me thoroughly love the "and God is dead, etc. etc." and on the hills the devil's camp fires burn.[23]

Lockwood, however, remained firm in his argument that the images had not been introduced earlier and would therefore clutter the final, dramatic impact of the opera.

Dear Russ, I know you'd wince at 'the end.' I tell you I did some tussling with it . . . but this is why I finally arrived at doing it the way I did; that your final lines for Jeff . . . would not carry, sung. Here is where, to my way of thinking, opera falls short of play. Those lines, were they introduced, [would have no] business being sung. No digressions. No refinements or intensifications embodying the slightest new angle. No God. No devil. No campfires. I am sorry as the devil . . . with this explanation goes my humblest apology.[24]

Lockwood's musical preoccupation seemed to be far removed from Honolulu that year, involved as he was with the new Denver project. Yet, his music made a memorable impact at the University of Hawaii, as related by former colleague, Norman D. Rian.

For many years I admired you and not from afar, because it was through your music that I learned to know you. And then there was that glorious and inspiring year for me when you were our visiting composer-in-residence at the University of Hawaii and I did have the opportunity to study with you. May you live and write forever.[25]

In addition to *Early Dawn*, Lockwood composed *O Lord, Our Lord* (1960) for Tenor and Strings during his year of residence at the University of Hawaii, and dedicated the work to the Music Department.

By 1960 the composer's published works exceeded one hundred in number, including five orchestral works, one work for band, fifteen larger choral works, forty-four anthem-sized works, four children's records (e. g., *Babar*, produced by the Franson Corporation), and two theater works.[26] The last category includes a lost work, *Sons of Coronado* (1959), which incorporates incidental and ballet music commissioned by the Cultural Institute of Spain in America.

The University of Denver, Operatic Works (1961-74)

Soon after his return to Denver in 1961, a teaching position with equal responsibilities to the Music and Drama Departments was offered the composer. At that time, the University of Denver's enrollment was around 6500, which included 138 undergraduate and thirty-nine graduate music majors in the Lamont School of Music.[27] Lockwood's position with the school, a rank of Associate Professor and title of Composer-in-Residence, provided the perfect opportunity to compose dramatic music, and he was soon busy on the third Lockwood/Porter joint effort, *The Wizards of Balizar*. Subtitled "A Comic Fantasy," the work is a lighthearted and fanciful story involving wizards, potions, jewels, and kings. The libretto is the type of which musical comedies are made, but the musical language often progresses from mild to strong dissonance—one of the reasons the work remains within the realm of "art" music.

The work opened on August 1, 1962, at the University's Little Theater. Three of its principal actors came from Colorado's Central City Opera Company, the group which had premiered Douglas Moore's *The Ballad of Baby Doe* six years earlier. The cast of *The Wizards of Balizar* is small, with only six leads and a miniature chorus. Appropriately for a chamber opera, Lockwood wrote for a small orchestra of thirteen players, including flute, oboe, clarinet, bassoon, trumpet, horn, strings, and two percussion parts. No act divisions are delineated in the one hour, forty-five minute work. One newspaper review depicted Lockwood's music as distinctive:

> Lockwood's music was written for a small orchestra . . . and though it starts with a sinuous, Egyptian atmosphere, [it] quickly develops its own pungent harmonies and clear orchestration.
> Even in broad moments of choral enthusiasm the orchestration contains color and rhythm that keep the powder dry.[28]

The composer and librettist would write two other works together, *No More from Thrones* (1962), a drama with music, and the opera *The Hanging Judge* (1964). Lockwood and Porter thus traversed many areas of dramatic terrain together: serious opera, comedy, and a play with music. Their friendship and their joint professional accomplishments were equally cherished by both parties, as Porter emphasized in this letter from 1971.

> I'll be damned if I know whether I admire you most as a person or as an artist. The problem is that over the last decade I have had such a marvelous experience with you in both roles that I would boggle at any necessity to make a choice.
> The event which first brought you here—*Land of Promise*—was, as it turns out, such a happy and lucky event for the University that it almost "persuadeth me to be a Methodist." And I think some of the most rewarding moments of my life were in the years that followed, as we worked together on so many things. I think that I most regret about the demands of the current scene is that they have literally precluded any continuing work in a job which I do dearly love and with a person by whom I am so stimulated. But there are years ahead and we'll get back together again![29]

As it turned out, *The Hanging Judge* would be their final collaboration, although Lockwood wrote music for the stage on two other occasions.

In 1964 the National Opera Association commissioned a new work for its annual convention to be held in Denver. The occasion brought about Lockwood's first collaboration with Donald Sutherland, then faculty member in the Classics Department at the University of Colorado at Boulder. Lockwood remembers Sutherland as a man of sharp wit, with a keen sense of nuance and a love for words.[30]

The opera *Requiem for a Rich Young Man* represents Lockwood's most successful operatic balance of text and music to date. The scope is small; the story itself is limited to a few ideas, presented by characters who, because of the satirical nature of the play, appear more as caricatures than as people. The music is sprinkled with programmatic commentary on the libretto, as in the recurrent "bump-and-grind" music suggesting the particular way in which the bereaved might console each other.

The second and last Lockwood/Sutherland combination was entitled *My Sister, My Spouse* (1972), a verse-drama with music. The music represents no more than one sixth of the total work and is therefore less integral to the drama than in opera. However, the play eventually provided creative material for another musical work. Later the same year, Lockwood excerpted a powerful portion of the text, "The Dialogue of Abraham and Isaac," and wrote a version for solo voice and piano.

Normand Lockwood, Genevieve McGiffert (director), and Donald
Sutherland (librettist) at the time of the 1964 premiere of *Requiem for
a Rich Young Man*. Photo courtesy of the Normand Lockwood
Archive.

The University of Denver, Non-Operatic Works

Lockwood retired from the University of Denver in 1974 as Professor Emeritus. In his thirteen-year tenure there, he had found the environment conducive both to composition and to performance of his new works. Appearing in all genres, not just opera, Lockwood's music exhibited an increased maturity and refinement. Advances in his operatic works took the form of musical contributions to the multi-dimensionality of the characters, and logically-evolved dramatic transitions. Other stylistic developments are equally linked to specific genres; for example, in the 1960s he began to incorporate extended serial procedures in the chamber genre, especially in the works for winds. *Sonata Fantasia* (1964) for accordion is his most complex serial work of the period. Commissioned by the American Accordion Association, it remains an important contemporary work for this instrument.

The choral genre is represented by no fewer than four important works, including a rescoring of his *Carol Fantasy* (1949), originally for SATB choir and orchestra, for SATB and band. One of his best-known pieces, this twenty-three minute work has been performed as far away as Jakarta, Indonesia.[31] Lockwood was also sought for commissions such as the one that initiated his *Choreographic Cantata* (1968) by the Reuter Organ Corporation and the National Meeting of the American Guild of Organists. The work was published by the Augsburg Publishing House in 1970.

Similarly, keyboard pieces, songs, and orchestral works are represented, the songs having caught up with the progressiveness of the other genres, as seen in the twenty-three-minute song excerpted from *My Sister, My Spouse*, "The Dialogue of Abraham and Isaac." The work progresses in a free, declamatory, non-tonal style, and features a parlando style achieved through complex rhythmic notations and shifting meters. Critic Anne Warriner commented,

Professor Lockwood's strength lies in his delicate use of long, thin strands of steel-like chords pliantly interwoven, sometimes supporting the drama as close as a shadow in inverted thirds, sometimes flung free, and most often sounding the sparse, stark freedom of the dreadful mountainside. [32]

Also highlighting his Denver years is Lockwood's return to the mass media, a KRMA-television documentary commemorating the centenary of Abraham Lincoln's death entitled *The Immortal Image* (1965). Finally, his *Oboe Concerto* (1968) was commissioned by former Denver Symphony Orchestra oboist Richard Pointer, and premiered by the Orquesta de la Universidad Nacional Autonoma de México (Mexico City) under the baton of Eduardo Mata.

The once-shy Lockwood made many friends while on the faculty of the University of Denver, proven by the many works dedicated to several of his faculty colleagues: Ramon Kireilis, clarinetist; David Karp, pianist; David Kaslow, hornist; and Robert Davine, accordionist. One former University of Denver associate of his, theorist Richard Parks, offered support for Lockwood's receipt of the honorary Doctorate of Humane Letters rather succinctly in 1977.

I heartily approve of the project, and hope it comes about. While I consider it, in a sense, impudent for me to "recommend" Normand Lockwood, I am most grateful for any opportunity to speak to his accomplishments and qualities. Thank you for thinking of me. [33]

In a manner consistent with his entire academic career, Lockwood inspired young composers with his perspicacity and wisdom, as recalled by former University of Denver student Kevin Kennedy.

[Of all my composition teachers], none seemed so egoless, so selfless, so genuinely interested in the student as Normand. Never did his past accomplishments or present projects intrude on the time he was dedicating to his students in class. Never did he seem interested in anything but the business at hand, that business being to move his students from the level they had reached to some higher level based on their respective talents and individual musical language.

What I learned from Normand was economy. It is difficult for a student composer to let go of some of those notes, some of those unnecessary extra beats, but the results of his considerate, always gentlemanly, help were to improve the work. . . . The importance of craftsmanship was thus insinuated into your consciousness and, over my three years anyway, eventually productive of a style that seemed to me more direct and more immediately concise.[34]

Lockwood's unobtrusive teaching style also made an impression on former student Sharon Lohse Kunitz.

Seldom did he tell us a specific answer, but made possible suggestions. Maybe only one note or rest would solve the problem. Even today when I compose and I hit a problem spot, I try to sit back and objectively view the over-all situation, recalling the various ways in which we would evaluate our problems and create solutions.[35]

Denver represents a gratifying combination for Lockwood, a place where he found both personal and professional enrichment. After a long delay because of his unresolved first marriage, he and Vona K. Swedell celebrated their nuptials on April 23, 1976. Through his relationship with her, the composer built a home which matched the permanence of his successful teaching position. He was locally recognized as a noteworthy artist and he flourished under the acceptance offered by the

Denver community. Honors came from both local and distant regions: in 1971 he received the "Governor's Award" from the Colorado Council on the Arts and Humanities, and in 1974, the year of his sixty-eighth birthday, he received an honorary Doctor of Music degree from Berea College in Kentucky, and retired as Professor Emeritus from the University of Denver.

Chapter Five

Retirement and Reflection

Retirement, Denver (1974-present)

Retirement brought about no significant change in Lockwood's composing, judging from the many works completed since 1974. His orchestral works from this period include two symphonies and several concertos. His choral compositions have remained in demand, represented by his *Mass for Children and Orchestra* (1976-77), commissioned by the Colorado Children's Chorale of Denver, Colorado Council on the Arts and Humanities, and the National Endowment for the Arts; and *Donne's Last Sermon* (1978), commissioned by the Classic Chorale of Denver. Chamber music resurfaces in his oeuvre, including a return to the string quartet genre after nearly four decades. New solo songs and keyboard works are also numerous.

In 1979 the University of Denver bestowed upon him the Doctor of Humane Letters degree. In 1981 he was once again honored by the National Academy of Arts and Letters, receiving their Marjorie Peabody Waite Award in Music. His eightieth birthday in 1986 was marked by all-Lockwood con-

Normand Lockwood (1990). Photo courtesy of Vona Lockwood.

certs in Denver and Carlsbad, New Mexico. Nearly a hundred fond letters of support from friends such as John Powell of the BBC in London commemorate several of these occasions.[1] Maintaining the vitality of his nexus to academic life, he visited Southeast Missouri State University as composer-in-residence as recently as 1989.

Commissions in his retirement represent the continuation of longstanding affiliations with the American Guild of Organists, the Cleveland Museum of Art, and Broadcast Music, Incorporated. Local organizations such as Denver's Classic Chorale and Community Arts Orchestra repeatedly turn to Lockwood for new works. A list of large-scale pieces alone, composed during retirement, includes three choral works, two keyboard pieces, two chamber works, two solo songs, two organ works, and six opuses for large instrumental ensembles, four of which are concertos. His total works have surpassed the four hundred figure, and he is still generating new music.

One of the large-scale choral works, *Life Triumphant* (1975), is a touching amalgam of Lockwood's various stages in choral composition. It is dedicated to the memory of Thor Johnson: champion of Moravian music, sometime faculty member at the University of Michigan, and prominent conductor-advocate of American music. Johnson had conducted the premieres of two of Lockwood's greatest choral works, *Children of God* and *Prairie*. To honor the memory of the man who interpreted his works with such great perception, the composer wrote in his most sensitive style, returning to texts by Walt Whitman and interpolating Moravian hymns with all the maturity and intelligence his life experiences had accorded him.

Normand Lockwood now reaps the benefits of a lifetime of exemplary teaching, noteworthy compositions, and cherished friendships. His associates, former students, and friends, pursuing their own careers in various parts of the country, have created a network of admirers that spans the continent. While commissions continue to appear, this lively octogenarian does not wait for the demand, but creates simply because he is, first and foremost, a composer. He continues to derive immense satisfaction from the process of composition, pursuing new compositions and, especially, new approaches to twelve-tone writing, with unquenchable curiosity. Because of this unending quest, he exudes an extraordinary youthfulness, drawing equally inquisitive, new admirers around him as a magnet might attract diverse metals. As this biography goes to press, he is putting the finishing touches on a new, large-scale work for mezzo soprano and full orchestra entitled *Medea Redux*, after the play of Euripides as translated by Simon Goldfield.

Like his *Medea Redux*, some of the finest works he has composed in his retirement are unsolicited, and many have never been performed. His wealth of experiences, including successes as well as failures, has taught him that popular art music is not necessarily good art music, and he is quite content with that maxim. As he stated in 1979,

> I write for the shelf—that's a good place. Some works emerge from the shelf and get performed. Some please and some don't. But that doesn't have anything to do with quality: some lousy things are popular and so are some good things.[2]

In his long life, Normand Lockwood has forged a style which is as wide-ranging and kaleidoscopic as his existence has been, and in fact, his constantly changing "modus operandi" has allowed him to find success in many varied environments. Not surprisingly, he has juxtaposed the past and the present in his retirement works. While commissions are often generated by former students and old friends, the resultant works are products of a contemporary, vital Lockwood. The new continues to fascinate him, as evidenced by his 1986 work for acoustic instruments and synthesizer, *Coming of the Spirits*. In the much-heralded spirit of his native country, Lockwood has, throughout his life, creatively merged a wealth of influences, ideas, and locations. The end result, Lockwood's distinctive amalgam, is one achieved by only a few of the many who attempt it: a productive and consistently progressive life as a composer.

Normand Lockwood and American Music

Normand Lockwood's early and middle career followed a path that seemed destined to bring him success as a composer in the United States of the middle twentieth century. Born of a remarkably musical and cosmopolitan family, he traveled more extensively in his first twenty-five years than many individuals do in a lifetime. In the two decades from 1925 to 1945, he would fulfill all the prerequisites for compositional success: three years' study with Nadia Boulanger, receipt of the Rome prize and two Guggenheim fellowships, procurement of various prestigious academic positions, and the establishment of a flourishing career in New York City. While the influence of his well-connected family, and especially his father, cannot be denied in his early career, he soon proved himself worthy of all those benefits through his tenacious pursuit of the art of composition. Until he left the Northeast, he was met with considerable national success. An understanding of the disparity between Lockwood's abundant compositional gifts and his relative obscurity today requires an examination of several factors.

Lockwood's innate shyness may have fundamentally affected his career. Former Oberlin student William Hoskins offered one negative appraisal of the composition teacher he otherwise admired.

There were some . . . Lockwoodian traits which it would have been better not to have learned. His attitudes reinforced my own publicity-shyness; I could never bear to become the

self-promoting salesman which a successful American composer almost has to be—and in that, I was a true disciple of N.
L. He was always shy and tentative in putting forward his own
compositions, and this attitude could not have helped but cost
him some career opportunities along the way.

Running his own works down in public was another trait
which was undesirable to copy. The event I remember best was
a Columbia University Library concert in the spring of 1945.
On this occasion, the works were string quartets by Normand
Lockwood and Norman Dello Joio. In the discussion [fol-
lowing the performance] Dello Joio came over as young, brash,
and aggressive in defense of his work. When it was Normand
Lockwood's turn, he . . . [gave] some information about the
form of the work, finally settling down on the Finale, which he
said had been the most difficult, . . . [and adding] "and that is
perhaps why it fails."[3]

Indeed, Lockwood recalls a 1940s encounter with Henry
Cowell that reinforces Hoskins's evaluation: "[Cowell] spoke
of the piece, *Weekend Prelude*, in terms gratifying enough. But
he took exception with its ending, and I jumped at the opportunity to agree with him."[4]

The vagaries of critical response to his music might have
caused Lockwood some distress during his early career. On the
one hand, he was frequently reinforced by a fair amount of
public acclaim. Occasionally, however, his perceived
shortcomings were noted in mixed or ambivalent critical
responses to his works. An extreme example occurred on the
night of *Prairie's* 1953 premiere, when composer Ross Lee
Finney vehemently attacked Lockwood's composition.
Whether the event changed his own opinion of the work or not,
the memory is still a uncomfortable one for Lockwood.[5]
Reproaches such as these must have made a tremendous impact
on the ever-sensitive composer, but historical perspective
suggests many reasons for the varied responses to Lockwood's

unique musical language, still in its developmental stage in the 1940s and early 1950s.

One explanation is the renewed emphasis on Germanic compositional ideals in this country precipitated by the emigration of Hindemith, Krenek, Schoenberg, and countless other prominent artistic figureheads in the late 1930s. Even the composer of *Rodeo* and *Lincoln Portrait*, Copland, capitulated to serialism after 1950. At the same time, Roy Harris maintained his connection with his American roots, and Virgil Thomson promoted French music in his role as music critic of the *New York Herald Tribune*. Small wonder that critical reviews of Lockwood's music would offer a variety of opinions—for some, his harmonic language seemed "deliberately ugly,"[6] while others described it as "boldly dissonant, rough, [and] energetic."[7]

The move to San Antonio in 1953 created a solution, as well as a complication, to Lockwood's compositional advancement. On the one hand, he effectively removed himself from the white heat of New York criticism and the vagaries of a public swaying between the conflicting, but fashionable ideals of neo-Germanicism and Americanism. He was free to pursue his own path without undue comparisons to the luminaries of the New York scene; however, his exodus from the East marked a chain of events that would change his life forever.

His familiar surroundings were replaced by a new environment, his thirty-year marriage effectively ended, his lifelong personal mentor died, and in 1955, his academic career stalled for two years. Like the Romantic hero who is ennobled by adversity, Lockwood finally achieved his maturity as a composer as a result of these trying events of the 1950s. However, the supreme irony of the 1950s is that, while his exit from the New York scene ultimately signaled his coming of age as a composer and the integration of his compositional style, the relocation just as effectively curtailed his practical opportunities for performances in the preeminent musical centers of the country. His opportunities for national acclaim diminished drastically at the very time that Lockwood was best prepared to maximize them. From that time, Lockwood was truly a master of his own fate, and he achieved great success, but he did so primarily on the regional level.

Lockwood on Lockwood

Composers are notoriously reticent to characterize their own styles, and Normand Lockwood is no exception. While he would undoubtedly refuse to offer a comprehensive statement on his style and work method, pertinent comments are scattered throughout the abundant paper trail that documents his career. In 1989, on the topic of constructing a good melody, he said,

> Some people make a graph—it should be high here, low here. I threw that out the window. Approach every melodic line on the basis of its own inherent character. There are many great melodic lines that don't "fill the bill" at all [i. e., that do not follow any formula]. It must make its point. If it's wrong, change it to make it right.[8]

The last statement articulates one of Lockwood's most important compositional philosophies, that a composer knows intuitively when a work is finished. For him, part of the process of creation is recognizing what is wrong, and having the skills to remedy the problem. In this way, he functions as his own teacher, internalizing the method of evaluation that many of his former students appreciated in his studio.

In 1962 he wrote an illuminating article concerning his favorite textual source, the poetry of Walt Whitman. His belief that composition, as well as listening, is an intuitive process, is clear.

Composers have a certain preparation for understanding Whitman. Whitman defies the laws of poetry much as a great deal of music defies laws of composition.

Who, listening to *La Mer*, can deny the presence of organization despite—or rather beyond—its loose program? I remember being in my youth moved and satisfied by the *Petroushka* of Strawinsky . . . and nobody told me that this was 'episodic' and not a 'homophonic' form!

These enter the ear and reach the music-loving soul with appeal to the same sense of form—the same desire for form—that classical form does. These and Whitman alike hold an appeal that is empirical. THE SOUND OF MUSIC. THE SOUND OF LANGUAGE. THE THING ABOUT MUSIC THAT MAKES YOU GO ALONG WITH IT. THE SOUND OF POETRY THAT CARRIES YOU ALONG ITS STREAM. THE SOUND OF THEM BOTH, THAT EVOKES THOUGHTS AND IMAGES AND FEELINGS. THAT OPENS AVENUES, VISTAS, HOWEVER FAMILIAR OR STARTLINGLY NEW. THIS THE POETRY OF WHITMAN DOES TO A HIGH DEGREE.[9]

In these words Lockwood offers an explanation of his seemingly spontaneous structures, evident in all phases of his career. As the composer, he is the sole judge of the logic of his structures; this belief prevents him from relying on the opinions of others, or on the degree of exposure his works received. He is, in the final analysis, an instinctive, individualistic composer who cannot exhaust all the compositional possibilities in a given system or structure—whether it is tonality, serialism, or sonata form—precisely because he refuses to be governed by them. In so doing, he creates for himself an unending, exponentially expanding set of possibilities. The tireless pursuit of the new within the old has occupied him for many years, and will doubtless continue to do so.

In Lockwood's mind, one criterion of rightness is memorability, as he expressed in the 1950s,

> In all media in which I have been composing I have been making an increasing effort to write music which, it seems to me, the memory will retain, once it has made its impression through the aural and motor senses. This concerns me more than adhering to one or another acknowledged system of tone relations or structural design, or to any formalized concepts. Another way of putting it, I try chiefly to write in such a way, and with a degree of clarity, that what is played, sung, and heard will "stick"—at least in my own memory, and not solely through my ability (or absence of it) to find logic (or absence of it) in what appears to the eye on the printed page.[10]

Incorporated in this passage is his opinion regarding systematic compositional systems. In 1991 he offered more information.

> There have been a great many fashions—"isms." I never hooked on any, but I was interested, of course. There is a big differentiation between what interests me and what I necessarily like. Twelve-tone writing draws me itself, not the idea that I have to do it. With anything, there is a danger of getting too pedantic.[11]

In Lockwood's continuing experiment with the avoidance of tonality, he often turns toward the direction of twelve-tone writing. However, his adherence to one of the most important techniques in twentieth-century compositional technique has always been moderate, and never rigid. For him, tone rows rarely encompass all twelve pitch classes. Additionally, Lockwood relies on a fixed-octave position in the rows; because a row maintains a melodic shape, it becomes memorable for the listener. Schoenberg's system has thus served for Lockwood, and for many American composers, as one of several methods assimilated in an eclectic compositional style.

Finally, economy of means has been his guiding premise in his most successful works. As he expressed with regard to choral music, "There is nothing like understatement."[12] In setting one of John Donne's sermons, he remarked, "I was as economical as possible."[13] He not only pursued it in his own music, he also appreciated it in works of others. In 1947 he wrote a review of William Schuman's ballet, *Undertow* (1946), that shows his admiration for his peer's austerity.

> It is especially arresting in its orchestration which, in spite of the orchestra's size, is economical and taut. Doubling occurs rarely and with discretion, resulting in striking instrumental sonorities and contrasts.[14]

Those properties he enjoyed most in Schuman's ballet are apparent in his own music, although they present problems of their own. A performer who brings a great deal of experience to the topic of Lockwood's music, Kevin Kennedy, offered an insightful summary of his style.

> In many ways his style is not immediately accessible, probably due to its economy of means. It is always easier to perform music that is excessive. An initial reaction may be that his music is dry, but further examination always reveals a clean, transparent, often haunting delicacy that lends itself to the very subtle romantic nuance on the part of the performer. Normand's music cannot be underestimated. It is not easy and cannot be "tossed off" at a performance. It requires much control, attention to detail, and careful concentration. His music is a challenge to performer and listener alike, but well worth the effort involved in producing a well-rehearsed performance.[15]

Perhaps for artists, justifying one's career choice is unnecessary. Lockwood composes because he is a composer. His own philosophy of the metaphysical nature of art adds another dimension to this answer.

> I don't think there is an end to any art. It started with the beginnings of human life as an expression of man, and it has extended from that time to this. If it doesn't extend, nothing will live. The classics won't live if we don't have vitality as a contemporary aspect.[16]

In this case, he equated life with art, supported by the wisdom of his advanced years. On another occasion, he reversed the analogy, comparing the processes of music with the workings of life.

> [Form in music] is rhythmic, I think—a sequence of events, just as in life—a year here, a decade there—it's not isolated, but in a context. Events often form a rhythm of life.[17]

Perhaps the simplest comment on his compositional motivation appears in a story he related in 1989 about his compositional mentor, Nadia Boulanger.

> A dear young girl sitting in the front row of a class meeting of fifty or sixty students at Southeast Missouri State asked, "Where do you get your inspiration?" Now, six months later, I haven't the vaguest recollection of how I may have answered that one! Of course I haven't found the answer—not any more than I had an answer to my father at age fifteen. I might have liked to have said in both instances, "Composing is an obsession." That's akin to what Nadia Boulanger said to me: "Zee musique, she must be like a seekness." (I'm sure Nadia wasn't aware of the excellent pun.)[18]

Whatever his motivation, Lockwood has exemplified his belief in composing as a way of life. In an artistic world with little room at the top, he stands as a remarkable example of an artist with an unshakable commitment to the creation of good music, in spite of popular recognition or lack of it.

PART II

THE MUSIC OF NORMAND LOCKWOOD

Chapter Six

Choral Music[1]

Overview

In Robert Stevenson's list of "established American [choral] composers," Normand Lockwood appears along with Samuel Barber, Aaron Copland, Ross Lee Finney, Lukas Foss, Howard Hanson, Alan Hovhaness, Norman Dello Joio, Peter Mennin, Vincent Persichetti, Quincy Porter, and Leo Sowerby.[2] Although only about one third of Lockwood's choral works have been published, he has gained perhaps his greatest recognition as a choral composer. Nearly 180 original works of varying lengths are extant, including 135 anthem-sized works, both sacred and secular.[3] Included in this category are several arrangements of folksongs, carols, and spirituals. Works of intermediate size, from eight to twenty minutes in length, number nineteen. Lockwood has composed twenty-two large-scale pieces, each lasting anywhere from twenty minutes to two hours.

Prior to his apprenticeship with Respighi in 1924, Lockwood was drawn primarily to choral works such as Delius's *Sea Drift* and Holst's *Dirge for Two Veterans*. While in Rome, however, he became fascinated with the chants he encountered in the Roman Catholic liturgies, and these memories soon influenced his choral style. Beginning with his earliest choral compositions in the 1930s and extending until the mid-1950s, Lockwood displayed his interest in chant through a homogeneous choral style that relied on the natural accents of the text, in a manner similar to text-dominated liturgical music. The words were also emphasized in his writings for four or more choral parts by his use of homophonic texture.

In the mid-1950s Lockwood began to incorporate more progressive inflections in his largely consonant choral language. Dissonances generated from octatonicism, tone rows, and bichords had been common in the prior instrumental works, but he waited until this time to assimilate these materials into the choral works. Thus from that time, Lockwood's compositional style has been largely unified from genre to genre, as he used new ideas in choral and instrumental works alike. In the large-scale works from mid-century, however, he continued to use 1930s-style choruses alongside more progressive movements, revealing the stylistic diversity that pervades his entire career.

In some of his later choral works, Lockwood has introduced a greater sense of understatement, reducing his musical materials to those he considers to be the most economical and expressive. In a work such as *Donne's Last Sermon* (1978), his most dissonant and challenging large-scale choral work to date, forces are reduced to four-part choir and organ, text is limited to one author, and musical language is highly unified.

Style

The words of Jacob Evanson are useful in a preliminary discussion of Lockwood's compositional process. While he was choral conductor at Western Reserve University in Cleveland,

Evanson wrote an informative, contemporary preface to *Dirge for Two Veterans*, Lockwood's 1937 choral piece published by Witmark. He discussed the modernist trend in American music as he saw it, the absence of professional choruses to perform such music, and the resultant dearth of new choral music. He felt that Lockwood was exemplary in the sparsely-populated world of modernist American choral composers.

Evanson's list of Lockwood's compositional techniques in *Dirge* is especially interesting because of its contemporaneous perspective. "Typically modern means employed" include "great rhythmic freedom; variety within the measure, even when restatements are made; chords of the thirteenth, eleventh, and ninth; single-toned and choral pedal-point passages; atonal succession of major triads; whole-toned scales; and parallelism."[4]

Evanson then made a statement which serves, over fifty years later, as a point of departure in the discussion of Lockwood's choral music:

> However, Mr. Lockwood's work is no mere bag of technical tricks. None of these devices protrudes itself, and emphatically should it be pointed out that in all likelihood they are used unconsciously by the composer in the process of his direct thinking in tone. Each technical device has been called into being for some expressive purpose demanded by the text.[5]

Lockwood concurs: "That's why I have trouble describing my music. I don't think of ways of describing it—I think of it in a sort of tonal language."[6] The fact that Lockwood "thinks in tone" is not distinctive; most composers would accept that description of their process. If his "thinking in tone" is indeed distinct to him, that distinction is one of degree. Lockwood, more than many composers, tries to honor the meter and syntax of the poetic source, although not necessarily the overall structure.

If Lockwood's choral works follow the organization of their texts, they are not, therefore, musically formless. Although the composer's primary concern is to render text, and not musical form, in a sensible and expressive way, his end result is formally coherent because of the underlying structure of the text. In his words, "The music takes off from the words and *becomes* the music."[7] Clearly, in Lockwood's mind, the musical structure is generated from the words, but in the process of "becoming," arrives at a musical form, however unconventional it may be. As is evident in the discussion of *Out of the Cradle Endlessly Rocking* to follow, Lockwood manipulated the form of the poem by freely excerpting from the Whitman original. Once that was done, however, he mirrored the structure of the remaining poetry with his musical structure.

Concern for the communication of the text has greatly influenced texture, as well as form, in Lockwood's works. His most prevalent texture is homophonic, with great attention given to proper rhythm and accentuation of the words. This style is favored by many of his contemporaries, as illustrated by Elliott Forbes's comment on Randall Thompson's music: "[He uses] individual choral colors to serve the successive word sounds, [taking] care for the natural rhythm of the spoken word."[8]

Lockwood's polyphonic sections most often take the form of two-part imitations and alternating statements by sections of the choir. One rationale for the use of such a transparent contrapuntal style lies with the sheer volume of text in most of Lockwood's works. If a composer sets a "Kyrie," which may consist of only six words, the literary import is not lost, even in complex polyphonic interweavings. But with a long Whitman text such as *Dirge for Two Veterans*, the words must be set carefully and clearly. Each line must receive only a moment in the limelight, otherwise the piece becomes unmanageably long. Another reason for the avoidance of counterpoint is Lockwood's concern for the individual import of each word.

"What in the world is the use of writing [independent] parts for the chorus—four or six-part writing is wasted. In such a texture, there would be no subtleties."[9]

At least two different literary aspects of text setting have concerned Lockwood: subtleties and details. Subtleties refer to non-literal, sonorous qualities of the words; they might be inspired by a poetic device such as onomatopoeia. For instance, in setting the phrase "All night long" from *Out of the Cradle Endlessly Rocking*, Lockwood exploited the similarly open vowel sounds of "all" and "long," and the repeated long sounds of the voiced consonants "l" and "n," in a protracted musical statement that underscores a seemingly endless vigil.

In another work, *This Moment* (1971), the composer depicted the second literary aspect, detail. Details are more precise than subtleties; they are musically descriptive evocations of specific images, as opposed to subtle suggestions. An example of pictorial detail—often called text painting—is found in Lockwood's use of a fragment of the well-known "Song of the Volga Boatmen" at the mention of Russia.

Regarding these literary elements, Lockwood remarked,

> One [text] may have a pervasive mood, which dominates the whole thing. In another, I will focus on bringing out certain details—of course, mood must be there, but I don't concentrate on it.[10]

Lockwood's musical structures depend to a great extent upon whether he chooses to depict subtleties or details. When he depicts details, he necessarily changes musical idioms as the text shifts from one thought or image to another. The result is an episodic form that he has used in all the oratorios, and in several intermediate and shorter choral works as well. In contrast to the great oratorio tradition of the Baroque period, which unified episodic subject matter stylistically, Lockwood's musical palette is much more varied and creates more stylistic contrast. If, instead of details, he chooses to render a mood, his text painting becomes more subtle and the form, more musically conventional, for instance, an ABA. The depiction of a mood may also figure prominently as one of the episodes in an oratorio or similarly constructed shorter work.

Representative Works

The choral works chosen to receive special emphasis in this chapter span the years 1937 to 1981 (Table 6.1). Although the works themselves are not discussed in temporal order, together they represent the variety of styles apparent in his oeuvre. *Prairie* serves as a relatively conservative initiation. The first two oratorios give slightly different views of his style at mid-century. The third oratorio, *Life Triumphant*, shows Lockwood's ability to assimilate disparate textual sources.

TABLE 6.1
Representative Choral Works in Order of Discussion

Title	Length
Prairie (1953)	Large Secular
Children of God (1956)	Large Sacred
Light Out of Darkness (1957)	Large Sacred
Life Triumphant (1975)	Large Sacred
Elegy for a Hero (1962)	Intermediate
Donne's Last Sermon (1978)	Intermediate
Monotone (1937)	Short
Because I Could Not Stop for Death (1981)	Short
Alleluia, Christ Is Risen (1974)	Short
Out of the Cradle Endlessly Rocking (1939)	Intermediate

Two intermediate works, *Elegy for a Hero* and *Donne's Last Sermon*, present points on his tonal gamut from relatively conservative to most dissonant. *Because I Could Not Stop for Death* represents Lockwood's development toward a more understated style in his later career. Works which depart from text setting as a primary consideration are illustrated by *Alleluia, Christ Is Risen*. The chapter closes with a detailed discussion of *Out of the Cradle Endlessly Rocking* because it epitomizes four important Lockwood characteristics: his preference for and response to the poetry of Walt Whitman, his initiation of the durable 1930s style that influenced his choral works for two decades, his favorite harmonic pattern,[11] and his scrupulous attention to subtleties which, together, create a mood.

Large-Scale Works: Secular and Sacred

Lockwood's best-known, large-scale, secular choral work is *Prairie* (1953), commissioned by the University of Michigan Musical Society. Lasting about thirty minutes in performance, it is written in eleven continuous sections. In *Prairie*, the chorus serves as the solo vocal instrument, which distinguishes the work from his oratorios, in which soloists are featured. The differences do not end there; the composer's musical style is much less dissonant in this secular work. Based on the Carl Sandburg poem of the same name, *Prairie* received an enthusiastic review by Louise Cuyler of the *Ann Arbor News:*

> Lockwood's *Prairie* . . . is as sinewy, stalwart, and relentless as the great mid-continent of America, which inspired both poem and music. The composer's idiom is relatively uncomplicated, and has a bold directness especially suited to this theme. . . . Lockwood is both a sensitive composer and a

practical craftsman, a combination which makes him articulate and comprehensible to a remarkable degree.[12]

Example 6.1, Motive resembling bird call, *Prairie*, MSC, "Look at Six Eggs," mvt. 8, p. 88, mm. 1-8.

Another critic felt that *Prairie* is "first-rate Americana, as authentic as its parent-text."[13]

The "uncomplicated" idiom to which Louise Cuyler refers is a patchwork of homespun, syncopated consonances, quartal fanfares, mildly dissonant bichords, octatonic scales, and the occasional sharper dissonance. The choir moves in declamatory homophony for the most part, although the delightful "Look at six eggs" (Section Eight) is written in an almost madrigal style which progresses from antiphony to imitative counterpoint (Example 6.1). The charm of this movement springs from Lockwood's use of literary detail: the main motive is a metaphor made from the intervals and articulation of the bird's song. Far more frequent in *Prairie*, however, is his homophonic choral style with folk overtones, as shown in the music which begins and ends the piece, "I Was Born on the Prairie" (Example 6.2). Folk elements such as eighth-quarter-eighth syncopations in the vocal bass part are reminiscent of such American folk tunes as "Lil' Liza Jane."

In *Prairie* Lockwood proves the value of an inspiring text for a composer who cherishes words. The music is as unpretentious as the language, and the composer seems very much at home with all of the episodes which comprise the work. Tender sentiment ("I am the Prairie, Mother of Men") is intermingled with joyous affirmations ("Look at Six Eggs") in natural, effortless balance. *Prairie* deserves the plaudits its premiere generated, representing Lockwood's primary compositional concern and strength—the musical setting of a text.

With regard to form in the large-scale choral works, Lockwood applied the word "rhythmic." He continued, "There is a rhythm in the wider sense, a sequence of events, [even in something as structured as a sonata], just as there is a rhythm [governing the sequence of events] in life."[14] This rhythmic form is derived from the element which is so important to the composer, the text. To the listener, the structure is a logical

Example 6.2, Homophonic choral style with syncopations, *Prairie*, MSC, "I Was Born on the Prairie," mvt. 1, p. 3, mm. 1-5.

progression, each event building on the previous one. The composer often unites the various parts by the use of characteristic sonorities, motives, and other devices, in a way so subtle as to be missed by the casual listener. In this respect, Lockwood's organization extends Romantic formal ideas, particularly those of the tone poem, while at the same time incorporating early-twentieth-century devices such as serialism.[15]

The large sacred choral works provide fertile ground for further discussion of his choral literature. An inherently episodic genre, oratorio, is made more so by Lockwood's particular eclecticism in *Children of God* (1956) and *Light Out of Darkness* (1957). Still, several consistent stylistic phenomena emerge in these works, apparently representing the composer's holistic concept of oratorio.

Thor Johnson conducted the Cincinnati Symphony and the Berea (Kentucky) College Choir in the premiere of *Children of God* on February 1 and 2, 1957. The work, for five soloists, mixed choir, children's choir, and orchestra, was written in response to a joint commission from the National Council of Churches and Berea College. In a review appearing in *Musical America* of April 1957, critic Mary Leighton commented, "Lockwood's oratorio had moments promising interesting developments that did not materialize. Rather it worked in segments in an idiom that presented no listening challenge."[16] Leighton took issue with Lockwood's episodic format in this review. Indeed, the oratorio suffers from its loose sense of integration; still, it presents moments of true inspiration. Although it is widely varied in its materials, it is dramatically pleasing as a whole.

The commission and presentation of this ninety-minute work commemorated Brotherhood Week in Cincinnati. Part One, containing a Prologue, seven Episodes, and an Epilogue, is subtitled "Am I My Brother's Keeper?" Its text is excerpted from the Old Testament prophets, excepting Episode Six, which is derived from the book of "Ruth." Part Two has an

Thor Johnson and Normand Lockwood at the 1957 premiere of *Children of God* in Cincinnati. Photo courtesy of Vona Lockwood.

identical movement structure to Part One; however, its text is restricted to the words of Christ and the New Testament Apostles and is subtitled "Who Is My Brother?" The text for both parts was adapted from the Revised Standard Version of the Bible by Clara Chassel Cooper, then a faculty member in Berea College's Psychology Department. Lockwood remembers that he had very little input regarding the choices of text. In his words, "It was watertight."[17]

Musical components which appear most frequently in *Children of God* have been described collectively by George Lynn as "Hebraicisms,"[18] a set of musical materials which calls forth the ancient atmosphere Lockwood desired for the presentation of the Scriptures. These Hebraicisms create the oratorio's pervasive mood. Part One opens with a motto consisting of a descending minor second interval, followed in measure six by a descending augmented second (Example 6.3). This configuration is an excerpt from the "Hungarian" or "Gypsy" minor, which often signifies Eastern European or Mediterranean cultures. The oboe continues the exploitation of the augmented second, followed by a chant-like pronouncement by the solo baritone, "God created man in his own image."

Example 6.3, Opening motto, *Children of God*, MS, pt. I, p. 1, mm. 1-6.

[Bsn]

Another strand of the ancient fabric occurs in Episode Two, "Amos," as the choir responds to the prophetic baritone with harmonic tritones. Open sonorities utilizing the perfect intervals are also frequent, but in *Children of God*, the "open" tritone typically signals tension or confusion. Open octaves occur in Episode Five, "The Lord is the Everlasting God," the first phrase of which culminates in another provocative pitch set, the whole-tone scale. These exotic compositional devices create a powerfully dark atmosphere.

Example 6.4, Baritone recitative with "ancient" devices, *Children of God*, MS, pt. I, pp. 13-14, mm. 75-86.

The recitative passages are governed by the same mood, as illustrated in the Prologue of Part One (Example 6.4). In the baritone recitative, the words "Cain said to his brother," are set on a portentous octatonic scale in descending order.[19] A later setting of the same words incorporates several melodic tritones.[20] In contrast, the men of the chorus respond with "Where is Abel your brother?" in open fifths. Christ's recitative in Episode Two of Part Two has a similarly dissonant flavor, often outlining a fully-diminished seventh chord and, again, exploiting the tritone. The lower tetrachord of the Phrygian mode provides similar material, as in Part Two, Episode Seven. Here the chorus opens with an octave, then the lower voices descend stepwise in a complete presentation of the Phrygian mode.

These materials—tritones, open perfect intervals, Phrygian mode, and the whole-tone scale—are woven in a tapestry which serves as the unifying backdrop for the oratorio. However, they are not the only family of sonorities to be found. Another set of sounds used frequently are melodic and rhythmic patterns common in the African-American spiritual. Such aspects appear in the form of occasional triadic, even pentatonic melodies which feature the lowered fifth or seventh scale degree. These are often combined with the eighth-quarter-eighth syncopation seen earlier in *Prairie*, but also common in the African-American vernacular tradition. The baritone recitative in the Prologue of Part One, marked "ballad-style," illustrates this new mood and also shows Lockwood's ability to write a folk-like melody, complete with a lowered-third-to-tonic phrase ending (Example 6.5).

Example 6.5, Baritone recitative with "spiritual" influences, *Children of God*, MS, pt. I, p. 9, mm. 54-55.

Ancient or folk-like moods in *Children of God* result from Lockwood's use of compositional devices. Another striking aspect of the oratorio, one which involves a less conscious manipulation of materials, and which appears throughout his choral genre, is his natural lyricism. The tenor aria "They Shall All Know Me" in Part One, Episode Four, spins a soaring,

Example 6.6, Lyricism in tenor aria, *Children of God*, MS, pt. I, pp. 82-84, mm. 405-416.

arch-shaped line; its brief visitation of the octatonic scale is well-suited to the poignant text (Example 6.6). Other lyrical moments occur in Episode Seven, Part One, "Ruth"; and in the simple children's chorus setting of the "Beatitudes" in Part Two, Episode Two. In the last-named movement, Lockwood displays his sure grasp of idiomatic children's choir composition and applies that knowledge in a combination with the mixed choir and orchestra. In lyrical places such as these, Lockwood gives freer reign to his introspective side than to the dramatic demands of the genre, and these contemplative moments seem to be a more comfortable mode for the composer. His lyricism is adorned with a well-developed gift of understatement, a facet of Lockwood's style which will be addressed further in conjunction with the shorter choral works.

For the oratorio chorus, Lockwood often prefers a lock-step homophonic style, so that the text is easily understood—echoing his 1930s choral style. For choral contrast, two-part imitation suffices to briefly change the texture from the more prevalent homophonic language. Not only is the latter used to present a textural and tonal contrast to the more dissonant recitatives, it often serves the same function when presented against a more active orchestral statement. Several elements, first apparent in Lockwood's works from the 1930s, emerge. First, closed-position chords are used to concentrate and intensify the varied vocal timbres inherent in a mixed chorus. Secondly, seventh chords of various types are abundant, and often appear in descending or ascending sequence. Third, the style is mostly homophonic, although Lockwood also gives great attention to linear construction within each voice. Finally, as mentioned before, word-stress is a prime consideration. Lockwood's use of his 1930s style in *Children of God* is charted in Table 6.2.

The "Paumanok" pattern is an adjunct to the 1930s style and a Lockwood trademark. Although there are several variants, the "Paumanok" pattern typically begins with a close-position

TABLE 6.2

Instances of the 1930s Choral Style in *Children of God*

Part I—Section	Text
Prologue	"Amen"
Episode 2	"Seek the Lord and Live"
Episode 3	"Return to the Lord"
Episode 4	"Amen"
Episode 5	"The Lord is the Everlasting God" (end)
Episode 6	"The Lord Recompense You"
Episode 7	"We Will Walk"
Epilogue	"Trust So the Lord"

Part II	
Episode 1	"Be Merciful"
Episode 3	"God Has Shown Me"
Episode 4	"We Are Fellow Heirs"
Episode 5	"See What Love The Father Has Given"
Episode 7	"The Field is the World"
Epilogue	"Behold, He Will Dwell with Him"
	"The Lord's Prayer"

Example 6.7. "Paumanok" pattern.

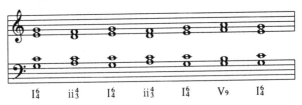

tonic chord in second inversion (Example 6.7). In *Children of God*, the pattern appears prominently in both principal sections, sometimes only as a choral fragment, and at other times as the opening of a full-blown anthem.

Beyond the harmonic structures inherent in the 1930s style, Lockwood's harmonic idiom includes frequent bichordal passages. Seen most often in festival movements, the style seems to represent Lockwood's desire to expand conventional tonality, to heighten the excitement of a "praise" anthem. The closing section of Part One illustrates this principle well. Here the choir and orchestra begin a tonal "Praise Hymn" which features firm, often root-position chords. After an extended recitative section, however, the choir returns with a new "praise" motive, now in F-sharp major, while the timpani, bassoon, and lower strings provide the tonic and dominant degrees of C major.

In a work as diverse as *Children of God*, unifying techniques may be well-hidden, but they indeed exist. As seen in Table 6.2, the 1930s choral style is used to bind the disparate elements together. The style is reserved for contemplative functions, or reflective thoughts, as in "See What Love the Father has Given Us." In contrast, the open sonorities discussed earlier are better suited to more dramatic functions, as in "Where is Abel, Your Brother?"

The composer's idiomatic choral writing implies an involvement with the medium that is just as intimate as his textual absorption. In fact, it is often difficult to determine exactly where three elements—his sympathy with the text, his knowledge of the choral medium, and his "direct thinking in tone"—intersect and merge. In a chorus such as "See What Love" from Part Two, Episode Five, Lockwood evokes the sentimental mood of a touching text by concentrating on its subtleties. Such an understated evocation is vastly different from the broad text painting he uses elsewhere; both devices are skillfully employed. To apply Archibald T. Davison's words, Lockwood has made "evocative not the words but what lies hidden within them . . . suggesting rather than describing."[21] When Lockwood limits himself to intimate, understated, and non-pictorial settings, the result is almost always a memorable chorus (Example 6.8). In these instances, his innate understanding of the choral medium is not overshadowed by excessive variety or density of materials.

Example 6.8, Intimate choral style, *Children of God*, MS "See What Love," pt. II, pp. 109-113, mm. 573-587.

The aforementioned traits are also evident in Lockwood's oratorio of 1957, *Light Out of Darkness*. The work was commissioned by the president of the board of Buffalo's Philharmonic Society, Robert I. Millonzi, in memory of his father, Phillip. The premiere, directed by Josef Krips, took place on February 18, 1958, at Kleinhans Music Hall in Buffalo. Lockwood found all aspects of Krips's conducting, and especially his tempo choices, to be appropriate and accurate.[22] Choir and baritone soloist Yi-Kwei Sze combined for a very successful premiere.

The performance also found favor with critic Berna Bergholtz, as she indicated in *Musical America* of July, 1958:

> Broad in scope, Mr. Lockwood's cantata reveals his high degree of musicianship and skill. Scored for full orchestra, organ, mixed chorus, and baritone solo, it is divided into five sections performed without pause. Dissonant passages are strongly contrasted in mood with those of calm and serenity. Demands on the performers are considerable and these were sustained with distinction.[23]

The piece is organized into five subdivided sections:

1a "God the Father has Delivered Us from the Dominion of
      Darkness"
1b "For in Him all the Fullness of God was Pleased to Dwell"
2a "We Are Afflicted in Every Way"
2b "I Love the Lord"
3a "The Word of the Cross is Folly to Those who are Perishing"
3b "Make a Joyful Noise"
4a "Why Doest Thou Stand Afar Off, O God?"
4b "Even If our Gospel is Veiled"
5a "We Look not to the Things that are seen"
5b "The Lord is My Rock"
5c "Alleluia."

A greater degree of motivic unification distinguishes this oratorio from *Children of God*. *Light Out of Darkness* opens with a fanfare involving F-sharp, G-sharp, and F-sharp, which later becomes the primary motive of the entire work. Section 1a ends with a harmonized, inverted version of the motive (G-F-G, not shown). Later in 2a, the English horn and bass clarinet have the same figure, again inverted (G-sharp, F-sharp, G-sharp). This statement is answered by the original motive. In 3a, the original motive is interspersed with its transposed inversion, and later in that section, the chorus sings the inverted form. Versions also appear in 4b, and in the final section of the work. This device allows Lockwood to achieve a formal cohesiveness that is less interrupted by stylistic variation than was *Children of God*.

Other innovations include a harmonic movement that is less predictable in comparison to the earlier work, as illustrated in 1b, a chorus entitled "For in Him all the Fullness of God was Pleased to Dwell." The chorus begins in C major, but the first phrase cadences on G, with C in the bass. The harmony moves through the major chords of E, A, and A-flat, while the low strings play a fragment of the whole-tone scale on C, thus destroying any inclination toward a tonal center.

Example 6.9, Tone row in oboe, *Light Out of Darkness*, MS, pt. 4a, p. 67, mm. 282-286.

Slow, lamentevole

[Ob]

Perhaps most startling to the listener acquainted with *Children of God* is the chorus in 4a, "Why dost Thou Stand Afar Off, O God?" To paint the desolate backdrop implied by the text, Lockwood wrote a melody for the solo oboe, built on a lyrical, twelve-tone row (Example 6.9). The soprano and alto sections share the second statement of the row alternately with the tenors and basses, and it is then presented a third time. Tone clusters appear next in dryly-articulated and crisply rhythmic woodwinds reminiscent of Stravinsky's *L'Histoire du Soldat* and *Octet* for winds. Presumably Lockwood used the dodecaphonic technique to generate pitch material, but he was not interested in writing a strictly serial movement. As he stated, "I could not care less if it's twelve-tone . . . it's the music that's important."[24]

An inventive rhythmic setting which appears frequently in Lockwood's oeuvre characterizes the gem of *Light Out of Darkness*, "Make a Joyful Noise" (Chorus 3b). Text-inspired word rhythms set in shifting meters make this C-major ensemble sprightly and engaging (Example 6.10). Trumpets and trombones provide the bridge to A major for the contrasting section of this ABA form. The B section begins with the same configuration of alternating meters as the A section, but is then extended. A false return of the A section in F major occurs, then A is repeated in the original key. The choral writing throughout is idiomatic, energetic, and concise.

Light Out of Darkness and *Children of God* show a similarity of compositional style, which is not surprising since their dates of composition are within one year of each other. Other oratorios reflect not only eras in Lockwood's career, but also another governing factor common to the genre: the demands of the originating commission.[25] Other multi-movement choral works which fulfill specific commission demands include *Land of Promise* of 1959-60, subtitled "A Dramatic Portrait of Rocky Mountain Methodism" and composed for the Rocky Mountain Methodist Annual Conference; and *Affirmation* of 1982, taking as its text the statement of faith of the United Church of Christ and commissioned by the Community Church of Honolulu for its fiftieth anniversary. In these two pieces, Lockwood created musical idioms particularly suited to their delineated texts.

Example 6.10, Rhythmic choral style, *Light Out of Darkness*, MS, "Make a Joyful Noise Unto the Lord," pt. 3b, pp. 55-56, mm. 223-231.

Intermediate Choral Works

Not all of Lockwood's choral commissions have been so clearly defined as those just mentioned. He enjoyed greater compositional freedom in his *Choreographic Cantata*, contracted in 1968 by the Reuter Organ Company for the 1968 American Guild of Organists Convention in Denver, Co.

Although the work features the obligatory virtuosic organ writing, it is most memorable for its extensive and colorful percussion component, contrasted with relatively traditional choral settings of five Luther/Bach chorales. Also integral to the piece is the element of dance, which was choreographed for the premiere by Charlotte Irey of the Dance Department of the University of Colorado at Boulder. In fact, the dance is so important to the piece that the composer included lengthy notes in the Augsburg edition regarding choreography.[26] In a manner typical of the composer, disparate elements are drawn together in *Choreographic Cantata* to a successful end—the music underscoring the implied movement with rhythmic clarity.

Another intermediate work, the twenty-minute *Elegy for a Hero* (1962) was originally entitled "Memories of President Lincoln," after the Walt Whitman original. The title was later changed by Shawnee Press with Lockwood's consent. Whitman's poetry has motivated Lockwood to compose his finest secular works and this piece is among the best the combination has yielded. In 1962, Shawnee Press published *Elegy for a Hero* for unaccompanied mixed voices. The work falls into three sections:

Part One
I.   "When lilacs last in the dooryard bloom'd"
II.   "Ever-returning spring"
III.   "O powerful western fallen star!"
IV.   "In the dooryard fronting an old farm-house"
V.   "In the swamp in secluded recesses"
VI.   "Over the breast of the spring"
VII.   "O how shall I warble"

Part Two
VIII.   "O Captain! my Captain!"
IX.   (Epitaph) "This dust was once the man"

Part Three
X.   "Come lovely and soothing death."

Textual lengths of the sections range from two lines in Section
II to six quatrains in Section X. Part One is modeled in the
1930s choral style described earlier: I, "When lilacs last in the
dooryard bloom'd," begins with the "Paumanok" pattern; II,
"Ever-returning spring" sets the words in natural rhythm and
with occasional dissonant harmony to enhance the rich chordal
writing which is fundamental to the 1930s style (Example 6.11).
Indeed, all the sections feature lush harmony. The brief "O
powerful western star!" (III), is nothing more than an A-major
thirteenth chord, presented in consecutive thirds. Section V,
"In a swamp" features occasional bitonality and the lower
tetrachord of the Phrygian scale, Lockwood characteristics
mentioned previously.
    The second large section of the piece begins with an ener-
getic, chantey-like setting of "Oh Captain! my Captain!,"
exhibiting a formal organization based on the stanzas of the
poem. In each return of the refrain, Lockwood varies the
mood from swaggering in the opening, through a militaristic
central section, to a subdued ending in which the death of the
"Captain" is realized. Lockwood followed this with a harmonized choral declamation of the epitaph, used by Whitman,
which appears on Lincoln's gravestone (IX, "This dust was
once the man").
    The final section, "Come lovely and soothing death," is a
fascinating moment in the piece, because Lockwood departed
from his predominant 1930s style and wrote a rare, fugal
chorus (Example 6.12). The tonal writing is unaffected and
simple, its imitations unfolding with almost textbook regularity. Unadorned as it is, the beautiful writing suggests a mood of
calm and serenity which would, perhaps, have been destroyed
by more active polyphony. To follow this exposition, the
composer returned to his more standard women-against-men

Example 6.11, 1930s-style writing, *Elegy for a Hero*, "Ever-returning Spring," pt. II, p. 7, mm. 1-5. Copyright (c) 1962 (Renewed) Shawnee Press, Inc. (ASCAP). International Copyright Secured. All Rights Reserved. Used by Permission.

Example 6.12, Contrapuntal writing, *Elegy for a Hero*, "Come Lovely and Soothing Death," pt. X, p. 29, mm. 1-20. Copyright (c) 1962 (Renewed) Shawnee Press, Inc. (ASCAP). International Copyright Secured. All Rights Reserved. Used by Permission.

antiphony. Finally, the text "Sooner or later delicate death" is painted subtly through the use of an appropriately delicate rhythmic setting.

A rousing hymn on "Prais'd be the fathomless universe" follows, again featuring the seventh-chord harmony of the 1930s style, enriched with bichords. Here is found the harmonic language which serves to unify this large piece, as shown by the return of pattern involving two chords at "The ocean shore," first used in section VII on the text "Sea winds blown." However, this device is merely a subtle reminder, and was not intended to be a literal "return." On the contrary, Lockwood has written, "I would not impose 'return' upon the poetry."[27] Another polyphonic chorus, with its syncopated subject in compound meter and its suggestion of the operative word of the text, "float" ("I float this carol with joy") provides a memorable close for the cantata.

Reviews contemporary with its composition describe *Elegy* as the sensitive and idiomatic choral work it is. A performance in Hartford, Connecticut, under the direction of Lara Hoggard, drew this critical response:

> Probably the outstanding performance of the evening was Normand Lockwood's 'Elegy,' a sensitive evocation of a poem by Walt Whitman. The chorus traversed its modern tonalities and delicate facets with disarming ease and assurance. . . .
>
> There was drama as well, drama of the most intense and absorbing nature.[28]

Although *Elegy for a Hero* shares many of the distinctive qualities of other 1930s-style pieces, it is also unique because of its contrapuntal sections and Lockwood's subtly sensitive text painting. Because its episodes span a narrower gamut that those of the oratorios, Lockwood's more sensitive style emerges.

In direct contrast to *Elegy* is a work written sixteen years later, *Donne's Last Sermon* (1978). Gerald Lepinsky, director of the Classic Chorale of Denver, commissioned Lockwood to compose the piece but gave no text specifications. In choosing Donne's final sermon, Lockwood created a challenge, particularly because of his overriding sense of responsibility to the words. Although, to him, the text "sings," it centers morbidly on images of death: "wormes," "corruption and putrefaction," and "winding sheetes."[29]

Predictably, the piece received its structure from changes of thought in the text, which Lockwood himself adapted from the prose. *Donne's Last Sermon* falls into five sections:

I.   "In all our periods and transitions in this life"
II.   "This whole world is but an universall churchyard"
III.   "Our birth dies in infancy, and our infancy dies in
        youth"
IV.   "But for us that dye now and sleepe in the state of the
        dead"
V.   "Even those bodies that were the temples of the holy
        Ghost"

Lockwood's textual choice for the commission shows his great respect for Donne's prose, as he indicated: "As a composer one has to try and recognize the shape of the phrases. Donne's phrases are so shaped . . . all you have to do is follow them."[30]

However, Lockwood exercised artistic license in the powerful postlude to the work. There he gathered all the Latin phrases used by Donne in the course of the sermon: "Exitus a morte" (an issue from death), "hebdomada mortium" (a weeke of death), and "Vermis Jacob" (Thou worme of Jacob). This departure from Donne's structure has the effect of an ancient litany, which both brings the sermon to a close and conjures the spirits which have influenced it (Example 6.13).

When the time came to set Donne's phrases to music, Lockwood stated, "I was as economical as possible."[31]   The

Example 6.13, Latin phrases, *Donne's Last Sermon*, MS, pt. V, pp. 44-46, mm. 4-7.

opening text is a preamble or prologue—"like Shakespeare, he tells us at the very beginning what the thing's about."[32] He continued about the opening: "singing is completely wrong for the dramatic idea—for what happens in the sermon at this point."[33] However, since he was bound to the medium at hand, he settled on an expanding chromatic motive for the ominous incantation at the beginning. The first phrase of the first movement illustrates his restrained "modus operandi" (Example 6.14). Utilizing rhythms generated by the words, the choir enters on an F-sharp octave which expands outwardly by half steps, then returns to F-sharp and descends chromatically. Regarding this device, Lockwood said, "Now that's a darned economical way of writing. The sopranos only go a minor third. It's sort of a mirror—but it's enough—that does it."[34] The work is integrated by means of this expanding chromatic motive.

Example 6.14, Expanding chromatic motive, *Donne's Last Sermon*, MS, pt. I, p. 2, mm. 1-7.

Text painting adds color to the pervasive darkness of this piece. The diminished fifth interval is utilized to depict "cruelty," and the organ accompaniment is thread-like under monotonous choral references to "winding sheetes." In "Vermis Jacob" he uses a pattern containing a minor second and a minor third. Its repetition and choral expansion suggests, perhaps, the sinuous motion of a snake charmer's object.

Lockwood is as fascinated with timbres as Donne was with colorful metaphors, and the composer effectively exploits the tonal possibilities of the organ in his setting of *Donne's Last Sermon*. The pedal ostinato in movement IV is indicated for principal sixteen- and eight-foot stops, dominated by a sixteen-foot bassoon stop—a very distinctive combination. This ostinato creates an unrelenting dissonance when combined with the more consonant choral statement.

The work is not limited to a simple depiction of the text, however. The composer, in effect, embellishes Donne's words in Movement V by including a musical clue to his own interpretation of the text. A phrase from the Martin Luther chorale, "Mitten Wir im Leben sind mit dem Tod umfangen" (Though we are in the midst of Life, Death ensnares us), is played on the organ. A more complete version of the same chorale was used in the previously mentioned *Choreographic Cantata*, which continues after the phrase it shares with *Donne's Last Sermon:*

Who then can save us from our woe
Save with grace unbounded?
Thou alone, O Lord.
. . . leave us not to languish in the bitter hour of Death
Kyrie Eleison.[35]

Such a penitent supplication never appears in Donne's text, but this brief instrumental reference to the chorale admits a glimmer of hope into an otherwise desolate topic. In fact, it challenges ever so slightly Donne's pervasive pessimism. To support the use of the chorale, Lockwood states, "In [Donne's sermon] he is not ever trying to spread doom and gloom. Even 'dilapidation' is (for me) only a physical condition, not a condition of the spirit."[36]

Donne's Last Sermon is, indeed, a venture into starkly dissonant, overwhelming darkness. When the text "sings," it does so with tremendous gravity. One such occurrence is in movement IV, "Dead march," where a twelve-tone row in the organ pedals is combined with static chords in the manuals, while the soprano and alto sections sing a clashingly dissonant unison line. Later in the same movement, however, the text is more colorfully presented in a dramatic contrast between a featured tenor section and the choir. The climax of the piece is prepared skillfully in a telescoping of the motive "vermis Jacob." These and other examples of Lockwood's craftsmanship make *Donne's Last Sermon* an intriguing piece, although the sheer volume of text overwhelms the music in many places. It is both Normand Lockwood's most dissonant and most unified large choral work.

Donne's Last Sermon and *Elegy for a Hero* present fascinating contrasts in Lockwood's choral genre. Text alone might account for the appeal of the first over the second. Certainly, Whitman's poetic text should produce vastly different results than Donne's prose sermon, especially from a composer so bound by his allegiance to the words. *Donne's Last Sermon* was written when Lockwood was seventy-two years old, seasoned with the maturity of a fruitful career replete with tonal or nearly-tonal choral works. Presumably, the challenge presented by a gripping, if macabre, text motivated the composer to try his hand at a distinctive musical rendering. In 1954, Samuel Barber had chosen the prose of Søren Kierkegaard as the text of a choral work, and few other choral composers had attempted such a demanding task. Perhaps another gift of the mature composer is to see beauty where others find only morbid fascination.

Shorter Choral Works

In this final sub-group of the choral works, texts have been drawn from authors and poets as diverse as Carl Sandburg for *Monotone* (1937), Dante for *O Our Father Who Art in Heaven* (1938) and *Hymn of Paradise* (1960), and Emily Dickinson for *Because I Could Not Stop for Death* (1981). However, from the 1920s to the present, one poet has captured Lockwood's attention—America's "Good gray poet," Walt Whitman.[37] In 1959 the composer wrote about this fascination. "It is only that, starting with my first setting of his poetry, which was in my young days, I have come to see more and more in him, and this is why I turn to him from time to time."[38] Indeed, Lockwood has turned often to Whitman, setting portions of the poet's "Inscriptions" (Lockwood's *I Hear America Singing*), "Starting from Paumanok" (*My Comrade*), "Song of Myself" (*What is the Grass?*), "Sea-Drift" (*Out of the Cradle Endlessly Rocking*), "Drum-Taps" (*Give Me the Splendid Silent Sun*), and "Whispers of Heavenly Death" (*Darest Thou Now, O Soul*).

Lockwood shows his responsibility to the text no matter the author or poet. Throughout his career, he has wisely chosen texts which, alone, create an almost palpable atmosphere. In so doing, he has created opportunities to exhibit his own strengths in text setting. *Monotone*, written in 1937 and based on excerpts from Carl Sandburg's work of the same name, is one such work. A ponderously slow tempo and sustained pitch in the bass part contribute to the non-changing atmosphere, while the upper parts occasionally depict a detail of the text. Word-generated rhythms, concerted choral statement, and bichordal, seventh-chordal, and modal harmonies are the elements from which *Monotone* is created.

Emily Dickinson's *Because I Could Not Stop for Death* inspired a solo song in 1938 and its adaptation for four-part chorus in 1981. The choral work was written to honor his daughter Angie, who died in 1980, and it represents a more mature Lockwood style, extremely subtle in the late stages of his evolution toward greater musical restraint. The inexorable mood of death is depicted in several ways. First, the lower three voices present interwoven ostinati in D minor, as a seemingly endless accompaniment to the solo line given to the soprano section (Example 6.15). In the middle section the bass voices continue to provide this droning accompaniment as the upper three voices present the text, often in open harmonies. The rounded form brings back the ostinati of the beginning, and the piece ends soberly on a D-to-A interval which includes a dissonant E. *Because I Could Not Stop for Death* is a restrained work, both in harmony and in the absence of overt text painting.

At the opposite end of the descriptive spectrum are those works which clearly depict details such as *This Moment*, based on a Walt Whitman text. Here Lockwood appears at his least restrained, indulging in broad pictorial descriptions of the countries mentioned. At the presentation of Russia, he quotes the "Song of the Volga Boatmen"; France and Germany are similarly suggested.

Equally representational, yet less obviously so, are the "Americana" choruses. *America!, O Democratic Nation*, subtitled "A Patriotic Anthem," features bombastic, homophonic writing with shifting meters and mild dissonance. Another Americanist poem, Whitman's *I Hear America Singing*, is noteworthy because of its rhythmic energy, a quality which is absent in the more typical 1930s style choruses such as *Apple Orchards* of 1952. However, the piece is stylistically identifi-

Example 6.15, *Because I Could Not Stop for Death*, p. 1, mm. 1-8. Copyright (c) 1981 by Jenson Publications. International Copyright Secured. All Rights Reserved. Used by Permission.

To Angi (October 19, 1935-March 21, 1980)

BECAUSE I COULD NOT STOP FOR DEATH

SATB, A cappella

EMILY DICKINSON

NORMAND LOCKWOOD

Example 6.16a, "Paumanok" pattern in *For a Child's Room*, Westminster Choir College 1949, p. 3, mm. 1-7. Used by Permission.

Example 6.16b, "Paumanok" pattern in *Apple Orchards*, p. 3, mm. 1-4. Copyright (c) 1950 (Renewed) Shawnee Press, Inc. (ASCAP). International Copyright Secured. All Rights Reserved. Used by Permission.

able as Lockwood's by its eclectic mixes of successive seventh-chord harmonies and tender, modal lyricism.

Many shorter choral works exhibit the 1930s style identified earlier: full, seventh-chord sonorities in a homophonic setting. The "Paumanok" pattern is just as prevalent as it was in the oratorios, seen in, among others, *For a Child's Room* of 1949 and *Apple Orchards* of 1952 (Examples 6.16 a and b).

Lockwood's greatest choral gift is his ability to write idiomatically for any choral medium, a skill he manifests in several choral styles. He occasionally chooses to write choral pieces which are not wholly homophonic and do not rely on poetic structure or text accentuation as much as the 1930s style. Whether it is the syncopated statements of *Praise to the Lord* (1958), the timpani-influenced use of voices as instruments in *Rejoice in the Lord* (1970), or the energetic counterpoint of *Alleluia, Christ is Risen* (1974), such techniques add variety to an otherwise largely homogeneous choral oeuvre. Other characteristics of the last-named work are its strophic form, displaying lively sixteenth-note figurations, joyous syncopations on "Alleluia," and one extremely striking shift from the newly-tonicized G-sharp major back to the home tonality of G major (Example 6.17).

Out of the Cradle Endlessly Rocking

Instead of retaining one choral style for the whole piece, many of Lockwood's short and intermediate choral works are episodic. In this respect, they are miniature versions of his oratorios. In such a piece, the composer carefully depicts a combination of moods and details, highlighting the poetic text as the work unfolds. As with the oratorios, unification is achieved by repeated harmonic or melodic motives; seldom does he repeat an entire section unchanged. *Out of the Cradle*

Example 6.17, Non-homophonic choral style, *Alleluia, Christ Is Risen*, pp. 1-2, mm. 1-10. Copyright (c) 1974 by Rongwen Music. Reproduced by permission of the publisher.

Example 6.17, continued.

Endlessly Rocking is the best of these—and rare among the episodic works because it includes a "refrain" of sorts in response to Whitman's original structure. Both the "Paumanok" pattern and other aspects of the 1930s choral style are evident in his 1938 setting of this poem.

Lockwood admits that the selection of the text took a great deal of time. Less than half of the lines in Whitman's *Out of the Cradle Endlessly Rocking*, the first poem in the "Sea Drift" set, were chosen. The resulting piece differs in theme from the original poem, which had focused on the narrator and his projected grief. In the process of text selection, Lockwood excised the most concrete portions and created a statement about loss and memory of happier times, which focuses on the primary "characters," the two birds.

For creative inspiration, the composer acknowledges his debt to Frederick Delius's 1903 setting of the same text. In comparison to Delius's version, however, Lockwood's is more intimate and understated, the latter being written for a cappella mixed choir, as opposed to Delius's dramatic solo baritone, choir, and orchestra.

Out of the Cradle Endlessly Rocking is valuable as an illustration of his early preference for understatement, which was manifested more frequently as his career progressed. Suggestion usually takes precedence over statement when he renders a Whitman text musically. His use of the "Paumanok" pattern is a perfect example of the sensitive and apt use of something so isolated as a tonic chord in second inversion (a prolonged anticipation of the root position chord) to suggest an expectant mood (Example 6.18).

Lockwood's fondness for the pattern stems from an aural preference—to him, the second inversion triad sounds more in tune than the root position. In his words, "the third is a very out-of-tune affair . . . with a root position chord, the overtones are out of tune with the upper notes of the chord."[39] An additional reason for preferring the second inversion, and one

Example 6.18, "Paumanok" opening, *Out of the Cradle Endlessly Rocking*, p. 3, mm. 1-7. Copyright (c) 1939 (Renewed) by G. Schirmer, Inc. International Copyright Secured. All Rights Reserved. Used by Permission.

G. Schirmer, Octavo No. 8316

To the New York World's Fair

Out of the Cradle Endlessly Rocking*

For Four-Part Chorus of Mixed Voices
a cappella

Walt Whitman   Normand Lockwood

*This composition was awarded the "World's Fair Prize", offered by G. Schirmer, Inc., for a choral composition suited to high-school singers, the jury consisting of Messrs. Samuel L.M. Barlow, Peter Dykema, George H. Gartlan, Roy Harris, and Hugh Ross.

which speaks directly to his subtlety, is its "mood"—as he says, "When I want it 'off the ground,' I write it like that. If I had written root position chords, we would have had Brahms."[40]

The prelude-like quality of the opening lines are perfectly depicted by Lockwood's "off the ground" writing. The music is static, never venturing far away from the second inversion, C major sonority of the first chord. The diatonic chords are written in close position, thereby presenting the wide range of the mixed choir in a narrow focus.[41]

1(23) Once Paumanok,
       When the lilac scent was in the air and fifth-month grass
         was growing,
       Up this seashore in some briers,
       Two feathered guests from Alabama, two together,
5   And their nest, and four light-green eggs spotted with
         brown,
       And ev'ry day the he-bird, to and fro [near at hand]
       And ev'ry day the she-bird crouched on the nest, silent,
         with bright eyes.

After a short sojourn into the realm of A-flat major, texture and tonality change at line six, beginning a transition to the next stanza. Lockwood gratefully acknowledges the suggestions of his former teacher, Nadia Boulanger, which resulted in a change in the penultimate chord in the section from a D-major chord to open D octaves[42] (Example 6.19).

Lockwood perceived Whitman's poem as "strikingly analogous to sonata-allegro form."[43] In such a framework, the next stanza functions as the contrasting thematic idea:

8(32) Shine! Shine! Shine!
       Pour down your warmth, great sun!
10   While we bask, we two together.
       Two together!

Example 6.19, Boulanger's suggested changes marked in Lockwood's hand, *Out of the Cradle Endlessly Rocking*, p. 5, mm. 1-8. Copyright (c) 1939 (Renewed) by G. Schirmer, Inc. International Copyright Secured. All Rights Reserved. Used by Permission.

Winds blow south or winds blow north,
Day come white, [or night] day come black,
Home, or rivers and mountains from home
15   Singing all time, minding no time,
While we two keep together.

The first line is set brightly on D octaves, then high thirds, to sustain the impact of the repeated word. Two-part contrapuntal writing follows, featuring more harmonic thirds. Both these paired devices seem to underscore the partnership of the subjects. Line fifteen returns to the "Paumanok"-inspired opening section.

A dramatic change of direction in the action occurs in the next stanza.

17(41) Til of a sudden,
       Maybe killed, unknown to her mate,
       One afternoon [forenoon] the she-bird crouched not on the
           nest
20   Nor returned that afternoon, nor the next,
       Nor ever appeared again.

As a consequence, the choral writing is more varied. Tenors and basses passionately decry lines seventeen and eighteen, moving through many dynamic changes in the space of four measures. The rest of the stanza is set with minimal imitative counterpoint, a procedure favored by Lockwood when contrast is needed, but text is too important for the confusion of complicated imitative statements.

22(52) Blow! Blow! Blow!
       Blow up seawinds along Paumanok's shore;
       I wait and I wait till you blow my mate to me.
  (56) All night long [on the prong of a moss-scalloped stake]
  (58) Sat the lone singer wonderful causing tears.

> He called on his mate,
> He poured forth the meanings which I of all men know.

Line twenty-two brings a return of the refrain, which again settles on the "Paumanok" chord. Lockwood pays particular attention to the setting of "All night long" in the next section by sustaining a B-flat minor seventh chord over the next eleven measures to suggest the seemingly endless vigil of the he-bird. Says Lockwood, "the consonants in this line are so liquid, it lends itself very well to a seamless sonority."[44]

At line twenty-eight, open fourth and fifth intervals (D to A and its inverse), subtly suggest bird calls in stretto fashion.

> 29(71)   Soothe! Soothe! Soothe!
>   Close on its wave soothes the wave behind,
>   And again another behind embracing and lapping, ev'ry
>   one close,
>   But my love soothes not me, not me.
>   Low hangs the moon, it rose late,
>   It is lagging—O I think it is heavy with love, with love.

The third appearance of the refrain diverges from its counterparts in lines eight and twenty-two. Here, he writes a rocking octave passage in the bass voices to suggest the "eternal rhythm, the staticness of the ocean."[45] The cadence at the end of line thirty-two is beautifully overlapped with the beginning of a transition which prepares the surge of emotion in the last return of the refrain:

> 35(81)   Loud! Loud! Loud!
>   Loud I call to you, my love!
>   High and clear I shoot my voice over the waves,
> 38   Surely you must know who is here, is here,
>   You must know who I am, my love.
> (111)   Hither my love!
>   Here I am! here!

The dramatic pinnacle of the piece is intensified with Lockwood's now characteristically tenacious writing, alternating between an upper register C octave and a diminished fourth interval. The composer's intuitive, suggestive sense shines forth in his choice of the G major-seventh sonority on line thirty-eight. The effect is startling in its freshness and clarity; the hebird is beside himself with grief. A surprising harmonic shift from the previous undulations around a G-sharp minor-seventh chord to a "pure" E minor triad on line forty-one begins the unwinding process into the next section.

42(95) O throat! O trembling throat!
        Sound clearer through the atmosphere!
(114)   This gentle call is for you my love, for you.
(119)   O darkness! Oh, in vain!
        O, I am very sick and sorrowful.
(123)   O throat! O throbbing heart!
        And I singing uselessly, all the night.

Dissonance is now introduced in the rocking harmony; sickness has replaced passion in the bird's sorrow. Line forty-two throbs first musically as soprano, alto, and bass parts have a mixture of sustained pitches and disjunct leaps (Example 6.20). In this section, Lockwood edited the poem to his greatest extent, in order to heighten the drama.

49(125) O past! O happy life! O songs of joy!
        In the air, in the woods, over fields,
        Loved! loved! loved! loved! loved!
        But my mate no more, no more with me!
        We two together no more.

When this "sonata" reaches its musical return at line forty-nine of Lockwood's text, the "Paumanok" pattern has taken on a poignant flavor, in contrast to its more hopeful, first-stanza

Example 6.20, Text-painting on "O throat! O trembling throat!", *Out of the Cradle Endlessly Rocking*, p. 18, mm. 1-14. Copyright (c) 1939 (Renewed) by G. Schirmer, Inc. International Copyright Secured. All Rights Reserved. Used by Permission.

appearance in a major tonality. Explained by Lockwood, "I'll put that in human terms—we now know the disappointment of that idea—what it could have been, and what it wasn't."[46] The piece ends with the now barren C sonority, stripped of its chord tones as the he-bird was deprived of its mate.

Lockwood feels that *Out of the Cradle Endlessly Rocking* is "right" poetically, dramatically, and musically. Critics and conductors must have agreed, because the piece won the World's Fair Prize offered by G. Schirmer in 1939. Soon after its publication, it was performed by the Knox College Choir (1941), the Harvard Glee Club and Radcliffe Choral Society (1942), and later by groups as diverse as the Westminster Choir College Graduate Choir (1950) and the George Lynn Singers of Denver (1959).[47]

* * * * *

Words of the composer's long-time associate, the late George Lynn, launch a summary of Lockwood's style:

> If there is a "stock-in-trade" for Lockwood, it is in the color of specific sounds, the *how* of a pitch as opposed to the *when* or the *what* of a pitch. It is his wont to give each word-meaning a particular sonority, while his basic sonority is forged out of lyricism.[48]

As Lynn states, timbre is a prime consideration for Lockwood; however, his concern for the text is even greater, and care in selecting timbres follows naturally from this concern.

As described by Jacob Evanson, Lockwood's particular response to a text is a mental translation of linguistic imagery to musical language—a "direct thinking in tone." Form in the choral works, as well as texture, is directly related to this attitude toward text. Similarly, two of Lockwood's operating modes, depicting a pervasive mood or specific details, is text-influenced. For Lockwood, text not only serves as the catalyst for a choral piece, it is the overriding "raison d'etre" for the work from start to finish. Every choice he makes, whether rhythmic, melodic, harmonic, formal, dynamic, or textural, seems traceable to this conviction.

The oratorio *Children of God* points out another typical Lockwood style characteristic—episodic structure. In that work, he uses a family of exotic or ancient components to create many "episodes." One such passage uses elements from the African-American folk tradition. An episode which occurs frequently enough to be recognized by the listener as an organizational element, the 1930s choral style, sometimes complete with the "Paumanok" pattern, represents another set of sounds present in the oratorio. In contrast to *Children of God*, later oratorios such as *Light Out of Darkness* feature more motivic unification, less tonal harmony, twelve-tone rows, and more diverse rhythmic writing. *Life Triumphant* is a notable example of Lockwood's fascination with the poetry of Walt Whitman, as it was combined with disparate text sources. Intermediate choral works such as *Choreographic Cantata, Donne's Last Sermon*, and *Elegy for a Hero* show, not only the influence of a commission on Lockwood's compositional process, but also his range of materials from Luther/Bach chorales, to unrelieved dissonance, to the 1930s choral style.

In the shorter choral works, Lockwood's penchant for Whitman is seen again, as well as his depiction of mood and/or detail. The pervasive 1930s style is another characteristic which appears consistently in the oratorios, interrupted only occasionally by a more rhythmic, non-homophonic style of choral writing. Finally, *Out of the Cradle Endlessly Rocking*, one of the composer's most popular pieces, is a culmination of his many choral presentations, including his careful approach to a Whitman text setting, episodic structures, concern for isolated sounds within and out of context, his alternation of mood with detail, and his 1930s "Paumanok" style.

Chapter Seven

KEYBOARD WORKS

Piano Solo and Duo

Overview

Normand Lockwood's piano works fall into three categories: thirteen written as a result of his piano lessons with Otto
J. Stahl prior to 1924, twenty-three from the years 1924 to 1974
including seven student works from 1924 and 1925, and eight
works composed since his retirement in 1974. The early-stage
works through 1925 are little more than compositional assign-
ments, incorporating various contrapuntal inventions and
small character pieces. Because they do not represent the adult
composer, those early works will not be addressed in this
study.[1] The *Piano Concerto* (1973), Lockwood's sole work for
piano and orchestra, is discussed in the chapter on music for
large ensembles.

Lockwood's second stage of piano composition was initiated
by his *Sonata* (1927), which shows signs of his more mature

style. In the remaining years of his second compositional period, Lockwood's tenures at Oberlin College (1932-43) and the
University of Denver (1961-74) were the most productive. The
Oberlin works include *Dichromatic Variations* (1935), a seven-
movement work based on the octatonic scale; *Sonata* (around
1935) which utilizes modal writing and major-against-minor
chords; *The Ninety and Nine*, a chordal, syncopated work
written for a dance performance in 1937; a lost work for dance
entitled *American Heritage; Sonatina* (1939), a tone piece
which features triple-staff notation; and *Six Piano Pieces*,
(1943) featuring both quartal and octatonic writing.

Between his Oberlin and Denver tenures, Lockwood wrote
three pieces: a study of sorts, full of Copland-like "Americana"
and bearing the composer's description, "Of Dubious Value"
(1950s); another 1950s work entitled *Piano Piece;* and the
bichordal *Lyric Arabesque*, published by Merion Music in
1956. Seven works were written while he was a faculty member
at the University of Denver, beginning with *Hamburg* (early
1960s) for two pianos, based on the hymn tune of the same
title, and followed by *Six Short Pieces for the Small Hand*
(around 1961), featuring tone rows and chromaticism. The
eclectic *Sonata for Two Pianos* (1965), a three-movement work
utilizing dodecaphonic principles, was composed next, followed
by the 1968 work, *Encores*, with five diverse movements
dedicated to several faculty players. *Fugue Sonata* (1969)
features a contrapuntal style and was composed as incidental
music for a dramatic work produced at the University of
Denver entitled *Summertree;* the five-movement *Fantasia*
appeared subsequently in 1971, again featuring polyphonic, as
well as hymn-style writing. The University of Denver piano
works conclude with *Series and Variations* (1974), which opens
with a six-note theme and concludes with seven short variations
of the theme.

The works from Lockwood's retirement years grow in
number as he continues to compose for piano. Often, these

pieces take the form of colorful miniatures, sometimes honoring friends in the profession. *Alternations* (1975), which was
later re-cast into a piece for trumpet and piano called *Adaptations* (1984), is the first. Others include *Lyric Poem*, arranged
in 1977 from a 1948 work of the same title for alto and piano
(another of the "Paumanok" works)[2]; the atonal *Eight Details
and Summary* (1982); and *Pieces of Eight* (1985), in which each
movement focuses on a single compositional device such as
pentatonicism or major/minor chords. More recently, he has
completed a set of miniatures entitled *Little Suite for Piano
(Five Out of Appalachia)* (1990), a brief *Etude* based on sixteenth notes in shifting meters (1990), and a graceful study in
timbres called *Farfalle* (1991). To honor American music
historian William K. Kearns on the occasion of his 1991 retirement from the University of Colorado, Lockwood wrote an
Ivesian solo entitled *A Childhood Recollection: "Lunch at the
Putnam Camp,"* which incorporates bitonality and the quotation of vernacular song.

In the piano genre as a whole, Lockwood's dissonance levels
range from mildly pungent quartal chords to dodecaphonic,
starkly atonal sections—a characteristic shared with his other
instrumental genres. In Lockwood's mind, atonality is better
suited to instrumental pieces than to vocal works: "For piano,
orchestral, and chamber music, it's wonderful, . . . but I don't
feel that way about singers."[3]

Lockwood's serially-constructed piano pieces are often
based on tone rows constructed of like intervals, especially 4ths
and 5ths. Such a row forms the base of the subordinate theme
area in the first movement of the *Sonata for Two Pianos:*

E   G# D# A# C# F# A   F   C   G   D   B

3rd 4th 4th 3rd 4th 3rd 3rd 4th 5th 5th 3rd.

This homogeneity is often coupled with a fixed-octave position which makes the original shape of the row recognizable, even when stated in retrograde or in a circular permutation (starting with pitches other than the first). Thus Lockwood utilizes serial techniques to avoid tonality, but bypasses manipulations that would destroy the row's familiarity. In essence, he exploits serialism to create atonal "melodies."

With regard to his serial writing, Lockwood stated,

> I have to confess that I disguise it. Not always [do I] write it pointillistically, for heaven's sake. I mean, how can you tell the difference? But if you give it a lot of quality, you can tell the difference. However you do it, it should be memorable—I don't like the isolation of ideas too much because they don't stick—you don't take them in, and they don't stick.[4]

In the context used above, the term "quality" may be interpreted as memorability.

In his use of non-tonal materials Lockwood identifies himself with many other peer composers in the United States who consciously modified Schoenberg's strict serialism to form a less-structured native style. Vincent Persichetti labeled the style "free serial technique" and named Aaron Copland, Irving Fine, Wallingford Riegger, and Roger Sessions among its advocates.[5] While free serial technique plays an important part in Lockwood's musical language, the eclectic Lockwood rarely writes a movement that is wholly in this style. Instead, atonality is often only one of several musical strands appearing in a composition. For instance, in *Sonata for Two Pianos*, an arpeggiated, bitonal figure—a kind of Albertian figure gone awry—is followed by a highly developed tone row. This striking mix of old and new ideas will be examined in greater detail below.

The composer's works draw on non-traditional pianistic techniques in order to accommodate his musical ideas;

however, they are not formidable by contemporary standards. One of Lockwood's favorite pitch sets, the octatonic scale, is awkward technically. Similarly, clusters of notes which appear in every range of the instrument in close succession provide technical challenges. His unpredictable "toccata" figuration calls for an almost frenetic energy, as well as an unfailing memory for asymmetrical patterns. Other pieces are, for the most part, timbral explorations, and these show Lockwood's exacting concern for tone quality. He is also fond of rhythmically notated tempo variations, apparently so that he can control the degree of "ritard" or "accelerando" in the performance. In these cases, the pianist must be rhythmically adept, yet sensitive enough in performance to escape a mechanistic adherence to the beat. As a whole, Lockwood's pieces present a challenge for the performer but, as pianists who have approached them have found, they prove to be well worth the effort.

Stravinskian Influences

As evidenced in the *Sonata* for piano (1927), Nadia Boulanger undoubtedly exposed Lockwood to techniques used by one of her favorite composers, Igor Stravinsky. Lockwood later renounced the overt imitations of Stravinsky's style, admonishing would-be performers on the score itself: "This is a curiosity at best. Not to be performed!"[6] The *Sonata* includes at least three ideas of probable Stravinskian origin, and therefore stands as somewhat of a chronicle of his Parisian studies. These influences would eventually be further digested and refined, becoming individualized characteristics of the younger composer.

The first such influence, modality, is shown in a complete Dorian scale near the beginning of movement one. The clear presentation of this mode in scale form is followed immediately by an ornamental figure and a scalelike reference to G Phrygian mode. Lockwood's interest in modes persists in later pieces; *Sonata* of 1942 explores Lydian mode, and *Encores* of 1968 has tinges of Locrian mode.

Lockwood's metrically disproportionate themes, ultimately resulting in some of his most memorable thematic gestures, might also have been inspired by Stravinsky. The third movement of the *Sonata* (1927) is based on such an unmetrical, repetitive germ which is treated to successive expansion and development (Example 7.1).

Example 7.1, Non-metrical theme, *Sonata* (1927), MS, mvt. I, p. 1, mm. 1-8.

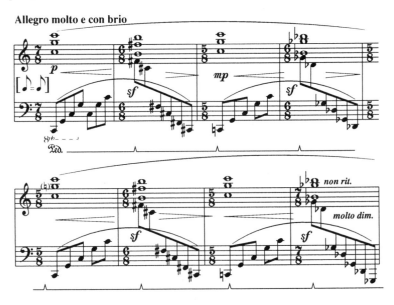

Lockwood's third Stravinsky-influenced device is the simultaneous use of parallel major and minor chords. This particular juxtaposition of lowered and natural thirds creates a jarring dissonance, and accounts for much of Lockwood's dissonant writing. He described such harmony as "Stravin-skian" himself with regard to the *Sonata for Two Pianos.*[7]

A fourth characteristic, Lockwood's fondness for the oc-tatonic scale, may have come from Stravinsky as well. Al-though the pattern is not prominent in the 1927 *Sonata*, it soon became one of his standard methods of avoiding diatonically derived sonorities. Lockwood's term for this alternation of half- and whole-steps was "dichromatic," and it was first seen in a piano work named *Dichromatic Variations* (1935) (Example 7.2). The octatonic scale is prominent in every genre of Lockwood's output, whether instrumental or vocal. Other style characteristics such as quartal and bichordal harmony appear as often as octatonicism, but they are best described in the context of the pieces themselves.

Example **7.2**, Octatonicism, *Dichromatic Variations*, MS, Introduction, p. 1, mm. 1-4.

Representative Works

Lockwood's early style is exhibited in the 1935 *Sonata*, while another work, *Six Piano Pieces* (1947) represents his mid-career interest in miniatures. Finally, *Sonata for Two Pianos* (1965) rounds out his compositional progression, a compilation of his favorite devices in the medium of piano ensemble.

Sonata (1935)

Regarding the *Sonata* written in 1935, critic Charles Mills wrote, "Normand Lockwood's *Sonata for Piano* was one of the most curious of the serious works heard in [WNYC's Fifth American Music] Festival. It is very rich in good sonorities but most disappointing in total content."[8]   Mr. Mills's "good sonorities" may refer to the many Stravinskian devices—major/minor chords, octatonic fragments, and modality—which occur in the piece. Other style characteristics, especially quartal and bichordal harmonies, also contribute to the musical language in this twenty-minute work. This critic's opinion was apparently not shared by Lockwood's noted colleague, pianist Beveridge Webster, who chose to perform the work at Columbia University in 1947.

The three movements of the *Sonata* are designated: I. Singing, then lively and energetic, II. Gay, but with a folk-like melancholy, III. Fast. The first movement, a sonata form, begins with a straightforward, chorale-like melody in G major, harmonized by major/minor chords that do not function in a key (Example 7.3). The subordinate theme is inspired by the children's chant, sol-mi-la-sol-mi. After a transition built on diminished-fifth intervals, the first presentation of the subordinate theme occurs in a suggested B-flat major, against arpeggiated quartal harmony in the accompaniment. Providing a majority of the movement's developmental material, the sol-mi-la-sol-mi theme is almost always presented bitonally, with increasing rhythmic, dynamic, and textural intensity.

The simple folk-like tune in G Lydian mode upon which the second movement is based (Example 7.4), recalls many of the modal movements of Bela Bartok's *Mikrokosmos.* The open, rocking accompaniment emphasizes D, the functional domi-

Example 7.3, Chorale-type Theme 1, *Sonata* (1935), MS, mvt. I, p. 1, mm. 1-15.

Example 7.4, Lydian Theme 1, *Sonata* (1935), MS, mvt. II, p. 10, mm. 1-4.

[Lydian theme, antecedent]

nant while simultaneously thwarting a purely Lydian modality by incorporating a piquant F-natural. Major-seventh harmonies provide a richer backdrop for the second part of the theme, presented, as with the entire *Sonata*, in bars of varying lengths. The second movement, abundant in soft dynamics and judicious use of pedal, is a delicate alternation of the two brief parts of its single theme.

Arpeggiation of bichordal ideas in a surprising, irregular framework comprises the first theme of the last movement (Example 7.5). The "germ" of the theme occupies seventeen sixteenth notes over two uneven bars (labeled A), then is expanded to the length of eighteen sixteenths (labeled B), and finally twenty-two sixteenths (labeled C), before the group is repeated. The second time, the minuscule opening germ is further contracted to thirteen sixteenths, followed by fourteen sixteenths, and finally a repetition of the twenty-two sixteenths of the previous third phrase. This method of composition, progressively but minutely varying motivic germs, contributes to the organic coherence of the first theme of this sonata form.

The third movement's contrasting theme is strongly accented, metrically uneven, and pentatonic, retaining the energy of the first theme. The theme erupts in percussive accents, punctuated by minor seconds, bichords, and ostinati. Lockwood's writing is rich in the varied manifestations of his harmonic language and progressive rhythms, but cohesiveness is ultimately overpowered by diversity in this work.

Example 7.5, Bichordal, rhythmically irregular Theme 1, *Sonata* (1935), MS, mvt. III, p. 1, mm. 1-11.

Six Piano Pieces (1947)

The central portion of Lockwood's career brought with it a greater appreciation for subtle, intimate piano pieces than is evident in his earlier works. Although written during a period when he was more involved in the composition of large-scale works, *Six Piano Pieces* of 1947 is one of the first manifestations of this later characteristic. The correspondence concerning it is equally significant. Pianist and scholar John Kirkpatrick, then at Cornell University, received the set early in 1947. Lockwood had sent them with the hope that Kirkpatrick would include them in a venture called the Music

Press Piano Series. While he chose not to publish the pieces in the largely pedagogical enterprise, Kirkpatrick offered Lockwood both praise and meticulous suggestions for improvement.[9] Lockwood characterized Kirkpatrick's remarks in a later statement.

> John Kirkpatrick's perceptive, incisive, and painstaking remarks are a masterly lesson.
> I never revised these pieces . . . he refers to his commentary as being "springboards or stickpins" in and for the future—which, indeed, they were and still are.[10]

Although Kirkpatrick felt that the pieces were too "erratic and unshapely" for the series, he also confessed that his comments were "not from anybody that's fussed with composing, but from a purely 'laity' viewpoint."[11] Kirkpatrick said of "Colloquy," a tonal melody accompanied by a quartally-based, arpeggiated ostinato, "[It] just misses being a very beautiful piece"[12] (Example 7.6). In reviewing the piece, the pianist questioned the tempo and the lack of a time signature, in particular. Another piece, "My Favorite Scale," is based on the octatonic scale, presenting and developing various converging

Example 7.6, Opening, Six Piano Pieces, MS, "Colloquy," p. 3, mm. 1-11.

patterns of the scale set in a swinging rhythm. The texture is sparse in the piece, usually involving only two-part polyphony, which allows Lockwood the spatial freedom to contrive a particularly piquant flavor through chromatic juxtapositions. Kirkpatrick's response to this innocently irreverent piece was, "I should think that here would be a proper field day for unpredictable whimsy."[13]

Sonata for Two Pianos (1965)

An amalgam of the many pianistic styles favored by Lockwood, the *Sonata for Two Pianos* was commissioned by Southern Colorado State College (now the University of Southern Colorado). In this work Lockwood exhibited his love of the collage principle, juxtaposing dodecaphonic writing in the second movement with a bluesy third movement. Lasting fifteen minutes in total, the movements are designated: I. Allegro, II. Adagio, III. Moderato, leggiero, and IV. Allegro scherzoso.

In the first-movement sonata form, an arpeggiated theme in C major is contrasted with a tone-row-based second theme.[14] The first theme is presented by the two pianos in canon, creating bichordal harmonies. The second theme's row, as discussed earlier, focuses on intervals of the third, fourth, and fifth, and is accompanied by arpeggiated seventh chords and bichords (Example 7.7). Forming an extension of the second theme group, the row is immediately presented in imitative retrograde. A three-note subset—C-sharp, E, and F-sharp—accompanied by major/minor chords, becomes the transitional material that leads to a restatement of the first theme in C major. The closing section consists of a new, four-pitch set that is extended in energetic sixteenth-notes. This new theme is later presented with cluster chords and finally appears in augmentation.

Example 7.7, Tone row in octaves, Theme 2, *Sonata for Two Pianos*, MSC, mvt. I, p. 3, mm. 10-12; p. 4, mm. 1-3.

In the development section, Lockwood manipulates the original row of theme two in various ways. First, the entire theme is presented in temporal diminution. He then begins a series of circular permutations, beginning with pitch 2, proceeding through the row, and placing pitch 1 at the end. Further similar permutations begin with pitches 3, 5, 6, and 7, each presenting the entire row. As these operations take place, the music becomes increasingly dense in dynamics and harmony.

After a return of theme one in C major, the transposed second theme returns. Lockwood changed the first two notes of the transposition, resulting in a row which lacks the pitch A and which duplicates C-sharp. When the arpeggiated first theme returns, E major/minor is placed against C major/minor. The movement ends with further manipulations and fragmentations of the row, and finally half the row is stated, then mirrored to create twelve tones—a serial technique that dates back to Berg and Webern. The close of the movement is a rhythmically dispersed ritard: notated in successive quarter, dotted quarter, and finally half-note values. An excellent example of Lockwood's "non-pointillistic" dodecaphonic writing, this movement alternates active, almost jarring bitonality with lyrical atonality.

Example 7.8, Opening row and reharmonized hymn tune, *Sonata for Two Pianos*, MSC, mvt. II, p. 15, mm. 1-7.

The "Adagio" movement treats its original row in a mysterious, ethereal way, often stating subsets in harmonic clusters in order to vary the linear timbre. In contrast to this row, a hymn tune is presented in dissonant homophony (Example 7.8). The Geneva, or Yattendon hymnal, (a hymnal of the Anglican church), served as the source of this tune. Both the expressive flavor of the movement and Lockwood's dissonant hymn setting recall works of Charles Ives, such as the *Fourth Violin Sonata* (*Children's Day at the Camp Meeting*). The same hymn tune appears in the last movement of the *Sonata for Two Pianos*, as well.

In fresh, almost defiant, contrast to the more cerebral structures of the two preceding movements, the third, "Moderato, leggiero" is a lazy jazz piece. Blue notes, ragged eighths, and the ever-present octatonic scale are interspersed with a Gershwin-like pattern of short notes reminiscent of the familiar locomotive section of *Rhapsody in Blue* and its rapidly repeated sixteenth notes (Example 7.9). Tinges of dissonance and rhythmic asymmetry, particularly in the five-bar theme, make it a relaxed, yet suitable companion for the rest of the *Sonata*. The movement closes with a series of non-metrical bichords.

Example 7.9, Gershwin-like sixteenths, *Sonata for Two Pianos*, MSC, mvt. III, p. 21, mm. 1-2.

The final movement, yet another sonata form labeled "Allegro scherzoso," begins with a motive that is similar to one in the third movement of the *Sonata* (1935). A modal solo melody, artfully constructed of mostly open intervals, alternates with the metric construction: 2/4 + 3/8 + 2/8. The theme consists of four alternations of each component, resulting in an appealing mixture of the predictable with the irregular.

The transition to the second theme group exhibits an energy particular to instrumental music of this century (Example 7.10). This motoric sixteenth-note figure makes unexpected directional twists, presenting a technical challenge for the performers, who play the material in dialogue. The rhythmic impulse generated by rapid directional shifts at high speed creates an almost frenzied energy level in this transition. Of this passage Lockwood said, "It depends on where you make your turns. Where you make them is something I consider more often than anything else [in this style of writing]."[15]

Example 7.10, Transition to Theme 2, *Sonata for Two Pianos*, MSC, mvt. IV, p. 27, mm. 1-6.

For the second theme Lockwood returns to the Geneva-Yattendon hymn of the second movement, using only the second half of the hymn tune. Both thematic ideas are highly developed in the movement, and eventually they are combined with the ever increasing momentum of the sixteenth-note figure. To close the movement and the sonata, Lockwood wrote a presentation of the hymn tune shared by the two pianos.

All of the piano works, regardless of size, have in common an attention to detail which demands that nearly every note be articulated in a specific way. In *Dichromatic Variations* (1935) and *Fugue Sonata* (1969), Lockwood used three or four staves of music for solo piano in order to make the pedaling clear to the performer. Lockwood's great care with the quality of the isolated sound, as well as its contextual function, is predictable enough to classify as a component of his musical signature. He not only treats the piano as a purely technical instrument, he also exploits all of its idiomatic textures, difficult as they are to produce. His piano accompaniments show the same attention to detail as the solo piano works (Chapter Nine).

Bichordality, modality, quartal writing, dodecaphonic writing, major/minor chords, organic development of themes—all of Lockwood's repertoire of compositional techniques appear in the solo piano works. Most often these elements follow each other in rapid succession, but occasionally, they occur simultaneously. Perhaps, as John Kirkpatrick has observed about Charles Ives, Lockwood assumes the transcendentalist view of an ultimate unity beyond all diversity.

Organ Works

Overview

In contrast to his early interest in composing for the piano, Normand Lockwood waited until mid-career to write his first work featuring organ. His initiation to this genre occurred in 1951, when he received a commission from Columbia Broadcasting Service to commemorate the tenth year of continuous Sunday Broadcasts by noted virtuoso, E. Power Biggs. Oddly enough, this honor was bestowed upon Lockwood without the benefit of any compositional evidence in the medium, a testament to his reputation as a composer of other works. The resulting *Concerto for Organ and Brasses* was premiered by Biggs in 1952 and published by Associated Music Publishers, Inc., in 1953. It was recorded in that same year by Remington Records with Marilyn Mason as the soloist. The 1951 concerto was the first of three similar works for the instrument. Lockwood's *Concerto for Organ and Chamber Orchestra* was completed in 1973 and his *Second Concerto for Organ and Brasses* was composed in 1977. The three organ concertos will be discussed at the end of this section.

Excluding the concertos, the organ genre is comprised of twelve works. Seven are small in scale—five minutes or under in duration; two, *Festive Service for Organ* (1976) and *Twenty-Five Organ Preludes* (1979-80), are sets of short pieces; and three are extended works—the *Sonata for the Organ* (1960), *Processional Voluntary* (1965), and *Fantasy on Jesus, My Joy* (1972). All except one of these twelve, *Quiet Design* (1953), were composed after Lockwood's move to Denver. Over one third of the organ works, five pieces, are based on hymn tunes—a reflection of the typically ecclesiastical use of the instrument.

Although the piano works are relatively unknown, the organ works have had public exposure through various media. Three of the works have been published in part or in their entirety, and the two 1950s pieces, the first concerto and *Quiet Design*, have been commercially recorded. The first concerto alone has been performed throughout the U. S. by at least ten different organists.[16] Its recording, coupled with its readily attainable accompanying group of three trumpets and two trombones, make it a favorite among organists who are drawn to twentieth-century music.

Performers have played important roles in the composition of these pieces, since Lockwood wisely solicited accomplished organists for their expertise concerning registrations. The substitution for and combination of ranks is a standard skill required of accomplished soloists, and Lockwood gained from the expertise of his dedicatees, organists such as E. Power Biggs, Marilyn Mason, Phyllis Selby Tremmel, and Roy Carey. In her monograph on Biggs, Barbara Owen related an interchange between Biggs and Lockwood concerning the ensemble balance in the *Concerto for Organ and Brasses*. Lockwood wanted to improve the balance between the brasses and organ, and Biggs responded,

> I think your comments on the way the work sounded result from . . . characteristics of organ tone. Actually an organ doesn't really create a lot of sound, and is easily covered by other instruments. This is just as true with much larger instruments than . . . [with smaller organs]. Antiphonal contrast of the instrumental ensemble and organ is always effective, in the Handelian manner, but as soon as the brasses all combine with the organ they tend to drown it out, except for full organ percussive-like chords.
>
> I've noticed this to be true in other works where one, two or three contrapuntal lines on the organ tend not to hold their own

against the orchestral fabric. On the piano they would sound through impact.[17]

According to Owen, Biggs advised Lockwood to retain the original scoring, since he felt that the work would be effective as it was.[18]

Organs vary more from location to location than any other musical instrument. Consequently, the judgment of an accomplished player is invaluable to a composer of organ music. As Lockwood stated in 1976, "The organ's a strange instrument to write for. A composer is up against it; he has to write a work that will hold water under almost any circumstance."[19] For this composer, individual ranks or small combinations "hold water" better than mixtures or full registrations. Concerning *Festive Service for Organ*, he stated, "I don't like to hear the organ too full all the time, because it inundates one and you don't hear anything anymore."[20]

Lockwood's organ works show a similarity to the piano works in their widespread avoidance of a functional tonic. In the organ pieces, serial compositional techniques occur more frequently than any other device, but like the piano pieces, bichords, quartal writing, chromaticism, and octatonic passages also contribute non-tonal materials with great frequency. In both genres, Lockwood focused on counterpoint or the linear aspect of homophonic music more often than a purely chordal style. Dissonance in the organ works far outweighs the occurrence of consonant passages, which is in keeping with Lockwood's procedures in the piano works.

Representative Solo Organ Works by Decade

1960s Organ Works

Because they were begun later in his career than any other genre, the organ pieces are the least diverse as a whole. The earliest work, *Quiet Design* (1953), is the most musically traditional, constructed contrapuntally of two, and sometimes three imitative parts. Works written in the succeeding decade, the 1960s, exhibit characteristics which would continue to be manifested throughout the genre. The first of these opuses is *Sonata for the Organ* (1960), a three-movement work in traditional forms, utilizing dodecaphonic and chromatic materials. Lockwood's tendency to write intervallically homogeneous tone rows, consisting of fewer than twelve different notes, is evident in the first theme of the first movement. In this theme, the pitch E is missing, while the pitch C is repeated. Pairs of half steps furnish the row with memorable emblems. The row is almost an entire chromatic scale, octave-displaced, and broken into four chromatic subsets (labeled a, b, c, and d), and re-assembled, as shown below:

G A♭ C D♭ A B♭ B D C E♭ F F♯
  a   b   c   d.

The second movement of the *Sonata* is also serially constructed, based on a four-note set—G♯, C, G, and E—and the final movement features yet another tone row. These rows are treated as if they were themes in traditional forms; however, in the development sections Lockwood often uses specifically serial manipulations.

Stopping on a Walk to Rest is the first of two works composed in 1963. Its rhythmically free fantasia style features the eclectic combination of a tone row, quartal writing, and a charming, triadic bird call (Example 7.11). The sparse scoring indicates Lockwood's interest in the isolated timbres of the organ. In the other 1963 work, *Processional Voluntary*, a unique stop, the "State Trumpet" of large cathedral organs is designated. This single-movement work, which was published

Example 7.11, Triadic bird call, *Stopping on a Walk to Rest*, MSC, p. 4, mm. 1-2.

in 1973 by Waterloo Music, is written in four through-composed sections, and draws from octatonic, bichordal, and modal materials.

1970s Organ Works

The next decade saw seven organ works produced, beginning with the *Fantasy on Jesus, My Joy* (1972). This ten-minute work is composed in five movements, all of which are based on the familiar chorale, "Jesu Meine Freude." Baroque contrapuntal procedures intermingle with dissonant, bichordal, and quartal harmonies in Lockwood's fresh approach to a time-honored theme. The first section of the fifth movement, "Ground, Canon, Chorale," is based on an octatonic scale in iambic meter. A two-part canon is placed over the continuing ground, which is followed by the chorale, reharmonized on F-sharp (Example 7.12). The next opus from Lockwood's prolific 1970s is the small-scale *Duo sopra pedale* of 1973, an AAB form featuring a canon at the interval of a second, over a pedal point. In the *Toccata* of 1975, Lockwood returned to serial procedures, adding a chromatic, accompanimental ostinato which is developed progressively over the course of the piece.

Example 7.12, Reharmonized "Jesu, Meine Freude" over octatonic ground, *Fantasy on Jesus, My Joy*, MST, mvt. V, p. 14, mm. 10-15.

A commission from the Denver Chapter of the American Guild of Organists launched the next work, *Festive Service for Organ* of 1976. A set of service music suitable for use in worship or in concert, the concert version is ten minutes in duration. Movements include a "Prelude," "Introit" (based on the hymn tune "St. Gertrude"), "Litany," "Fanfare," "Offertory,"

"Benediction," "Postlude," and "Exit" (based on the hymn tune in retrograde). *Festive Service* is a joyous piece, its first movement evoking clanging church bells (Example 7.13). For the "Introit," Lockwood borrowed from his own choral anthem, *The Heavens are Telling* (1974), also based on "St. Gertrude." This hymn tune is best known for its accompaniment of the

Example 7.13, Irregular ostinato creating church-bell effect, *Festive Service for the Organ*, MSC, mvt. I, p. 2, mm. 1-12.

text, "Onward, Christian Soldiers." As in *Fantasy on Jesus, My Joy*, Baroque forms and styles traditionally identified with the organ are used throughout *Festive Service for Organ*, and especially in the passacaglia tune found in the "Offertory."

Following chronologically is Lockwood's *Canonic Toccata* (1979), which is uniquely scored for two organs. Another commission from the Denver Chapter of the American Guild of Organists, it is a dialogue featuring some of Lockwood's favorite devices: chromatic, octatonic, and quartal materials. The toccata figure evolves asymmetrically and therefore resembles the toccata sections of other instrumental works including the *Piano Concerto*, first movement (Example 7.14).

Example 7.14, Asymmetrical toccata figuration, *Canonic Toccata*, MSC, p. 2, mm. 1-2.

1980s Organ Works

Twenty-Five Organ Preludes (1979-80) features some of Lockwood's finest organ writing. His focus on a single thematic idea in each and use of limited musical materials make these preludes distinctive in his organ genre. Ranging in length from fifty seconds to two and one half minutes, they are artfully written and would make worthy, accessible additions to any service organist's repertoire. The first prelude, "Stille Nacht," is a lovely paraphrase of the Franz Gruber tune with harmony rarely more complex than ninth chords. In prelude Number 7, "Love Divine" ("Hyfrydol"), Lockwood crafted an ingeniously modulating bass line against ostinati in the manuals.[21] Other preludes in this set exhibit the composer's breadth of expression: the atmosphere of Gregorian chant in Number 16, "Ostande Nobis"; the lively rendition of the "L'Homme Armé" tune in Number 18; and the lullaby treatment of Number 24, "Jesus, Jesus, Rest Your Head," in compound meter. Numbers 1, 4, 5, 9, 13, 15, 18, and 20 of the *Twenty-Five Organ Preludes* were published in 1981 by Augsburg Publishing House under the title *Eight Preludes for Organ.*

Three Chorale Voluntaries for trumpet and organ (1982) begins with a largely homophonic, dissonant treatment of the chorale "Es ist genug," which incorporates Lydian modality. Less harmonically pungent is the contrapuntal "Aus Meines Herzens Grunde," unique because it bears the F-major key signature throughout. Most of Lockwood's instrumental works have no key signature, since they are written without reference to a functional tonic. In the final movement, "Ein' feste Burg," the trumpet embellishes the popular hymn tune with driving sixteenth notes. *Three Trumpet Voluntaries,* published by Wilshorn Music, adds fuel to the hypothesis that, by 1982, Lockwood had found both a profitable enterprise and a creative outlet in the composition of music for the sacred service.

Two of the *Twenty-Five Organ Preludes* were dedicated to Lockwood's sister, Albertine L. Reynolds and, in his next work of 1982, he created a title from that sentiment. *Postlude for Albertine* is a reharmonization of the "Old Hundredth" hymn tune, preceded by two pages of highly ornamental, pentatonic prelude. Finally, and with an appropriate title for the culminating work in the genre, *World Without End. Amen.* (1985) is a motivic, serially-composed tone piece lasting only about ninety seconds. Opening with ten successive thirds in arpeggiated fashion, the main thematic material is successively abridged, an inverse of his "organic" style prevalent in the piano works.

Organ Concertos

Overview

The three organ concertos form a homogeneous group for several reasons, but primarily because of the abundance of Baroque procedures they exhibit. The second movement of the *Concerto for Organ and Brasses* (1951) is based on a passacaglia, while fugal and chorale-style writing characterize the outer movements. The first two movements of the *Concerto for Organ and Chamber Orchestra* (1973) are entitled "Sinfonia" and "Ciacona," and the latter features the continuous variation style of the chaconne. Finally, each of the three movements of the *Second Concerto for Organ and Brasses* (1977) follow Baroque organizational practices: "Partita," "Canzona," and "Ricercare Scherzoso." An additional neo-Baroque feature is Lockwood's use of a homophonic chorale style in parts of each concerto. Many of these sections are not based on pre-existing chorales, while others, such as "Langdon" in the 1977 work, are actual hymn tunes treated in chorale style.

Performing forces for the first and third concertos differ with respect to one instrument only. The 1951 work calls for two each of trumpets and trombones, while the 1977 work requires an additional trumpet. In these works, the brass writing assumes two forms: the homophonic chorale style mentioned above, or an exalted, declamatory counterpoint. The middle concerto is scored for two each of flutes, oboes, trumpets, and horns, with string section, timpani, and tubular chimes. Again, chorale and contrapuntal sections are abundant. A most striking scoring of the "Rondo" theme features a rhythmic dialogue between timpani and organ pedals.

The first and third organ concertos are linked by more than their similar instrumentation. Although the 1951 work was conceived for and premiered by E. Power Biggs, it was performed on the Remington recording by organist Marilyn Mason. Mason met the composer at Union Theological Seminary as a graduate student, during his tenure on the composition faculty. Twenty-six years after the date of the first concerto, Mason, then chair of the Organ Department of the University of Michigan at Ann Arbor, commissioned Lockwood to write another work with the same scoring. The two concertos for organ and brasses are, therefore, inextricably linked to the gifts and energies of this noted artist. Lockwood undoubtedly owes numerous performances of the early work to Mason's talents, as exhibited on her recording.

All three concertos exhibit harmonic language which is greatly influenced by octatonicism and chromaticism, as well as bichordal, quartal, and serial techniques. The resulting dissonant timbres of the organ create a much more relentless impression than the same constructions on piano, possibly because of the natural sonic decay (or "decrescendo") that occurs when harmonies are played on piano. Lockwood, consequently, was careful to write more sparsely for the organ than he did for piano, to avoid the driving effect of dissonance without subtle, indigenous shadings he would have created on the piano. Speaking of the *Concerto for Organ and Chamber Orchestra*, he pointed out, "Notice how widely-spaced the parts are. I don't like it to sound messy, unless, of course, you're writing about a river bottom."[22] Additionally, he offered, "Different octaves are important—they keep out of the way of each other."[23]

Lockwood's organ registrations were usually dictated by the specifications of the premiere instrument. In the Associated Music Publishers' 1953 edition of the first concerto, Lockwood addressed registration only in general, leaving specific stops to the discretion of the performer. There he indicated only that each manual and the pedals should be "forte," and recommended couplers. The two unpublished concertos provide for as much freedom, although he specified the occasional "gemshorn" or "scharff" stop when a particular color was desired. In Lockwood's mind, problems of texture and clarity could best be addressed in the process of composition, rather than registration. Timbral differences on the organ are only relative, as he observed with respect to a flute and reed combination, "Something like this sounds homogeneous, whereas [the same sound] in instrumental ensemble is heterogeneous."[24]

The composer's technical requirements for the organist are somewhat less demanding than those for the pianist. Contrapuntal themes that make appearances in the pedal part, do so briefly. If the pedal part is featured, it is rarely demanding rhythmically or technically. The portions written for manuals offer their greatest challenges in the clusters, arpeggiated or chordal, which contribute to the almost continual thread of dissonance inherent in the works. Inevitably, running figures based on the symmetrical octatonic scale require that soloists adjust their conventional fingerings and pedal techniques.

Concerto for Organ and Brasses

Jacket notes which accompany Remington's 1953 recording characterize the *Concerto for Organ and Brasses* as "contemporary musical language shaped in rugged baroque design."[25] As mentioned earlier in this chapter, its dedicatee, E. Power Biggs, premiered the work on the Contemporary American Festival of the Air on April 27, 1952, in a broadcast sponsored by the Alice M. Ditson Fund of Columbia University.

The overall flavor of the 1951 work is dominated by the pervasive influence of the octatonic scale, beginning with page one (Example 7.15). Here the scale takes on macabre overtones, perhaps because it accompanies the reiteration of the pitches C, B, C, and A: the same pattern as the opening of the ancient "Dies Irae" sequence. The organ's opening statement is followed by brasses in chorale style (Example 7.15, mm. 8-10), and these two ideas alternate as primary and secondary material throughout the movement, which ends remarkably on a strong C tonality.

The "passacaglia" of the second movement is a descending chromatic scale in the pedals, with an ornamented version of the same in the manual and brasses. Its "pianissimo" designation helps to create an overwhelming sense of melancholy. This mood is relieved in the third movement, a fugue with an octatonic subject. A chorale-like tune provides contrast to the counterpoint, presented in unison brasses. Later, the first-movement chorale theme, C-B-C-A, appears in the brasses, this time harmonized and temporally augmented.

Example 7.15, Registration; octatonic bass line in Theme 1, chorale-style brass Theme 2, (with composer's annotations), *Concerto for Organ & Brasses*, mvt. I, p. 1-2, mm. 1-16. Copyright (c) 1953 (Renewed) Associated Music Publishers, Inc. (BMI). International copyright secured. All Rights Reserved. Used by Permission.

To E. POWER BIGGS
COMMEMORATING TEN YEARS OF CONTINUOUS BROADCASTING

Concerto for Organ & Brasses

Example 7.15, continued.

Concerto for Organ and Chamber Orchestra

The *Concerto for Organ and Chamber Orchestra* is immediately striking because of the twenty-two-year evolution in
Lockwood's compositional technique since the composition of
the first concerto. Still, the older concerto is not forgotten,

because the first theme of the later work is an almost exact quotation, in inversion, of its earlier counterpart. Major/minor chords are added to the harmonic palette, and quartal fanfares also become prominent. The effect of these additions is to dilute the influence of the ubiquitous octatonic scale, thereby creating more harmonic depth. Notable among the movements is the "Tema con variazioni," based on a delightful melody honoring the dedicatee and commissioner of the concerto, Walter Blodgett, then curator of the Cleveland Museum of Art (Example 7.16). The theme, which features a distinctive fifth leap, is alternated with fragments of the octatonic scale in this linear movement. The chimes close the movement with several complete statements of the theme. Lockwood's second organ concerto was performed only once, at the Cleveland Museum of Art in April of 1974.

Example 7.16, "Walter Blodgett" derivation and theme, *Concerto for Organ and Chamber Orchestra*, MSC, mvt. III, p. 58, mm. 1-7.

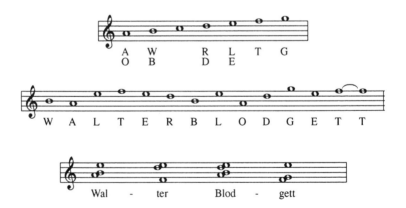

Example 7.16, continued.

Second Concerto for Organ and Brasses

The finest of the three concertos, the *Second Concerto for Organ and Brasses*, exhibits a composer even more at home with the medium. Modal harmonies offer a refreshing shift from widespread dissonance, and themes are not only well-constructed, but are also well-developed. These three facts contribute to a whole which is less dissonant and more structurally cohesive than the sibling works which precede it.

Always the subtle humorist, Lockwood provided brief notes on each movement in a tongue-in-cheek "Scholarly Appendage" at the end of the score (Example 7.17). As evident in the cryptogram on "Langdon," Lockwood's 1970s period is characterized by a fascination with serial composition. Still, he manages to present this motive in a form which is as engaging for the listener as it is idiomatic for the brasses (Example 7.18).

Movement one opens with a series of harmonies played by the organ, based on the second phrase of "Langdon"[26] (Example 7.19). He punctuated these harmonies with quarter-note rests, bearing in mind the sonorous church which would be the

Example 7.17, "Scholarly Appendage," *Second Concerto for Organ and Brasses*, MST, p. 49.

Scholarly Appendage

I Partita

Herein occur fragments of, and the entire tune, "Langdon," a characteristic 18th-century compound of the grave and the frivolous. (See *Grove's* HYMN, 5th Edition, Vol. IV.)

II Canzona

In this movement the tune is obscure although inverted fragments serve remotely as melodic sources.

III Ricercare scherzoso

The principle subject is a cryptogram on the letters of the tune:

Hence, an arrangement of the resulting four-tone motive:

Example 7.18, Brass introduction on "Langdon" cryptogram, *Second Concerto for Organ and Brasses*, MST, mvt. III, p. 24, mm. 1-10.

site of the performance.[27] What follows in movement one is somewhat episodic, but in the course of the episodes "Langdon" is treated to exhaustive development, thereby unifying the movement's many branches.

The "Canzona," movement two, is based on one of Lockwood's memorable tone rows, the first presentation of

Example 7.19, Second phrase of "Langdon," reharmonized, *Second Concerto for Organ and Brasses*, MSC, mvt. I, p. 2, mm. 1-22.

which is designated for a cornet stop on the swell manual. The distinctive leaps between pitches 2 and 3, 4 and 5, and 5 and 6, (ordinal positions), in combination with its 6/4 meter, give this row-based theme an identity which is not disguised by serial manipulations.

Opening with the cryptogram on "Langdon," the final movement, like the first, features extensive use of developmental techniques. An illustration of this occurs midway through the movement, where the main theme is fragmented and developed in a brass tone specified as "blatant," while the organ plays bichords (Example 7.20). That passage leads to one featuring imitation of the fragments, now with brasses using a "natural" tone. The chorale from movement one returns to give the concerto a rounded structure, before the piece ends on a B/F# bichord.

*   *   *   *   *

The most distinctive attribute of the organ genre is its relatively widespread popularity among performers. Lockwood's attempt at reducing the harmonic complexity in these works had the dual effect of making the works accessible to the listener and the performer alike. They have been featured often on recitals, frequently performed by their dedicatees. An all-Lockwood organ recital consisting of the *Preludes*, the *Sonata*, and *Three Chorale Voluntaries* and organized by organist Roy Carey, took place at New Mexico State University at Carlsbad in 1985. Similar events were a result of Lockwood's liaison with the Denver Chapter of the American Guild of Organists. Organist Phyllis Selby Tremmel has been recognized in dedications more than any other performer, playing many of his compositions while on the faculty of Colorado Women's College in Denver. As Lockwood

Example 7.20, Fragmentation of main theme, *Second Concerto for Organ and Brasses*, MSC, mvt. III, p. 38, mm. 1-5.

remembered, "[She has been] of enormous help to me in organ compositions, with her suggestions—going over what I've written, discussing registration."[28]

Paradoxically, the most popular work, *Concerto for Organ and Brasses*, does not represent the composer at his mature best. The work is, nonetheless, interesting in timbre and motive—intriguing, yet accessible enough to place it within the reach of most serious performers. Lockwood's other organ concertos await discovery by those interested in challenging, yet idiomatic, works for organ and instruments.

Chapter Eight

Chamber Works

CHAMBER WORKS
EXCLUDING STRING QUARTETS[1]

Overview

In a manner consistent with his eclectic interests, Normand Lockwood has composed forty-eight works for chamber ensembles of widely varying instrumentation. Although he obviously enjoys the almost endless timbral combinations possible in chamber music, he has shown a marked preference for woodwinds, composing seven works for heterogeneous woodwind ensembles, and ten more for mixed instrumentation that includes woodwinds. He has written on four occasions for unaccompanied instruments, once each for harp, oboe, cello, and accordion. Thirteen opuses include piano. These chamber works, varied as they are, offer an excellent opportunity to address Lockwood's instrumental style in some depth.[2]

Lockwood's chamber genre represents twenty-seven multi-movement works, nineteen single-movement opuses, and two arrangements of folk tunes. In some, he utilized more traditional elements of music such as sonata and ABA forms, and fugal writing. Others, however, are more spontaneous in organization and depict a mood or extra-musical idea. The terms "absolute" and "descriptive," respectively, will be used in the subsequent discussion to differentiate these two types. Works written in a single movement, as well as multi-movement works, appear in both categories.

Often the multi-movement descriptive pieces have miniature movements, as in *Eight Trumpet Duets* (1969) or *Four Excursions for Four Basses* (1976), which contains four movements: "An outing," "A stroll in the Cemetery," "On a holiday," and "Of an evening." Another pair of descriptive pieces bear separate titles: *Le Chateau Overture* and *The Church at Ripton* (1949). These two miniatures, scored for two flutes, oboe, horn, two violins, viola, and string bass, together last only about five minutes. *The Church at Ripton* features only one primary thematic idea and depicts its mood through a slow tempo, homophonic writing, and the use of woodwinds as distant church bells. The resultant flavor, a sort of New England "Americana," might be compared to "The Housatonic at Stockbridge," the final movement in Charles Ives's *Three Places in New England.* Rare examples of a tonally non-challenging Lockwood are found in these two pieces.

Lockwood uses absolute structures in about half of the chamber works—including fourteen multi-movement works. Understandably, their titles are equally traditional: *Quartet in Three Movements for Four Cellos, Clarinet Quintet, Three Canons for Flute and Clarinet,* and *Suite for Solo Cello.*

Chamber music, with its focus on individual players, allows Lockwood to apply his fascination with subtly differentiated sounds—Lockwood's result is often an almost microscopic analysis of the possibilities of each musical event. In the choral medium, this characteristic was evident through his focus on individual words and word parts (e.g., vowels and consonants). In his chamber music, the composer successfully exploited these possibilities through colorful, lucid dialogue and crisply-articulated polyphony, as well as full-bodied, lyrical melody.

Materials

All of the distinctive musical materials used by Lockwood in the chamber works may be seen in his other genres, but with greater density in the chamber works. The early instrumental pieces are progressive in comparison to the homophonic, more consonant choral and vocal pieces written prior to 1950. Compositional devices such as the octatonic scale replace text as a primary structural factor in the chamber works. As early as 1933, the year in which his *Suite for Solo Cello* was written, the composer relied on this colorful, symmetrical scale for motivic, as well as transitional, material (Examples 8.1 and 8.2). Octatonic pitch patterns remain important throughout his life, figuring prominently in seven chamber works, including the most recent *Atànos* for two flutes (1986).

Example 8.1, Transitional octatonic scale in *Suite for Solo Cello*, MS, p. 1, mm. 15-20.

Example 8.2, Octatonic scale as embellishment in *Suite for Solo Cello*, MS, p. 2, mm. 1-3.

Quartal chords and arpeggios are equally prominent in Lockwood's chamber pieces, as seen in his *Piano Quintet* of 1939. In the first movement of this piece Lockwood blended quartal and triadic structures in the string parts, while the piano sustains unrelated pedal tones (Example 8.3). Quartal harmonies also abound in two 1960s pieces for woodwinds, *Fun Piece* and *Three*, and in a later piece for flute and guitar, *Tripartito* (1980).

Example 8.3, Quartal and triadic chords in *Piano Quintet*, MS, mvt. III, "Adagio," p. 13, mm. 1-4.

Modalities, including Phrygian, Lydian and whole-tone fragments, appear particularly in the two distinctively "impressionistic" works, *Litany* (1938) and the *Piano Quintet* (1939) (Example 8.4). Subtle modal allusions are also evident,

Example 8.4, Lower tetrachord, Lydian mode in *Litany*, MS, p. 3, mm. 6-10.

such as the Phrygian interplay between G-natural and G-flat in the key of F minor in *Quartet in Three Movements for Four Cellos*. More entirely modal is the first of *Three Chinese Tunes* (1930s), which is based on the pentatonic scale.

Ethnic materials of varying origins are used by Lockwood to season several of the tone pieces. The second movement of *Diversion* (1950), scored for clarinet, two violins, and cello, is entitled "Slow blues," and contains several "blue note" manifestations of its title. A piece dedicated to composer Otto Luening, *Flute Piece for Otto*, also uses the rhythms and pitch structures of jazz. In another vein, the previously mentioned *Fun Piece* for woodwind quintet is built around a motive with Hispanic ornamentation (Example 8.5). Tonal materials of an Eastern variety are found in three pieces: *Three Chinese Tunes* (1930s), *Native Quarter, Tunis* (1944), and *Revery* and *Kissinger in Egypt* (1970s). In the last-named pair of pieces, written for clarinetist Ramon Kireilis, the augmented second interval is used extensively to suggest the exotic Middle East.

Example 8.5, "Hispanic" motive in *Fun Piece*, MS, p. 3, mm. 3-8, flute and oboe parts.

As he does in the other genres, Lockwood occasionally looks to rhythm alone for musical interest in the chamber works.

Atànos (1986) is representative of his ability to integrate a series of shifting meters into a cohesive rhythmic whole. *L'Homme Armé*, written in 1955 for trumpet and piano, is another work with consistently fascinating rhythmic structures. Lockwood's three-movement rendition of the ancient melody opens with a rhythmically irregular piano accompaniment to the trumpet's melody. Later in the same movement, the piano is metrically organized in three half-note units, while the trumpet plays in 6/4 meter (Example 8.6). The middle movement, "Adagio molto," features a syncopated interpretation of the tune, and in the final, ABA-structured movement, "Allegro," Lockwood created more engagingly asymmetrical music (Example 8.7).

Example 8.6, Polymeter in *L'Homme Armé*, MS, mvt. I, "Andante con moto," p. 4, mm. 1-6.

Example 8.7, Mixed meters in *L'Homme Armé*, MS, mvt. III,
"Allegro," p. 10, mm. 1-10.

Lyric Poem (1977), originally scored in 1948 for alto voice
and piano, bears a final Lockwood characteristic—the
Paumanok pattern. Roots of the 1977 version for cello and
piano go back further than 1948, to the 1939 choral piece, *Out
of the Cradle Endlessly Rocking*.[3] Lockwood used this distinctively consonant sound in nearly every genre of his output.

Serial Pitch Organization

Lockwood uses tone rows for generating pitch content in the
chamber works; however, he does not adhere strictly to
serialism as a compositional discipline. Even his twelve-tone
rows consistently present a melodic contour which departs

from the inherently non-specific octave positions of serialism. In this practice, Lockwood is in good company—so many native composers adopted and digested dodecaphonic practices in a non-strict way that Vincent Persichetti coined the term "free serial technique" to describe their work.[4]

Many of Lockwood's twelve-tone pieces fall into an ABA structure, representing first a presentation of the principal set of pitches, then a series of manipulations of that set, and finally an embellished regathering of the scattered opening set. Certainly, such a process is fundamental to traditionally structured instrumental works, being similar to sonata form. Even if they are not composed in ABA form, Lockwood's eight dodecaphonic pieces usually fall into some absolute structure.

Only one descriptive piece in Lockwood's chamber genre contains a tone row, but its use is an isolated phenomenon, since the context of the piece is not twelve-tone. In "A Stroll in the Cemetery," the second movement of *Four Excursions for Four Basses* (1976), a lugubrious melody in triple meter is based on an incomplete row lacking G-sharp. Dodecaphonic chamber works with absolute structures include the *Suite for Solo Cello* (1933, revised 1979), the *Clarinet Quintet* (1959), *Sonata Fantasia* for accordion (1964), *Five Pieces for Unaccompanied Oboe* and *Sonatina for Oboe and Piano* (both from the 1960s), *Sonata for Flute and Piano in Two Movements and Coda* (1968), and *Mosaic* for flute and accordion (1970).

The original row of *Sonatina for Oboe and Piano* exhibits Lockwood's lyrical treatment of a twelve-tone set (Example 8.8). Even in the first measure, the composer reinforces the

Example 8.8, Lyrical treatment of an twelve-tone set in *Sonatina for Oboe and Piano*, MS, mvt. I, "Contemplativo," p. 1, m. 1.

concept of the row as a melodic unit by fragmentation and restatement. This row is treated motivically throughout the movement, and contrapuntal dialogue of these fragments characterizes the development, before a more cohesive statement of the row ends the section.

Another effective treatment of dodecaphonic materials is found in *Five Pieces for Unaccompanied Oboe*. In this suite, the composer states short motives, followed by sequential repetition of those motives, thus completing the row (Example 8.9). Often motives are not subsets of the row at all, as seen in measures six and twelve, where Lockwood states a fragment of the octatonic scale. However, the ordering of the original row seems to have been derived from the octatonic scale, so its use actually becomes a means of unification, as well as diversification.

Example 8.9, Sequential motivic treatment of twelve-tone row in *Five Pieces for Unaccompanied Oboe*, MS, mvt. I, "Lento commodo," p. 2, mm. 1-6.

Lockwood's most memorable dodecaphonic chamber pieces are based on rows which have a distinctive linear shape or a striking intervallic content.[5] *Mosaic*, a single-movement work for accordion and flute, displays a row with both of these qualities. Written in 1970, it is one of Lockwood's most cohesive chamber works.

Mosaic is based on the following row:

From the opening of the piece, the row is presented in a conjunct melodic form, creating a memorable shape which "peaks"
on the second beat of every measure. Another distinctive
aspect of the row is the many melodic perfect fourths incorporated within it. The row commences with four consecutive
fourths, the first of which is enharmonically spelled. Pitches 9
and 10 prescribe another fourth, and the row ends with yet
another. Adding further interest is the fact that melodic intervals change as melodic direction changes. Standing at the onset
of the first change in melodic direction, the second beat of the
measure contains two minor-third intervals, and the perfect
fourth interval on beat three motivates the final change in
direction.

Such a distinctive row might pall after repeated manipulative
treatments—the accordion plays it twelve times in the first
twelve measures of the piece. However, the composer altered
each of the accordion's ostinato-like restatements to avoid
potential redundancy. His treatment is, in fact, a permutation
of the row to accommodate the sustained flute notes over the
first twelve measures, which together form a rhythmically
augmented version of the row. In measure two, for instance,
the flute sustains pitch 2, and for the accordion, Lockwood
substitutes pitch 1 in the place of pitch 2, and then proceeds
with pitches 3 through 12. The end result of this permutation
is an ostinato which is, at the same time, static and constantly
changing.

In measures thirteen through twenty-four of the piece, the
organizational procedure is much the same. However, the
accordion has the rhythmically augmented row in bass tones,

Example 8.10, Alternating harmonic and melodic forms of row, *Mosaic*, MS, p. 3, mm. 1-2.

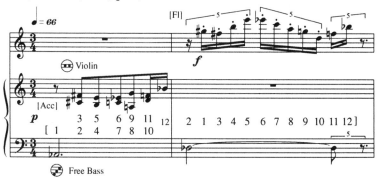

while the remainder of the row is supplied, first, harmonically by the accordion, then, melodically by the flute (Example 8.10). In the next three short sections of the piece, the row is treated in various ways, beginning with a contrapuntal treatment of the row's retrograde. Next, the flute plays a cadenza which features retrograde versions of the row, as well as permutations similar to the ones found in the opening of the piece.

When the melodic registration and voicing signal the return in the ABA structure, Lockwood writes his most complex manipulation of the original row (Example 8.11 and Table 8.1). The basic procedure of this permutation is the retrograde of the row occurring in long notes in the flute (the first pitch of every set). Lockwood then shuffles the retrograde of the row in each individual measure to accommodate the changing initial pitch of the measure, avoiding a consistent pattern.

Such a sustained focus on one set of pitches must have called for a marked change in direction in Lockwood's mind at that point; in the final nine measures of the piece, he departed from the original row altogether. Perhaps to reflect the freer pitch content, this last segment also uses rhapsodic, non-metrical rhythms. A row is presented in partial canon, but its similarity to the original row of the piece is remote.

Example 8.11, Permutation of the original row in *Mosaic*, MS, p. 6, mm. 7-10.

[12 1 11 10 9 8 7 6 5 4 3 2   (1) 11 1 10 9 12 6 7 8 5 2 3 4

(12) 10 12 11 9 8 7 6 5 4 3 1 2   (12) 9 12 11 10 8 7 6 5 4 2 1 2

TABLE 8.1

Manipulations of Original Row, *Mosaic*

↓Flute	Accordion→												Measures
12	1	11	10	9	8	7	6	5	4	3	2		1
11	1	10	9	12	6	7	8	5	2	3	4		2
10	12	11	9	8	7	6	5	4	3	1	2		3
9	12	11	10	8	7	6	5	4	2	1	3		4
8	12	11	10	9	7	6	5	4	3	2	1		5
7	12	11	10	9	8	6	5	1	4	2	3		6
6	12	11	10	9	8	7	6	1	4	3	2		7
5	12	11	10	9	8	7	6	3	4	2	1		8
4	12	11	10	9	8	7	6	5	2	1	3		9
3	12	11	10	9	8	7	6	5	4	2	1		10
2	12	11	10	9	8	7	6	5	4	3	1		11
1	12	11	10	9	8	7	6	5	4	3	2		12

Mosaic is typical of Lockwood's instrumental music in two ways: first in his distinctive use of dodecaphonic principles, and secondly in his unwillingness to be bound wholly by those principles, as shown in its rhapsodic conclusion. The closing section of *Mosaic* points to Lockwood's reliance on his own innate sense of musical propriety, a philosophy that takes precedence over any organizational procedure.

In 1969 Elise Bennett, then chair of the Composer's Commissioning Committee of the American Accordionists Association, provided valuable comments on his writing from a performer's perspective.

> The accordion seems to lend itself admirably to such harmonic devices as . . . serial or twelve-tone-row lines. There seems to be more of an evenness of quality throughout the instrument's range than is present either in winds or strings.[6]

Her remarks were directed toward his earlier *Sonata-Fantasia* (1964) which her group had commissioned, and which was published by Pagani Publishers in 1965. Apparently, Lockwood's two accordion compositions were enthusiastically received by professionals in a field which had been largely neglected by serious composers.

Contrapuntal Organization

Whereas Lockwood avoided intricate counterpoint in his texted works because communication of the words was paramount, he regularly wrote polyphony of varying complexity in the chamber works. *Three Canons for Flute and Clarinet* (1941) consists wholly of canons at the octave. In the next decade, he wrote the *Clarinet Quintet*, in which a fugue subject in the first movement is based on a twelve-tone row. The work was commissioned by the Cleveland Chamber Music Society for its May Festival of Contemporary Music, and performed there in 1960 by George Silfies, clarinetist of the Cleveland Orchestra and the Oberlin String Quartet. One critic noted,

> This is a splendid work, decidedly contemplative in nature and yet quite intense. There is admirable writing for clarinet in it, seemingly as totally integrated with the strings as a clarinet can be.[7]

A work with traditional structures, the *Quintet* features another tone row in the second movement. Lush homophony alternates with intricate counterpoint in the final movement, a non-dodecaphonic theme and variations.

The final movement of the 1984 *Trio for Violin, Cello, and Piano* provides an opportunity to examine Lockwood's contrapuntal procedures further. Subtitled "Duettino fra gli archi" (Little duet among the bows), it opens with a "contemplative"[8] duet between the two string instruments which lasts for thirteen measures. Labeled "Vivace," the "Fuga" which follows is notated in the following time signatures: 3/8, 3/4, and 6/8. The accented articulation of this subject is one of its more memorable features (Example 8.12).

Tonal materials and structural procedures also contribute to the uniqueness of this fugue. The subject is almost wholly constructed of perfect fourth intervals, a reminder of Lockwood's penchant for quartal writing. The textbook regularity of the exposition, with entrances on F-sharp, C-sharp, and F-sharp, provides the listener with ample opportunity to recognize the subject in later treatments. A fourth statement of the subject in the piano leads to an episode in which the main idea is fragmented and stated in dialogue between the instruments. The subject is again treated in an expository way, leading to a "stretto" presentation of the subject in the piano.

A transitional passage in 3/4 meter recalls the quartal elements of the subject. Metric regularity, seen for the first time in this movement, dissipates the rhythmic tension created by the shifting meters of the opening. The subject then returns, however with a different character, as it is presented in the

Example 8.12, Fugue subject in *Trio for Violin, Cello, and Piano*, MS, mvt. III, "Fuga," p. 22, mm. 1-13.

Example 8.13, Rhythmic and octave displacement of subject in *Trio for Violin, Cello, and Piano*, MS, mvt. III, "Fuga," p. 29, mm. 1-12.

piano accompanied by dissonant chords in the strings. Another transition ushers the subject from the forefront. With accompanimental figures from the first episode in the strings, the piano is featured in the first section of the piece which is free of the subject, although its quartal genesis remains. Again, Lockwood provides a metrical respite from the unsteady opening by writing in a consistent 4/4 meter.

The return of the subject is masked by complex rhythmic and octave displacement of the pitches (Example 8.13). The motive of the 4/4 episode is recalled, and an "allargando" leads to the final, broadened section, grounded with an F-sharp pedal tone in the piano. To close the movement, Lockwood writes an "adagio molto" which recalls the pensive opening.

WORKS FOR STRING QUARTET

Overview

Normand Lockwood focused his attention on works for string quartet between 1930 and 1945, a fact that differentiates them from the other chamber works, composed throughout his career. Lockwood's tenure at Oberlin College (1932-43) has been his most fruitful period for string quartet composition, since half of his eighteen works for the medium were composed there. The genre as a whole falls into five subgroups, beginning with one work he wrote in his teens, *Andantino* (1922). Works lacking precise dates but stemming from the 1930s form a second group: *Adagio, Andante, String Quartet in C Major,* and *String Quartet in E Minor.* The Oberlin works reveal several discrepancies in the numbering of Lockwood's quartets, and they include *String Quartet in C Minor* (1933), *Adagio Intristito* and *Grazioso Teneramente* (1935), *String Quartet in D Minor, Number One* (1937), *Third String Quartet* (1937), *String Quartet Number Six* (1937), *String Quartet Number*

Seven (1938), *Informal Music Number One for String Quartet* (1940), *Informal Music Number Two for String Quartet* (1941), and *Nine U. S. American Folk Songs* (1941). *Serenades for String Quartet* (1945) is the sole work composed in New York. Forming a final group are works from his later career, including *Overture for String Quartet* (1987), *Quartetto Breve* (1990), and *String Quartet 1992* (1992), a work receiving its finishing touches at the time of this publication.

Devices such as the octatonic scale, quartal melodies and chords, bichordal writing, and shifting meters appear as frequently in the string quartets as in his contemporaneous chamber music. Tones rows abound in the works for other chamber ensembles, but are used only sparingly in the string quartets until they make an appearance in *Overture For String Quartet* and *Quartetto Breve.*[9] Chromaticism and "Stravinskian" chord clusters round out his tonal language in the quartets (Example 8.14).

A distinctive feature of the string quartet group is Lockwood's repeated use of cyclic organization, a hallmark of his Oberlin period. *String Quartet in C Major, String Quartet in E Minor, String Quartet in C Minor,* and *String Quartet Number One in D Minor,* have cyclic returns. Lockwood returned again to thematic integration of movements in his *Informal Music for String Quartet Number One.*

Youthful Quartets

These works represent Lockwood's youthful, somewhat experimental forays into quartet writing. Serving as preparations for the first full quartets are *Adagio,* a brief sketch based on a lyrical, nine-bar period, and *Andante,* which eventually became the second movement of Lockwood's *Third String Quartet.*

Although they represent the earliest stages of his stylistic development, the next works for string quartet exhibit charac-

Example 8.14, Stravinskian rhythms and quartal melody, *Third String Quartet*, mvt. IV, p. 19, mm. 1-32. Society for the Publication of American Music, 1946. Used by Permission, American Composers Alliance.

teristics that Lockwood eventually chose to make a standard part of his instrumental vocabulary.

String Quartet in C Major, a four-movement work, begins with a simple fugue, the subject of which features only the most basic of rhythms. The second movement, in B-flat major, is occasionally modal, and the third is a poignant song form in C-sharp minor. Foreshadowing a later Lockwood style is the rhythmically unpredictable fourth movement, which irregularly alternates quarter note values with a combination of dotted eighth and sixteenth notes, in two-part counterpoint.

A developing sophistication is evident in the *String Quartet in E Minor*, written in four movements. Particularly striking are the smoother transitions from theme to theme, and the shifting meters of the second movement, "Presto leggiero" (Example 8.15). The degree of cyclic organization has also been expanded from the simple gestures of the previous two quartets. The "Presto" theme appears not only as a bridge between the third and fourth movements, but is also developed later in the fourth movement. Contrapuntal writing is still a staple of Lockwood's quartet menu, used in the E Minor quartet as the structural base of the third, "Larghetto" movement, and in a long coda at the close of movement four.

"Number One" in the title of *String Quartet Number One in D Minor* has two possible interpretations: it may represent the first of two quartets in the same key, or Lockwood's feeling that it was his initial serious attempt in the genre. In it, the themes are well-developed and distinctive, surpassing even further their earlier, somewhat academic counterparts. The *pizzicato* dissonant quarter notes in the opening theme of the first movement evoke a primitive and sinister mood. The second and third themes of its rondo structure contrast strikingly with each other and the first theme. Diversity between themes is heightened in the second movement, and the third movement features an opening fugue and a cyclic return of the first movement. While the *String Quartet Number One* shows many positive developments in the composer's abilities, he still searches for methods of integration, a challenge which he met quite effectively in his next quartets.

Example 8.15, Shifting meter theme, *String Quartet in E Minor*, MS, mvt. II, p. 5, mm. 1-13.

Mid-Career Quartets

The *Third String Quartet* (1938)[10] is dedicated to the Walden String Quartet, then in residence at the University of Illinois. Lockwood dedicated several works to the Walden Quartet and they retained his *Third String Quartet* in their repertoire for several years, drawing favorable reviews.

> The large audience at the Cleveland Museum of Art Auditorium was especially pleased with the Lockwood opus, the D Minor Quartet No. 2. In this the sharp irritations of the modern style were compensated for by a beauty of design and a richness of tonal color, particularly in the rather contemplative Andante and the Closing Allegro.[11]

> One of the best of some 45 American works in [the Walden Quartet's] repertoire is the String Quartet No. 2 in D minor [i.e., *Third String Quartet*] of Normand Lockwood.   . . . This is the work of a richly gifted composer, imaginative, distinctly personal, and skillfully wrought.[12]

Perhaps as a result of the exposure the quartet received by the Walden, the work was published for the Society for the Publication of American Music by G. Schirmer in the society's 1945-46 season.

The *Third String Quartet* signals an arrival in Lockwood's string quartet composition. Its length is more substantial, and proportionately, it resembles the traditional string quartet genre—the durations of the four movements are approximately six, five, four, and seven minutes, respectively. The greater length brought with it more developed musical concepts: striking themes full of developmental possibilities and integrative transitions. Even Lockwood's now familiar devices are presented with more assurance. The first movement opens with a ten-measure introduction featuring constantly-shifting meters—an overture which compels the listener to take notice (Example 8.16). The main theme is presented fugally, and contrasts with a highly ornamental second section.

Example 8.16, Shifting meters, *Third String Quartet*, mvt. I, p. 1, mm. 1-13. Society for the Publication of American Music, 1946. Used by Permission, American Composers Alliance.

To the Walden String Quartet

Third String Quartet

I

Score

NORMAND LOCKWOOD

S.P.A.M. 55

Copyright 1946 by Society for the Publication of American Music
International Copyright Secured
Printed in the U. S. A.

The second movement, an "Andante" in ternary form, had been written in the early 1930s and was revised for this quartet. The opening section is imitative, accompanied by downward-moving, diatonic counterpoint. Of this movement, critic A. J. Warner wrote in 1946,

> The contrapuntal style of the second movement of the quartet played last night was arresting, and it was easy to detect, during the performance of the score, the composer's predilection for choral writing.[13]

After the third movement, a lovely violin melody accompanied by quartal chords, the fourth movement bursts forth with random accents and dissonant second intervals. Both the irregular pulses and the contrasting theme, based melodically on fourths, recall Stravinsky's often brash early style. The movement is highly developed both rhythmically and tonally, its flexible shape proceeding naturally from one idea to the next. Momentum is propelled from theme to theme by octatonic fragments, and intensity is heightened by the sixteenth-note rhythmicization of the first theme in its return. Lockwood is indeed at home with string writing, ensemble interplay and dialogue, and high-pitched rhythmic energy in the *Third String Quartet.*

Ross Parmenter of the *New York Times* reviewed Lockwood's *String Quartet Number Six*[14] in 1952, when it appeared with works by Arthur Berger and Walter Bricht.

> The selections were not of a modernism that some people might consider "fearsome," and Mr. Lockwood's quartet was especially admirable in the beautiful texture it maintained throughout its three movements.[15]

Immediately striking about the *String Quartet Number Six* is the substitution of English for the dominant Italian musical terminology of his earlier works.[16] Although some Italian indications remain, Lockwood made an effort to "Americanize" his score with the following movement titles: 1. Slow, Sustained—Faster—Fast, energetic, 2. Singing, Folk-like, and 3. Fast: Light with digressions.

The first movement begins with an introduction that features sustained, close-position quartal chords and bichords. Its rondo structure features a principal theme in B-flat major against more quartal accompaniment (Example 8.17). The sole

Example 8.17, Melody with quartal accompaniment, *String Quartet Number Six*, MS, mvt. I, p. 2, mm. 20-21; p. 3, mm. 1-4.

contrasting theme of the rondo begins with repeated eighth-notes in the first violin, followed by an octave melody con-structed predominantly of melodic fourths and sevenths. Each theme returns several times, and the movement closes on an E-B open fifth.

Contributing to the folklike personality of the second move-ment are several dimensions of its theme: the sometimes purely pentatonic mode, syncopations, and the interplay between B-natural and B-flat (Example 8.18). The third movement is an

Example 8.18, Folklike melody, *String Quartet Number Six*, MS, mvt. II, p. 9, mm. 1-7.

extended romp, spiced with occasional "blues" chords. As a whole, the *String Quartet Number Six* is fresh thematically, well-developed, and consistently idiomatic for strings.

String Quartet Number Seven seems less balanced than *Number Six*, as indicated in Lou Harrison's review of 1946.

> At a recent program of the ISCM [International Society for Contemporary Music] Forum Group . . . Vivian Fine's *Three Pieces* for Violin and Piano and Normand Lockwood's *Seventh String Quartet* were each *eclectic*, Miss Fine's selectedly so and Lockwood's *abandonedly* so.[17]

Eclecticism in itself does not warrant negative criticism. In the words of composer Lejaren Hiller, "Stylistic heterogeneity and healthy eclecticism have always been characteristic traits of American music."[18] Indeed, William Schuman's *String Quartet Number Three* (1939), shares many of the characteristics considered eclectic in Lockwood's quartets: dissonance created by a simultaneous use of major and minor chords, diatonic melodies, contrapuntal expositions, episodic rondo forms, and non-diatonic triadic movement.

Diversity alone does not account for the weaknesses in *String Quartet Number Seven*. A more likely catalyst for Harrison's observation might be Lockwood's blatantly incongruous insertion of a jazzy rag in the middle of the second movement, after the unrelieved dissonance of the first movement (Example 8.19). If Lockwood's diversity damages the piece, it is a matter of degree, not of substance. The two-movement quartet appears to be an experiment—a desire to move away from his more secure style which, perhaps, reached a culmination in the *String Quartet Number Six*. In any case, the later work stands out in relief against the other mature works for string quartet, even the *Overture* of 1987, which was unified by dodecaphonic techniques.

Example 8.19, Ragtime writing, *String Quartet Number Seven*, MS, mvt. II, p. 14, mm. 5-10.

Following the numbered string quartets in chronological order are the two pieces entitled *Informal Music for String Quartet*, written in 1940 and 1941, respectively. Their structures are those of the string quartet genre, although the lengths of the movements are abbreviated. *Informal Music for String Quartet Number One* exhibits chromatic writing and ABA form in the first movement. A set of twelve variations forms the second movement, the theme of which is a cyclic revisitation of the first movement. Accompaniment figures which embellish the variations become more rhythmically active as the movement progresses. The third movement is a swirling, seamless, unresolving "Song" in ABA structure. Bichordal harmonies characterize the "Rondo" that closes the piece.

In *Informal Music Number Two* (1941), Lockwood "exploited 'blues' and other nostalgic and simple Americana in a deft and sophisticated way."[19] Although the movements each last only about five minutes, the themes are distinctive and the transitions are well-crafted and energetic. In the first movement, the pentatonic, metrically shifting tune in the first violin is interrupted by dissonant punctuations in the other instruments which either destroy the consonance of the melody, or form dominant-seventh harmony with it (Example 8.20). The addition of syncopated sixteenths make its return especially vernacular in spirit. To contrast, the subordinate theme features "pizzicato" walking bass notes in the cello part, against mildly dissonant chords. When the second theme is restated, the chords are quartally inspired, and because they are written an octave higher, they heighten the excitement which characterizes the entire movement.

The second movement, "Adagio sostenuto," features a cello melody, accompanied by descending parallel major chords in second inversion. It provides a languid, unruffled respite from the energetic outer movements. The contrasting thematic idea features static chords which accompany a melody—chilling in its quality—in the highest register of the cello.[20] After a homophonic section, dissipation of rhythmic energy brings about a resolution.

The final movement, "Allegro molto," opens with a nontonal melody built around several melodic fourth intervals and octatonic fragments (Example 8.21). Forming the two-part counterpoint with the main theme is an eighth-note figure which expands downwardly, and then upwardly, in a chromatic fashion. The melody and counterpoint is stated again, then homophonic accompaniment is added. A syncopated, triadic tune provides material for the subordinate theme, while the first theme remains in the first violin in rhythmic augmentation

Example 8.20, Main theme, *Informal Music Number Two*, MS, mvt. I, p. 1, mm. 1-20.

Example 8.21, Quartal and octatonic theme, *Informal Music Number Two*, MS, mvt. III, p. 13, mm. 1-24.

Example 8.22, Syncopated, triadic theme, *Informal Music Number Two*, MS, mvt. III, p. 16, mm. 6-17.

(Example 8.22). When descending seventh chords accompany a repetition of this section, the flavor is strongly jazz-influenced.

The return of the main theme occurs in a *stretto* fugue which also features the original eighth-note counterpoint. As before, the well-wrought transition makes good use of the contrapuntal idea; first, to intensify, and then, to disperse rhythmic and dynamic energy. The return of the subordinate idea is extended by the insertion of full, tranquil chords. A final return of the main subject rounds out the movement, fragmenting and dissolving into trills, triplets, and crescendi.

Compared to the Oberlin works, the set of miniatures entitled *Six Serenades for String Quartet* (1945), shows freer dissonance, achieved by the use of major-minor chords. Structurally, they are simple song forms. An unsigned review appearing in the *New York Herald-Tribune* on January 14, 1953, stated

> Mr. Lockwood's *Serenades* were the gems of the evening. Each one was quiet, short, and unobtrusive, and witty, too, and of course, perfectly written for strings. None of the *Serenades* is particularly advanced in style, but so natural is the musical impulse that style, as it should be, is beside the point.[21]

Late-Career Quartets

Written in 1987, the *Overture for String Quartet* is unique in two ways. First, its compositional date represents a return to string quartet writing after a break of over forty years. Also, it introduces dodecaphonic writing in the works for string quartet; Lockwood's creative treatment of the original row is worthy of comment. After a four-measure introduction, the opening set is partially presented, interrupted by an incomplete retrograde of those pitches, and finally completed. The remaining three-quarters of the piece features an alternation of the introductory figuration with non-imitative contrapuntal material based on subsets of the row. The introductory material is then used as modulatory material and as an accompaniment to the row. Lockwood's ubiquitous octatonic scales and bichords also make appearances toward the end of this piece.

In *Quartetto Breve*, Lockwood also relied on serial procedures and the sonorous, fluid writing that drew praise in the mid-career works. The work is written in two movements and coda, an overall structure that was also used in a 1969 work for flute and piano.

*   *   *   *   *

The earliest string quartets are a record of Lockwood's experiments in the idiom. By the time of the *String Quartet Number Six* and the two sets of *Informal Music for String Quartet*, he had settled in a style that featured the eclectic use of folk materials, quartal and bichordal harmony, octatonic scales, and shifting meters. Texturally, the composer preferred either fugal counterpoint, dialogue which featured instruments in pairs, or pulsing, often off-beat chords to accompany an "espressivo" melody. Long melodic lines, as well as motivic germs, supply thematic material. His clear structures most often resemble classical models, with movements following traditional fast/slow/optional movement/fast plans. The large-scale outer movements are often written in a modified sonata allegro form, and frequently begin with a contrasting introduction.

The year 1945 brought Lockwood's concentrated string quartet period to a close, perhaps because he preferred the greater timbral possibilities of a mixed chamber ensemble, or his liaison with the Walden Quartet had changed. His career points to the fact that new locations brought new challenges and opportunities, and his output indicates that Lockwood began once again to concentrate on his choral writing soon after his move to Union Theological Seminary in 1945. In a career so long and prolific as Lockwood's, the string quartets provide an unusual opportunity to trace a relatively brief period of his development in a single medium.

The works for chamber groups other than string quartets present an altogether different side of the composer with respect to form and tonal materials. While some works are traditionally structured, the tone piece category presents rather rhapsodic organizations. Because his chamber compositions permeate his career to a greater extent than the string quartets, he gave his particular version of twelve-tone serialism more attention in this medium.

Within the sparsely-populated context of mid-century chamber composition in the United States, Lockwood is revealed as a moderate: less formally spontaneous than Miriam Gideon, less directly Americanist than Ross Lee Finney. Like Otto Luening, timbre to Lockwood was important as an element of form. He shares with Irving Fine a manifestation of Stravinsky's crisp, clear-cut articulations and rhythmic vitality bequeathed to him via their common mentor, Nadia Boulanger.

Lockwood's uniqueness, however, stems from his fascination with juxtaposition, presenting as he does, twelve-tone rows in the same piece with vernacular jazz. In that respect, the works for chamber ensembles are representative of his entire compositional output. They are, in fact, the perfect medium for a composer who enjoys the combination of a wide range of musical colors, since the medium itself is an amalgam of a variety of musical timbres.

Chapter Nine

Solo Songs

Overview

Normand Lockwood has written solo songs during every decade of his career, beginning with a 1920s setting of Walt Whitman's *Memories of President Lincoln*. Within this medium he has rivaled not only the variety and inspiration, but also the plurality of his own choral genre. His forty-eight short art songs, combined with twelve sets representing fifty-eight additional songs, form an impressive body of song literature. Four arrangements or sets of arrangements on tunes not composed by Lockwood also contribute to the total. Most notably in this category, he created instrumental accompaniments for tunes such as "Ol' Man River" and "It Ain't Necessarily So" for Paul Robeson's Columbia Recording, and the Irish melodies "When Irish Eyes are Smiling," and "A Ballynure Ballad" for a Century recording by tenor Christopher Lynch.[1]

In addition to the above-mentioned works, Lockwood has composed seven extended pieces, the shortest of which is ten minutes in duration, while the longest, the withdrawn *Hound of Heaven* (1937), is an hour long. *Hound of Heaven* was followed by *Mary, Who Stood in Sorrow* (1950), *Prelude to Western Star* (1951, rev. 1983), and *Fallen is Babylon the Great, Hallelujah!* (1955). Ten years later he wrote *The Dialogue of Abraham and Isaac* (1965), followed by *To Margarita Debayle* (1977). His most recent work of this scope is *Medea Redux* (1992) for mezzo soprano and orchestra.

Like most composers, Lockwood has taken great advantage of striking performing talents around him, seemingly always surrounded by gifted singers.[2] The vast majority of Lockwood's vocal pieces are composed for soprano and piano, although he frequently omitted the designation on the manuscript itself.[3] However, he scrupulously notated any departure from his normal instrumentation or vocal choice, for instance, when the accompaniment was for organ, or the intended soloist was a contralto.

SHORT WORKS

Texts

Lockwood's poetic muses reflect a facet of his compositional personality already noted elsewhere, eclecticism, which directs him both to concisely economical poetry and broadly dramatic, even florid, texts. Of his own literary taste he stated, "I don't like trashy poetry,"[4] and indeed, his poets include some of the greatest names in both recent and past history.

The poetry of Walt Whitman, so present in the choral genre, appears in two settings only: *Memories of President Lincoln* (1920s) and Four Songs—A Cycle (1977). More often, Lockwood turned to another type of American poet for his vocal pieces. Perhaps reflecting the sharpened individual focus of song as opposed to chorus, he chose a concentrated poetic style to replace expansive Whitman texts. Leading this group of preferred American poets is Adelaide Crapsey (1878-1914), an important figure in the poetic renaissance which took place in this country in the early twentieth century.[5] Lockwood used eleven of her poems in two sets, *Six Songs of Adelaide Crapsey* (1938), and *Five Cinquains of Adelaide Crapsey* (1945).[6] Crapsey's brevity is evident in the fourth song of the second set, "Arbutus":

> Not spring's thou art,
> but hers, most cool, most virginal
> Winter's, with thy faint breath,
> thy snows rose-tinged.[7]

In league with his contemporaries Ernst Bacon, Aaron Copland, and John Duke, Lockwood turned to another native female for song texts: Emily Dickinson. Her allegorical verse, as brief and direct as Crapsey's, is featured in Lockwood's *Three Verses of Emily Dickinson* (1938), which includes "The Murmur of a Bee," "Because I Could Not Stop for Death," and "Elysium." Dickinson's well-known preoccupation with death is evidenced in the third of these verses. The death of Lockwood's middle daughter, Angie, caused the composer to turn again to this song in 1980. His arrangement of the 1938 work for mixed choir was dedicated to her memory.

Lockwood set other American poetry to music, including four of Robert Frost's simple rural poems, two of e. e. cummings's distinctively structured works, the metaphysical *Catskill Eagle* of Herman Melville, E. B. White's pseudo-serious *The Red Cow is Dead,* Stephen Vincent Benet's epic *Western Star—Prelude,* and Sara Teasdale's romantic *Night Song at Amalfi.*[8] Lockwood, somewhat of a non-traditionalist himself, has been drawn to native poets who contributed to the "American revolution in poetic language"[9] begun by Whitman and Dickinson. In doing so, he placed himself among the most innovative of national song composers from the 1930s through the 1950s.

Although Lockwood "has shown a particular interest in setting American poetry,"[10] his search for poetic inspiration has led him abroad as well. Both his love of sparse texts and his cosmopolitan interests were indulged most notably in 1984, when he set *Four Poems of Liu Chang-Ch'ing*, an eighth-century Taoist poet. Lockwood shows in his musical setting his command of minute artistic detail, aptly depicting the poet's restrained mysticism with great subtlety. The third work in the set, "A Farewell to a Buddhist Monk," will be discussed subsequently in this chapter.

The extended solo works sample a variety of literary styles, including a narrative work, Benet's episodic *Prelude to Western Star.* Chapters eighteen and nineteen of the Book of Revelation, richest of all Christian scriptures in colorful, symbolic imagery, presented Lockwood with the gripping subject of *Fallen is Babylon the Great, Hallelujah! The Dialogue of Abraham and Isaac* is based on an embellished scriptural version of Abraham's test of faith written by Donald Sutherland, then head of the Classics Department at the University of Colorado in Boulder. In that work, the composer dramatically presented the parts of father, son, and narrator in an alternating style similar to that of Franz Schubert in "Der Erlkönig." The beautifully sensitive, sometimes theatrical *To Margarita Debayle*, after a poem of Nicaraguan Rubén Darío, relies on the translator Donald Sutherland as well as the poet for its haunting lyricism.[11] The poem recounts a meaningful visit between a charming girl child and an old family friend, complete with the gift of a fanciful story.

Turning again to Lockwood's shorter songs, the Book of Psalms also provided textual sources for vocal music. *O Lord, Our Lord* (1960), written for tenor and strings, is based on Psalm 8; *Prayer of David: Hear a Just Cause, O Lord* (1985) is based on Psalm 17 and is scored for mezzo soprano and organ, and *Observance: When Israel Went Forth from Egypt* (1985), also for mezzo soprano and organ, is based on Psalm 114. *Psalm 23* (1948) was scored for full orchestra and soprano, and premiered by the Young Men's and Young Women's Hebrew Association of New York in the year of its composition. The Song of Solomon inspired *Set Me as a Seal Upon Thine Heart* (1987), a rare example of dodecaphonic writing in the composer's solo songs.

Lockwood also paid homage to great literary and philosophical figures of pre-twentieth-century history, turning at least once each to Sappho, St. Augustine, Shakespeare, Ronsard, Blake, Wordsworth, Dostoevsky, and Schopenhauer. In his *Five Inspirational Lines* (1967), he even drew on words of Mozart and Beethoven for literary material. Yet, as attracted as he was to great poetry, Lockwood often found a striking concept or image in the works of lesser known figures that called for a musical setting, authors such as Joaquin Pasos, Eric Axel Karlfeldt, A. Mary F. Robinson, and F. W. Handley, M. D.

Vocal Lines

Both traditional and progressive elements mark the linear element of Lockwood's vocal pieces; his traditional side is seen in two types of vocal lines. First, in recitative-style declamations, he featured natural word-rhythms, higher pitches denoting stressed syllables, an accompaniment which interacts with the singer as if in dialogue, voluminous text, and a high degree of dramatic intensity. Second, he adopted the lyricism of a more ruminative aria style, often featuring mood-weaving ostinato accompaniments and a reflective atmosphere.

As his textual choices prove, however, Lockwood is not wholly a traditionalist. Accordingly, he used a third, more sparse linear style, created in response to the poetic styles of

Crapsey, Dickinson, and others. Here the poet's frugal use of words is subtly underpinned with equally concise, but suggestive accompaniments. Because the message of the poem is often hidden, understated, or non-existent in the literal sense, Lockwood does not attempt to clarify or illuminate. He matches and enhances the lack of specificity in the poetry.

The set entitled *Five Cinquains of Adelaide Crapsey* (1942), illustrates this third style well. The titles alone of the five cinquains are sufficient to set the imagination in motion: "Triad," "Trapped," "Anguish," "Arbutus," and "The Grand Canyon." While all movements illustrate Lockwood's sparse style, the emotive aim of poet and composer is most easily elucidated in the final poem, with its text

> By Zeus!
> Shout loud of this to the eldest dead!
> Titans, Gods, Heroes, come
> Who have once more a home.[12]

The piece is an exuberant piano solo punctuated by vocal exclamations in its first thirty-one bars. The instrumental writing revolves around octaves and a rhythmic/melodic germ presented in the first three bars (Example 9.1). A non-exact inversion of the germ appears in measures eight and nine, illustrating Lockwood's manipulative techniques throughout the piece. Doubled octaves evolve into a chromatic bass line against a recurring treble chord in measures thirteen through seventeen. Chords become thicker, and meters remain joyously unreliable as the singer proceeds with the text. Even with the new textual emphasis, however, the piano remains the focal point, inserting the germ as a punctuating refrain to the words "dead," "Gods," "Heroes," and "Home." Although the piece is abundant in energy, its precise message is left undefined. Intensity of emotion—whether it represents fear or awe in the

Example 9.1, Abstract style and motive in *Five Cinquains of Adelaide Crapsey*, MSC, "The Grand Canyon," p. 9, mm. 1-18.

beholder or the grandeur, sublimity, or massiveness of the canyon—is presented in the broadest of strokes, first by Crapsey, and then musically supported by Lockwood.

A prime example of Lockwood's recitative style is found in the extended work, *The Dialogue of Abraham and Isaac* (1972). The composer extracted its text from Donald Sutherland's play of the same year entitled *My Sister, My Spouse*, for which Lockwood had composed incidental music. Lockwood chose endlessly complex rhythmic notations, shifting meters, and high-pitched syllabic accents in his efforts to provide a natural setting of the prose text (Example 9.2). In its twenty-three minutes' duration, the piece settles into homophonic or metrical writing only occasionally, gravitating instead toward a freer, more declamatory style. Throughout the work, familiar devices such as quartal chords, major-minor chords, and tritones are abundant. Although the vocal line is sometimes tonal when viewed alone, the addition of the accompaniment destroys any feeling of tonality. Together these techniques create a profound atmosphere similar to those found in Lockwood's oratorios such as *Children of God*.[13]

The composer's devices are well-suited to the Sutherland text; the first half of *The Dialogue* follows the Biblical account closely. However, Sutherland then allows Abraham to explain his actions to his son. This explanation progresses into a rather cynical view of God from Abraham's standpoint.

> God is not human and you are in his hands.
> Here on this dreadful mountainside, here is the
> fact. The rest is only thought . . . You are in his
> hands which will release you only when they kill.[14]

Sutherland's new twist to the familiar near tragedy provided great opportunity for compositional expressiveness. At the beginning, Isaac protests and questions his father's actions, but once Abraham's explanations begin, "the child just sits there

Example 9.2, Recitative style in *The Dialogue of Abraham and Isaac*, MSC, p. 3, mm. 5-14.

and never speaks again. However we have not forgotten him—we know he is still there."[15] Such a text allowed the composer to explore a starkly dramatic application of his dissonant style.

Lockwood's aria style of vocal composition appears in many works and takes two forms: a traditional song form with independent sections, and a more through-composed, developmental structure. All of the four poems on texts of Pierre de Ronsard, written from 1939 to 1941, illustrate the first treatment. The second piece of the set, "Remembered Scenes," is a beautifully pensive melody, supported by rich, mood producing harmony (Example 9.3). Comprising three strophes and a coda, the song's tonality is inspired by the pentatonic scale, which, combined with the melody's recurring perfect fourth intervals and other repeated motives, accounts for the cohesiveness of the piece. A pedal tone E, changing to E-sharp, provides further dissonant unification, as it accompanies chords in G-sharp minor.

Undoubtedly, the most important attribute of these songs to a vocalist is whether or not they are idiomatic—"singable." June R. Boyd, a soprano who has researched and performed Lockwood's vocal pieces, made this positive assessment.

> Lockwood's vocal settings are singable. He knows what the voice can do and he writes to accommodate it. Extremes of range are used, but the singer is not required to stay in those extremes for a long time. Accompaniments are supportive of the voice. . . . His accompaniments set up the mood of the text and continue that mood. The listener to a Lockwood song can tell how he perceived a specific section of the poem by the way he set it musically.[16]

Example 9.3, Aria style in *Ronsard Poems*, MSC, "Remembered Scenes," p. 1, mm. 1-10.

Accompanimental Styles

Lockwood's textual choices have inspired several accompanimental styles. In the recitative style the accompaniments are somewhat predictable, serving to support spontaneous, rhapsodic vocal lines. To create these more unified accompaniments he uses ostinatos and both programmatic and nonprogrammatic recurring motives.

Ostinatos, in this instance, may refer to rhythmic and melodic patterns which repeat exactly, or merely similar patterns which create the same sustained result as an ostinato. Modified repetition provides both unity and variety, an attribute favored by the composer, who said, "[I try to] retain the character of a melodic line without resorting to repetition of exact pitches."[17]

A clear example of his modified ostinato technique is seen in *Ten Songs* (1939-40) for soprano and string quartet, with texts by James Joyce. A 1948 review characterized them as

> . . . finely schemed within the chosen medium, the vocal line being a natural extension of the shape and mood-content of the verses, and the string accompaniment, an accompaniment in the true sense, is an emanation harmonically, from the melodic line.[18]

The tenth piece is entitled "Sleep now, O sleep now, O you unquiet heart!", a perfect text for Lockwood's restless stepwise ostinato, which is treated in dialogue among the instruments of the string quartet (Example 9.4). In this case, Lockwood's ostinato presents a subtly agitated accompaniment for a rhythmically sparse vocal line.

An ostinato built on triads with added tones forms the singer's backdrop in the third song of the Emily Dickinson set, "Because I Could Not Stop for Death" (Example 9.5). The sonority is sustained in a well-defined, eight-measure pattern

Example 9.4, Stepwise modified ostinato in *Ten Songs*, MSC, "Sleep Now, . . . O you unquiet heart!" p. 35, mm. 1-16.

Example 9.5, Homophonic ostinato in *Three Verses of Emily Dickinson*, MSC, "Because I Could Not Stop for Death," p. 1, mm. 1-16.

which is repeated, varied, and extended. The presence of inexorable death is plausible in this somber accompaniment, parts of which were assigned to the lower voices of the choir in the 1980 choral version.

A more traditional accompaniment of repeating harmonic patterns is seen in *She Dwelt Among the Untrodden Ways*

(1939), on the well-known text by William Wordsworth. Rich in musical ideas, the piece features a sixteenth-note figure,

Example 9.6, Ostinato accompaniment in "She Dwelt Among the Untrodden Ways" (1939), MSC, p. 1, mm. 1-8.

beginning in measure five, that creates a wistful, unsettled complement to a lyrical melody (Example 9.6). The contrasting section of this ABA structure retains the sixteenth-note values of the ostinato, further delineating the four-measure octave phrase that announces both A sections. Lockwood used this poem for two different settings, but this version is the more interesting of the two. In comparison, the version he included in *Six Miscellaneous Songs* (1955) is more tonal, and the E-

Example 9.7, Repetitious harmonic accompaniment in *Six Miscellaneous Songs*, MSC, "She Dwelt Among the Untrodden Ways" (1955), MSC, p. 2, mm. 1-6.

minor accompaniment pattern repeats more exactly (Example 9.7). The two settings, viewed together, provide a common denominator in Lockwood's reading of the poem; musing over the lost Lucy is suggested by repeating harmonic patterns.

Example 9.8, Uses of the octatonic scale as a programmatic motto, *Fallen is Babylon the Great, Hallelujah!* MSC; (a) p. 5, mm. 5-6, (b) p. 9, m. 7.

(a)

(b)

When the text calls for a more flexible accompaniment, the composer often resorts to more self-contained devices for cohesion. In *Fallen is Babylon the Great, Hallelujah!* the octatonic scale is used a number of times for this purpose (Example 9.8). The first two appearances serve as mottos by which the allegorical, wanton nature of the sinful city is remembered, supporting the phrases "have committed fornication with her" and "who were wanton with her."[19] In a subsequent reference, the now programmatic leitmotif appears in ascending order, depicting the rising smoke of Babylon's destruction.[20]

Another of Lockwood's unifying devices became familiar in the choral works and was labeled the Paumanok pattern.[21] Lockwood's explanation of its reappearance in *Four Songs—A Cycle* for soprano, violin, and organ (1977) seems to declare a benediction on this particular harmonic configuration.

> The musical idiom peculiar to *Apple Orchards*[22] is one that has long been associated in my mind with settings of Whitman texts. It was born, so to speak, in the 30s in an unaccompanied choral work, *Out of the Cradle Endlessly Rocking* (1938, G. Schirmer). . . . I composed *Four Songs—A Cycle* for the soprano, Mary Anne Kirk, dedicating them to her. They are a cycle not only in the sense that the 4th song is a reprise of the 1st, altered somewhat and simplified, but in the sense that there occur snippets of the *Apple Orchards* idiom.
>
> This may be the last of the idiom for the reason that in its reappearance in *Four Songs* I believe I have finally found the lyricism that I had been searching for—this as a direct result of hearing Mary Anne Kirk's recital in Boulder [Colorado] on December 6, 1978.[23]

The text appears in Whitman's *Out of May's Shows Selected:*

> Apple orchards, the trees all cover'd with blossoms,
> Wheat fields carpeted far and near in vital emerald green,
> The eternal, exhaustless freshness of each early morning,
> The yellow, golden, transparent haze of the warm afternoon sun,
> The aspiring lilac bushes with profuse purple or white
>   flowers.[24]

Example **9.9**, Paumanok pattern as a leitmotif, *Four Songs—A Cycle*, MSC, "Apple Orchards I," p. 2, mm. 1-3; "Apple Orchards II," MSC, p. 13, mm. 1-4.

The song settings of *Apple Orchards* retain the "off the ground" quality created by the opening, second-inversion triad of the Paumanok pattern (Example 9.9). The piano part is written, for the most part, in the close-position style of the 1938 choral piece. Beyond that, "Apple Orchards I" from *Four Songs* employs some of the same rhythms of the choral work, and the harmony is remotely similar, but the solo piece features more non-triadic harmony. The two inner movements, "Winter's Foil" and "Halcyon Days," do not address the Paumanok pattern at all. "Apple Orchards II" is, indeed, a reverberation of the first movement, but the elimination of eighth-note rhythms in the opening creates a greater sense of peace. *Four Songs—A Cycle* represents a cycle in many ways: through its own ABCA structure, in combination with the other Paumanok pieces, and, less concretely, as a late appearance of a compositional leitmotif in the career of the composer. Lockwood considers it purely coincidental that the idiom reappeared in the 1987 quartet for solo voices, *We Are of God*, but it suggests that he has not yet laid that favorite combination to rest.[25]

Works unified by recurring devices appear in all decades of his song composition. Patterns of chord clusters interlace the fourth movement of *Five Cinquains of Adelaide Crapsey* (1942) and *To Margarita Debayle* (1977). A motivic germ provides the abstract setting of e. e. cummings's *sitting in a tree* (1943) with a reference point. The descending perfect fourth interval, manifesting Lockwood's fondness for quartal sonorities, occurs repeatedly in the first of *Ten Songs* with texts by James Joyce (1939).

One of his most widely integrated uses of a recurring musical idea is found in *A Song of the Virgin Mother* (1955). Based on a text by Lope de Vegas as translated by Ezra Pound, the ornamented fifth degree of the minor mode seems at first to be mere decoration (Example 9.10, measure 5). However, this trembling Hispanic ornament becomes connected with the phrase in each strophe, "Still ye the branches." Before the final verse, the piano plays a cadenza passage based on the ornament, elevating its status to the level of primary organizational unit (Example 9.11). The singer's final phrase, "Still ye the branches," is a further extension of the figure.

Example 9.10, Ornament as an organizational unit, *A Song of the Virgin Mother*, MSC, p. 2, mm. 1-8.

Example 9.11, Cadenza based on ornament, *A Song of the Virgin Mother*, MSC, p. 7, m. 7.

Tonal Languages

The diversity of Lockwood's songs allows for a great range of tonal languages. Bichords are sprinkled throughout the genre. The composer goes beyond occasional bichords to full-blown bitonality in the first movement, "Rosemary Leaves!", of the set of songs with texts by A. Mary F. Robinson. Throughout this two-page piece, the vocal line and treble staff of the piano are notated in G major, while the bass of the piano is given a sustained dominant chord in the key of B major. Although the conflicting key signatures seem capable of

Example 9.12, Opening tone row in *Set Me as a Seal Upon Thine Heart*, MSC, p. 2, mm. 1-14.

producing sharp dissonances, the main juxtapositions are C with C-sharp and A with A-sharp, which are only mild manifestations of bitonality.

Elsewhere with regard to tonal languages, the solo songs support the fact that Lockwood turns less often to dodecaphonic practices in vocal works than in instrumental works. One example of twelve-tone writing as a structural, instead of decorative, technique is seen in *Set Me as a Seal Upon Thine Heart* (1987). Written for soprano and organ on a text from the Biblical Song of Solomon, the song opens with a tone row played by the organ, with repetitions of six pitches (Example 9.12). The entire ABA structure of this song is based on the serial manipulative techniques found in the instrumental genres, whereas in *Prelude to Western Star*, the other notable serial piece, only the second movement is dodecaphonic, and in the context of the five-movement piece, it appears more as an episode than a structural statement.

In *Four Poems of Liu Chang-Ch'ing* (1984) Lockwood combines a distinctive texture with an evocative tonal language to match the extremely economical poetry of the sources. The observations of the set's sole performer to date, June Boyd, are especially valuable:

> [The musical style] is more pared down, suggesting the Chinese ideal of simplicity. The rhythms, although carefully notated, give a feeling of freedom and improvisation. These are not dramatic settings in the traditional sense, but are atmospheric settings which let the texts, simply stated, shine through. They have their own subdued drama.[26]

Whether inspired by Chinese ideals or his own highly developed sense of artistic economy, the composer filled these miniatures with subtle timbral phenomena and mood-evoking text settings. The first song, "On Parting with the Buddhist Pilgrim Ling-Ch'E," opens with a programmatic overtone effect in the piano that requires a few performance directives from the composer (Example 9.13). Although it is a depiction of "the low sound of an evening bell,"[27] the almost pentatonic bass cluster, held throughout by the pianist's right hand, also subtly suggests a half-heard reverberation of the ancient East. Elsewhere in *Four Poems of Liu Chang-Ch'ing*, pentatonic and whole-tone scales are the dominant tonal materials, rendering an ancient, changeless atmosphere.

Example 9.13, Performance notes on overtone effect, *Four Poems of Liu Chang-Ch'ing*, MSC, "First Song," p. 1, mm. 1-5.

Directions: Piano RH: Silently depress in advance and
hold down throughout the song

Piano LH:

Strike precisely together   Release precisely together
not harshly but firmly

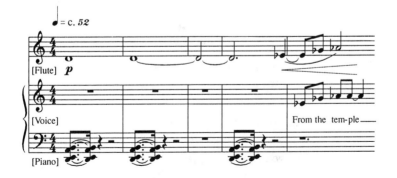

Example 9.14, Sparse writing in *Four Poems of Liu Chang-Ch'ing*, MSC, "Third Song," p. 7, complete.

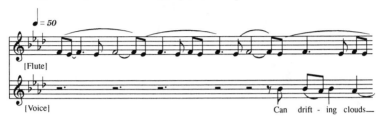

The text of the third song, "A Farewell to a Buddhist Monk" inspired a truly unique jewel within this delightful set.

> Can drifting clouds and white storks
> Be tenants in this world of ours?—
> Or you still live on Wu-chou Mountain,
> Now that people are coming here?[28]

The movement is not only a textual miniature; it is musically sparse as well (Example 9.14). The flutist plays only the two pitches of a whole step, while the singer centers on another major second, pitched a perfect fourth higher; the pianist does not play at all. The result is an exquisitely restrained moment of text and music, as precise as an ancient woodcut, yet also as symbolic. Ms. Boyd's term, "subdued drama," aptly describes this movement.

EXTENDED WORKS

Prelude to Western Star

The large-scale *Prelude to Western Star*, with text by Stephen Vincent Benet, is a fine example of the various musical ideas Lockwood brought to solo song composition. As episodic as the oratorios, it provides a synoptic glance at a large portion of his vocal style. The five movements are entitled "Americans," "The Stranger," "Star in the West," "I Make My Song," and "Lend Me Your Music." Originally composed in 1951 for soprano and piano, the 1987 revision features baritone instead, but otherwise differs little from the original.

"Americans" is a patchwork of many folk styles, illuminating musically what Benet discusses textually. In the opening, the baritone sings a syncopated, pentatonic melody: the "Americans" motive, cyclic for the work. The pianistic suggestion of a blue note accentuates a whimsical ostinato which features simultaneous D and D-flat pitches (Example 9.15, measure 16). In the course of the movement, programmatic references such as bass tremolos under parallel minor triads, depicting "The whistles of the great trains going west" are introduced. "New England's soul" is remembered with a chorale-like fragment, a folk-like tune frames "We're off to Californiay," and the

Example 9.15, Opening of *Prelude to Western Star*, MSC, "Americans," p. 1, mm. 1-19.

movement ends with a rousing tune featuring the dance
rhythms and pentatonic contours of the Western vernacular
style (Example 9.16).

Example 9.16, Western vernacular tune in *Prelude to Western
Star*, MSC, "Americans," p. 9, mm. 8-14.

"The Stranger" is an episodic setting which opens with a
pointillistic tone row. After piano and baritone state the row,
the "Americans" theme returns for the first of its cyclic re-
appearances. "The Stranger" is more a dramatic dialogue than
the aria-style first movement. Spoken words, pictorial phrases,
and even tempo indications call upon the performer to act, as
well as sing. Accompanying the text—

Example 9.17, Descriptive tempo indications in *Prelude to Western Star*, MSC, "The Stranger," p. 13, mm. 1-8.

He came and went. He liked our women's looks.
Ate lunch and said the sky scrapers were high,
And then, passed by, to the next lecture.

—Lockwood coaches the baritone with the words, "bordering on fawningly, condescendingly," and later annotates the score with "'rallentando,' dying of ennui"[29] (Example 9.17).

"Star in the West" and "I Make My Song," the third and fourth movements, are in recitative style. They are unified by motives and ostinatos, but both suffer from the weight of the voluminous text. Lockwood's flair for setting word rhythms is evident, but the concentration of this one style soon becomes overwhelmingly operatic, without the benefit of contrasting arias. The final movement, "Lend Me Your Music," provides a simple, lyrical contrast to the dramatic intensity of the previous movements, opening with the "Americans" motive once more. Recalling the guileless animation of the first movement, it provides a symmetrical close to the set.

To Margarita Debayle

Devices abound in *To Margarita Debayle* (1977), but the text and music are so well integrated that they seem to have been created simultaneously, instead of consecutively. Lockwood's musical renderings of the text based on Rubén Darío's poem, translated by Donald Sutherland, are descriptive extensions of its various dramatic levels.

A harmonic germ consisting of an E-flat major triad with an added A-natural serves as the primary means of unification in the piece. Beginning with the second measure of the keyboard introduction, the four-note set is presented in arpeggiated form. From this sonority is distilled the tritone which is associated with the child's name (Example 9.18).

Example 9.18, Arpeggiated harmonic motive, *To Margarita Debayle*, MSC, p. 2, complete.

The text at the opening is the old man's address to the child:

Margarita, the sea is bright,
and the wind
carries a subtle attar of citrous flowers;
I feel
in my soul a lark singing;
your tone of voice.
Margarita, I am going to tell you a story.[30]

Example 9.19, Tone row in *To Margarita Debayle*, MSC, p. 3, complete.

The first musical phrase of this text is a tone row, with repeated tones, and missing A-flat and F (Example 9.19). The construction of the row, which emphasizes half steps, and the opening tritone contribute to the haunting, almost mesmerizing quality of the vocal line. Such concentrated, sensuous music is almost mandatory, since Darío has called forth the human senses of sight, touch, smell, and hearing in this short section. When Margarita's name is spoken a second time, the tritone is reversed. As June Boyd has noted, "The 'diabolus in musica' has become, in Lockwood's hands, a warm and personal form of address for a special little girl."[31]

The story tells of a wealthy king and his daughter who follows her dream, journeys to heaven, and picks a star for her shawl-brooch. The musical ideas succeed one another in mosaic fashion, rapidly changing as the import of the text shifts. The king's music is pompously regal, featuring bichords in the accompaniment, word rhythms, and syllabic stresses indicated by high notes in the vocal part. The cluster from the introduction returns, now on a G-major triad, as the princess contemplates her sojourn. The narrator, constantly stepping in and out of the story, reminds the listener of the "real" child, Margarita, by singing a tritone on the text "Exquisite princesses are very much like you" (Example 9.20).

The princess's "traveling" accompaniment features a motive based on a perfect fourth, presented in the imitative accompaniment (Example 9.20, measure 8). In the vocal part, the universal children's chant, sol-mi-la-sol-mi, is suggested, and will later become the leitmotif for the princess. The king's bichordal music is remembered, as the narrator sings, "but the trouble was she went without Papa's permission." When the girl is confronted by her father, the octatonic scale is used as the base for the narrator's statement, "The princess never told a lie and so she told the truth" (Example 9.21).

The composer cleverly utilizes the princess's leitmotif to suggest her chagrin, even though it is not referenced in the text,

Example 9.20, Tritone motive and traveling music, *To Margarita Debayle*, MSC, p. 7, complete.

Example 9.21, Octatonic scale in *To Margarita Debayle*, MSC, p. 11, mm. 1-3.

by presenting it in strongly-accented eighth notes. When Jesus himself comes to her rescue, the triad-cluster of the introduction returns, suggesting that this has been heavenly music all along (Example 9.22). At the story's happy conclusion, the opening accompaniment and old man's line return, this time ornamented. To underscore the epilogue of the story, Lockwood wrote a comparatively tonal phrase which emphasizes the poem's nostalgic, final words:

> Now that you are going to be far from me,
> keep, little girl, a kindly thought
> of him who one day wanted to tell you a story.[32]

Example 9.22, Return of opening motive, *To Margarita Debayle*, MSC, p. 14, mm. 1-7.

To Margarita Debayle represents the song composition of Normand Lockwood at its romantic, colorful best. The wide array of musical ideas are arranged seamlessly into a cohesive work of art. Programmatic motives are only subtly suggested, and not stressed. The vocal line is non-tonal, surely, but at the same time its development is achieved traditionally by the use of repeating motives and sequences. The colorful accompaniment functions as a Wagnerian orchestra: to suggest ideas which are not stated in the text by use of leitmotifs. All the elements of the song create a spellbinding aura which draws the listener into the world of little girls and stories.

*   *   *   *   *

Lockwood's solo songs show his love for good poetry and his desire to render many different poetic styles musically. Although his taste runs in many different directions, his special gifts are admirably utilized in the setting of the exquisitely concise verse of Adelaide Crapsey and Liu Chang-Ch'îng. In response to these abstract texts, he composed many songs which depart from traditional vocal patterns, organizing them around short motives, subtle statements, or some ineffable mood.   His favorite devices—bichords, octatonic scales, dodecaphony,   and   quartal,   quintal,   and   modal harmonies—were used to create these motives.

The two other formats he chose are the traditional recitative and aria styles. In all these styles, the accompaniments often became the cohesive force behind vocal lines. Sectionalized song form was not abandoned if the text called for it; as he stated, "You must have respect for the structure of the text."[33]

Criticism of his style usually centers around his eclecticism; however, it is this tendency which makes his music so surprisingly fresh. Furthermore, Lockwood's mode of song composition is a response to the wealth of stimuli that flooded native composers in the first half of this century. As Ruth Friedberg states, these composers

> [worked] to integrate the newer twentieth century elements of flexible meter (the musical counterpart of free verse), Impressionism, neo-classicism, late Romantic chromaticism, and its serial derivatives into a language that [would] adapt to the prosodic and expressive needs of the poetic texts.[34]

Lockwood has contributed strikingly to what she calls "the staggering variety of their success,"[35] while remaining faithful to his own style and American heritage.

Chapter Ten

Instrumental Music

Overview

Instrumental music for larger ensembles is another compositional genre which spans Normand Lockwood's career. His earliest instrumental ensemble work, *Symphony in E* (1928-29), was completed during his period as a fellow at the American Academy in Rome, and his latest, *Pi March*, was completed in 1992.

Lockwood has composed twenty-eight works for instrumental ensembles, six of which have been lost or withdrawn: *Erie* (1936), *Variations on a Gitlin Tune* (1949), *Goin' to Town* (1950), *Bernie's Animal Orchestra* (1950s), *Triptych to the Memory of W. R. B. Willcox* (1958), and *Toccata for Brass and Percussion* (n.d.). The remaining works fall roughly into three stylistic periods—early, middle, and late—which generally reflect his overall compositional progression.

Four of the early works, dating from 1929 to 1949, are brief and less developed than the others: *Brass Music for Their Majesties' Entry* (1929), *Chorus Girl* (1940s), *Marche Breve*

(1946), and *Sleeping Beauty* (n.d.). The remaining early-period works are characterized by the ubiquitous use of bichordal materials and cyclic organization in a traditional fast-slow-fast symphonic structure. In these three-movement works, the outer movements are often sonata forms. Orchestral scoring is relatively sparse, even neoclassical, and chords are spaced widely. Included are *Symphony in E* (1928-29), *A Year's Chronicle* (1933-34), *Symphony* (1941), and *Weekend Prelude* (1944).

A gap exists in Lockwood's production of instrumental ensemble music from 1949 to 1965; none of the ensemble music written during that period survives. However, during his second active period of instrumental ensemble composition, from 1965 to 1979, Lockwood replaced the expansive, lyrical themes that had been so well suited to the sonata structures of the first period with melodies based on tone rows. Although bichords are still apparent in the music, other procedures such as quartal and octatonic writing are also prevalent. Jazz and oriental musics round out Lockwood's eclectic blend of styles. Due to this wealth of ideas, thematic density is high in the second-period works, and orchestrations are more complex than those in the first period. Three of these works are traditionally orchestrated and structured, indicating a continuing connection with his first-period compositions. Works included in the second period are *Symphonic Sequences* (1965), *Concerto for Oboe* (1967), *From an Opening to a Close* (1969), *Piano Concerto* (1973), *Symphony for String Orchestra* (1975), *Symphony for Large Orchestra* (1979), and *Panegyric for String Orchestra and Horn* (1978-79).

Lockwood alternated a leaner style with his earlier methods in his third-period works. Several of the seven instrumental works which comprise the category are constructed with clear, uncomplicated counterpoint and recurring motivic cells that replace the long, tone-row-based themes of the second period. On the whole, rapid shifts or juxtapositions between ideas occur much more rarely in the later years. With the exception of the *Concerto for Two Harps and Orchestra* (1981), the structures and orchestrations are non-traditional. The other works which stem from his latest compositional period are *Prayers and Fanfares* (1980), *Choreographic Suite for String Orchestra* (1986), *Return of the Spirits* (1986), *Lenten Sequence, Interval and Ascent* (1989), *Metaphors* (1991), and *Pi March* (1992).

Early Period Works

The twenty-minute-long *Symphony in E*, the earliest developed work in the genre, has never been performed. Except for an expanded section of six French horns, it calls for an orchestra of typically romantic proportions. The first of its three movements is a sonata-allegro form introduced by a solo violin melody, a rather intimate opening for a symphony. Later, the first theme of the movement appears ("Allegro mosso"), a gaily articulated, tonal theme in E major, centering on the dominant scale degree, B (Example 10.1). The colorful subordinate theme, with its augmented second melodic interval, is more specifically folklike. The second movement, a theme with variations, features a cadenza section written for percussion, harp, and two players at one piano. The third movement is another sonata form, thematically based on the octatonic scale and its resultant diminished triads and tritones. New ideas and devices follow one another in rapid succession, and although there are only two distinct themes, the movement's diversity inhibits its formal stability.

In 1933-34 Lockwood composed his second symphony, a work with the programmatic title *A Year's Chronicle*, supposedly a look at the events of one year in the artist's life. With it, Lockwood won Chicago's Gustavus F. Swift Competition.

Example 10.1, First theme in upper woodwinds and viola, *Symphony in E*, reduced from MSC, mvt. I, p. 7, mm. 1-7.

The work was performed on April 4, 1935 by the Chicago Symphony Orchestra under the direction of Frederick Stock. Again written for standard romantic instrumentation, in three conventional movements, it opens "casually,"[1] with the marking "senza espressione." The primary theme is a trumpet melody in C major, with a shift in tonality to A-flat midway through (Example 10.2). The subordinate idea is based on the then-popular "without a shirt" motive [2] (Example 10.3). Seeds of Lockwood's later eclecticism appear in another jazzy motive and impressionistic seventh sonorities later in the movement.

Example 10.2, First theme in trumpet with tonal shift in measure 4, *A Year's Chronicle*, reduced from MSC, mvt. I, pp. 1-2, mm. 1-7.

Already in this movement, the composer uses retrograde as a method of thematic development, although further serialization comes much later in the orchestral genre.

The second movement is a harmonically lush song form featuring descending seventh chords and chord clusters in the French impressionist style (Example 10.4). The symphony concludes with a "fugato" third movement, introduced by a thirty-one measure, partially quartal, fanfare. The fugue subject exploits melodic fourths, (Example 10.5), and its four-voiced exposition is played by oboe, bassoon, trombone, and Heckelphon, respectively. The entire movement is occupied with "fugato" and "stretto" presentations of the subject, interrupted only once by the cyclic return of sixteenth-note figuration from the first theme of the symphony. Chords from the fanfare which opened movement three reappear as a rounded close.

Example 10.3, Second theme in oboe, based on "Without a Shirt" tune, *A Year's Chronicle*, MSC, mvt. I, pp. 22-23, mm. 4-9.

Example 10.4, Descending seventh chords and clusters, *A Year's Chronicle*, reduced from MSC, mvt. II, p. 59, mm. 1-3.

Example 10.5, Fugue subject with prominent fourths, *A Year's Chronicle*, MSC, mvt. III, pp. 80-81, mm. 6-14.

Another work from Lockwood's early period is *Symphony* (1941), written in three movements and lasting about thirty minutes. Progressive elements include a surprising lack of key signature in the first movement and sophisticated uses of the octatonic scale, both common features of Lockwood's later compositional periods. *Symphony* is a cyclic work, with triadic main themes in its outer movements, and stressed bichordality in the third. The second movement, "Sostenuto," highlights the horn section, while strings and woodwinds supply a seamless, interweaving accompaniment. No record exists of the work's performance, although the score bears conductor's marks.[3]

Example 10.6, Main theme and octatonic alteration, *Weekend Prelude*, reduced from MSC, pp. 1-2, mm. 1-10.

The delightful, five-minute-long *Weekend Prelude* was composed in 1944. Although not expressly composed for the occasion, it was performed on a concert featuring the Music of Recipients of Awards and Honors, given by the American Academy of Arts and Letters and the National Institute of Arts and Letters on May 23, 1947. The work is traditional both in instrumentation and form, featuring a repeated exposition in its brief sonata structure. The opening juxtaposes A-flat major and a B-F-sharp open fifth, then rapidly shifts to a melody in B minor. In the subsequent restatement of the melody, the lower instruments bring about a shift in tonality from D major to E-flat octatonic (Example 10.6). Shifts of this kind occur frequently in the early pieces, as illustrated later in the same work, where the second tetrachord of the G major scale is changed to a whole-tone tetrachord in order to facilitate a series of modulations. *Weekend Prelude* is compact and precise, showing Lockwood's talent for composing in condensed forms.

Variations on a Gitlin Tune (1949) and *Triptych to the Memory of W. R. B. Willcox* (1958)[4] were withdrawn from Lockwood's primary rental agent, the archives of the American Composers Alliance, in 1970.[5] *Variations* was scored for "radio orchestra,"[6] while the eight-minute *Triptych* was written for narrator, flute, brasses, and percussion. The latter work, one of the few pieces resulting from Lockwood's year in Eugene, Oregon (1959-60), was commissioned by the School of Architecture at the University of Oregon. Texts came from writings of Emanuel Swedenborg and Henry George, arranged by Wallace Haydn.[7]

Middle-Period Works

The years between 1949 and 1965, unchronicled by orchestral music with the exception of *Triptych*, were years of tremendous growth and experimentation for Lockwood. During this period he began his tenure at the University of Denver, a location which ultimately proved to be as hospitable to instrumental composition as it was to opera. As a result, his first middle-period work presents a marked contrast to the more traditional works of his first period. Themes based on tone rows were developed and integrated with the whole piece to a much greater extent.

Example 10.7, Oboe theme with quartal accompaniment, *Symphonic Sequences*, MT, pp. 3-4, mm. 1-10.

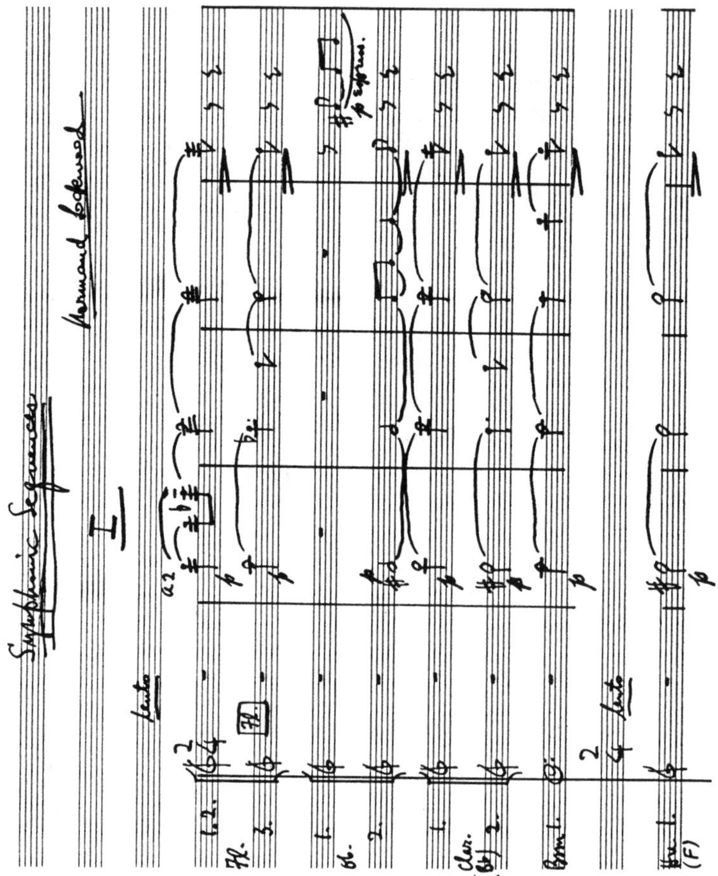

Example 10.7, continued.

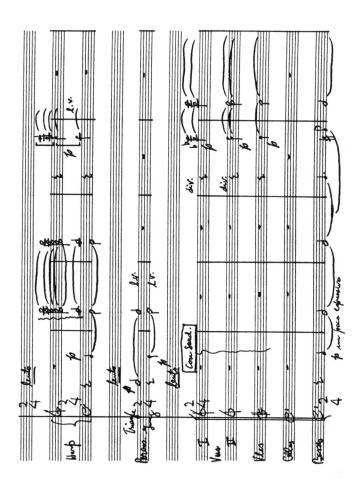

Example 10.7, continued.

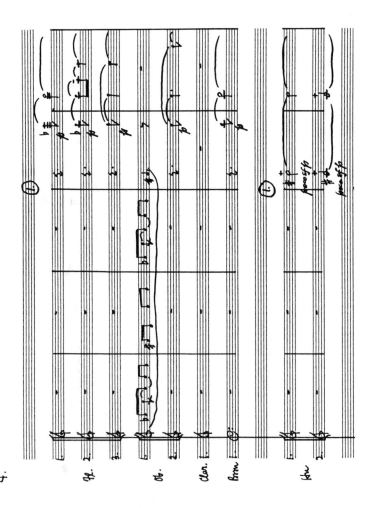

Example 10.7, continued.

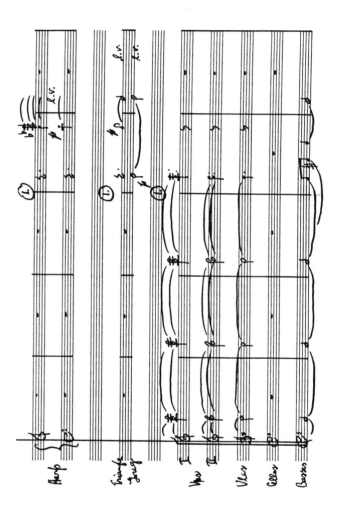

Symphonic Sequences, written in 1965 and lasting just over three minutes, was Lockwood's first Denver composition in the instrumental genre. These three miniatures, true to the title, incorporate harmonic, melodic, and rhythmic sequences. The theme of the first movement is played by the solo oboe, an instrument which becomes more prominent in his middle period, usually in connection with tone-row-based themes. Strings provide a quartal foundation for this theme (Example 10.7). Following the harmonic sequences of the first movement, the second movement exploits the technique of melodic sequence in a dialogue between oboe and bassoon. Sequential rhythms characterize the third, "Allegro," movement. The work was performed at the University of Denver in April of 1967.

That same year, Richard Pointer commissioned Lockwood to write an oboe concerto with the intent of playing the solo part himself. Formerly a faculty member at the University of Denver, Pointer was then professor of oboe at the Universidad Nacional Autonoma de México in Mexico City. The resultant work was premiered by the Mexican university's orchestra on April 19, 1968, and conducted by Eduardo Mata. Perhaps to emphasize the timbre of the solo instrument, Lockwood chose a unique instrumentation: no orchestral woodwinds and a brass section of horns only, accompanied by strings and a percussion section that makes prominent use of chimes. Another notable feature in the concerto is the oboe's free rhythmic, quasi-improvisational style, which persists until the third movement.

The row which forms the base of movement one is stated by the solo oboe (Example 10.8), and punctuated by dissonant chords in the orchestra. Manipulations of the row form a creative patchwork of several serial techniques, as shown in its first variation: a partial retrograde of pitches one through eight, followed by pitches nine through twelve in original order. The second movement, a warmly homophonic, but dissonant song

Example 10.8, Tone-row theme in oboe, *Concerto for Oboe*, MSC, mvt. I, p. 1, mm. 1-4.

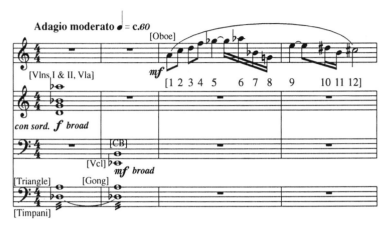

in seemingly unstructured rhythm, follows without a break. This meterless style, in combination with a self-generating melody based on a pivotal B-flat, contribute to the theme's improvisational quality. Toward the end of the movement, chimes and an F pedal point in low strings emerge from the orchestral texture, serving as the bridge to the third movement. The "Scherzo" is a "giocoso" melody spiced with piquant, idiomatic writing for the oboe (Example 10.9). The solo violin, and not oboe, is featured in a cadenza-like passage, which leads to a beautiful section in which the oboe floats out of the tutti orchestra texture, its phrases extending beyond those of the ensemble (Example 10.10).

Example 10.9, "Giocoso" theme in oboe, *Concerto for Oboe*, MSC, mvt. III, p. 49, mm. 1-4; p. 50, mm. 1-3.

Example 10.9, continued.

Example 10.10, Oboe contrasted with "tutti" orchestral texture, *Concerto for Oboe*, MSC, mvt. III, pp. 86-87, mm. 1-8.

Example 10.10, continued.

From an Opening to a Close (1969) is written for winds, percussion, and piano. Its three petite movements, entitled "Opening and Dialogue," "Fanfare and March," and "Hymn and Close," together last about seven minutes. Foreshadowing his late period, Lockwood is primarily concerned with timbre in this piece.[8] Chromaticism is emphasized in the thematic material for the first movement—an idea which is anticipated in the half-step, accompanimental clusters at the opening. Appearing first in the xylophone, the principal theme is a mostly chromatic passage that has been treated with octave displacement (Example 10.11). In the second movement, a four-note motive and its permutations are interspersed with disguised quotations of such vernacular tunes as "The Gang's All Here" and "Dixie." The oriental flavor of the final movement was inspired by the Japanese Shinto service, and Lockwood revealed this mood by using pentatonic modality and colorful commentary in the percussion. In the "Close" the piano supplies the ictus for a seemingly random set of percussion timbres. The care with which the composer constructed the primary themes in this piece, in combination with the colorful, often pointillistic use of the percussion section, makes "From an Opening to a Close" a memorable work, a fact supported by its relatively frequent performances.

Example 10.11, Octave-displaced, chromatic theme, *From an Opening to a Close*, reduced from MSC, p. 2, mm. 1-5.

Lockwood's concertos have always been composed with specific performers in mind. In the case of the *Piano Concerto* (1973), the intended executor was David Karp, the composer's friend and former colleague at the University of Denver. The dedication evolved into a happy collaboration, with Lockwood drawing as readily upon his knowledge of Karp's brilliant technique as on his own increasingly confident, middle-period style.[9] The two corresponded by letter between Denver and Dallas, Texas, where Karp was on the faculty of Southern Methodist University, before the piece's premiere.[10] Karp's sense of involvement in the piece is clear from his letter dated December 8, 1975.

> [The] chairman of the piano department at SMU and a wonderful person and pianist listened to a portion of the first movement . . . [and] turned around to me and said, 'This is some of the most exquisite keyboard writing I have heard and it is also some of the most expressive music . . . you play it as if you wrote it yourself.' Of course I responded: 'I feel as if I composed it, and am proud to be his dedicatee.'[11]

Cast in a three-movement structure, the work opens with an "Allegro" in sonata form. The main theme group consists of a dialogue between two elements: dissonant chords of varying durations in the orchestra, and a "toccata-like"[12] figure in the piano (Example 10.12). The toccata figure begins by outlining two consecutive perfect fourths, B-E-A. The resultant minor seventh interval, which forms the boundaries of the theme, contracts chromatically, meeting at E and E-flat, then expands chromatically to a B-B-flat major seventh. The movement's contrasting theme is stated by the solo piano—a more sensitive, yet still chromatic, section featuring a pianistic evocation of string harmonics. The closing theme returns to the brash rhythmic energy of the opening, only now featuring open,

Example 10.12, Toccata figure in piano and dissonant orchestra clusters, *Piano Concerto*, MSC, mvt. I, pp. 1-3, mm. 1-10.

Example 10.12, continued.

Example 10.12, continued.

quintal sonorities. The development addresses both themes, using octatonic and chromatic passages for transitional and developmental material. A cadenza built on an atonal embellishment of the second theme leads to the recapitulation. Both themes return, but they retain the increased rhythmic energy of the development section. The movement ends stridently on an F major/F minor/F-sharp minor compound chord.

The "Adagio" movement's foundational, twelve-tone row is ingeniously constructed to emphasize the two prominent intervallic elements of the entire concerto: the minor second interval (underlined below), and two types of the fourth interval (indicated below by breaks in underlining).

C F♭ F B B♭ A E E♭ A♭ G D C♯

Because Lockwood relied on a fixed octave position in most of his rows, their intervallic relationships remain unchanged in subsequent repetitions.

The first statement of the row is followed by woodwind imitations of a three-note motive (Example 10.13). This small set will later be expanded, and become the subject of the movement's main section. Before that occurs, however, the piano states an octave-displaced version of the original row. Finally, the contrapuntal theme is stated and imitated by the piano—its three opening pitches are a transposition of the three-note motive. This movement is thus organically constructed of a few sparse ideas, against a persistently atonal structure. Instrumentation is equally austere; flute, oboe, clarinet, bassoon, and cello complement the timbre of the piano. Eventually, the opening row returns in the solo instrument, leading to an extended pointillistic ending against the backdrop of an ethereal "tremolo al punto" in the strings.

Following without a break, the "Scherzo" is a "tour de force" for both composer and performer. The metrically shifting

Example 10.13, Woodwind motive and resultant contrapuntal piano theme, *Piano Concerto*, MSC, mvt. II, p. 61, mm. 1-14.

Example 10.14, Polymetric trumpet theme and quartal piano rendition, *Piano Concerto*, MSC, mvt. III, pp. 75-76, mm. 1-16.

theme, shared by trumpets and timpani, is composed of only
four pitches, which emphasize both the fourth and minor
second building blocks of the concerto (Example 10.14). The
piano enters on a quartally-influenced, harmonic rendition of
the theme, transposed to C-sharp. A "tutti" presentation of the
theme follows, then the piano embarks on the first of several
passages which suggest the improvisational skills of a jazz
pianist. Immediately following is a "scorrévole" section, which
juxtaposes the often quartal eighth notes with a sequentially-
extended, sixteenth-note pattern in the solo piano.

Example 10.15, Jazz combo section, *Piano Concerto*, MSC,
mvt. III, pp. 102-103, mm. 8-16.

During the development section, a "jazz combo," comprised of clarinet, horn, bass, and piano, breaks away from the constraints of the traditional orchestra to supply a mood change (Example 10.15). Harmonic underpinning defines several pitches as "blue" notes, while the horn sustains "choralesque"[13] tones in a delightfully fresh, mixed-genre section. The chapel is again suggested when the entire "Old Hundredth" hymn tune is presented as a "cantus firmus" in a subsequent section. The recapitulation, which features a re-harmonized and fragmented return of the first theme, spares none of the pianist's energy, igniting all players into a shower of virtuosic fireworks.

Example 10.15, continued.

The *Piano Concerto* is undoubtedly one of Lockwood's
finest works. All of the marks of his maturity are evident: his
forthright, unabashed juxtaposition of unrelated vernacular
and "serious" elements; his sensitive use of quartal harmonies,
tone rows, and pointillism; and his organically-constructed
main themes. Critic Glenn Giffin elaborates on the Lockwood
style in reviewing a 1988 performance by Karp and the University of Denver Orchestra.

> Lockwood obviously wrote the piece for a pianist with good
> fingers. The last movement, in particular . . . is something of a
> Bach-meets-Bartók affair, running figures interrupted by dense

Example 10.15, continued.

chords—and even a little bit of swing thrown in. . . . Beyond the
craft of the piano writing, which is always forthright and asser-
tive, Lockwood has an unusual sense of instrumental color.
The whole has a finely chiseled neo-classic sound about it which
Karp projects with unaffected bravura.[14]

Karp has also performed the piece at Southern Methodist
University and in Oklahoma.

The remaining two works falling into Lockwood's middle
period are his 1975 *Symphony for String Orchestra* and *Symphony for Large Orchestra* of 1979. The earlier work was
commissioned by Broadcast Music, Incorporated, for its
annual Chamber Music Conference, held in Bennington,
Vermont. *Symphony for String Orchestra* is written in one
dissonant sonata movement, sporting many permutations of
the main theme, and organic developments in which passages,
several measures long, are often generated from one short
motive. Octatonicism provides the harmonic milieu, while the
equally familiar device of chromatically expanding motives is
used to generate the themes. However similar their musical
materials appear, this piece lacks the integration and
memorability of the *Piano Concerto.*

In the more cohesive *Symphony for Large Orchestra*,
Lockwood opens the first movement with a descending, non-
tonal melodic gesture. This section functions not as a theme,
but as a pivotal factor used throughout the movement
(Example 10.16). The passage represents his non-serial use of
a pitch set, since the opening motive is not a row, and bears no
resemblance to the complete row which occurs later in the
piece.   Here, as in other atonal works, the composer
appropriated any technique that suited his intent, but never felt
compelled to adhere strictly to a style.   Modality, chromaticism, octatonicism, and serialism flesh out his tech-

Example 10.16, Opening non-tonal motive, *Symphony for Large Orchestra*, reduced from MTC, mvt. I, pp. 2-3, mm. 1-8.

Example 10.17, Chromatic timpani cadenza, *Symphony for Large Orchestra*, MTC, mvt. III, pp. 90-91, mm. 3-16.

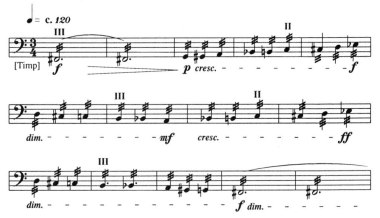

nical repertory in the sonata-like outer movements, while the minute "Interlude" that separates them focuses on contrapuntal statements of a theme exploiting the minor second interval. The third movement's chromatic timpani cadenza is as intriguing for the listener as it is as unusual for the player (Example 10.17). The subsequent combination of celesta, chimes, and bichordal strings adds color to the ethereal atmosphere initiated by the timpani.

The *Symphony for Large Orchestra* was written for T. Gordon Parks, conductor of the Community Arts Symphony of Denver, and was premiered by his group on November 21, 1980. The composer provided descriptive program notes for the occasion.

> The harmonic idiom travels along an axis between polytonal and atonal poles. The melodic idiom is one of diatonically related intervals and shifting modes with the latter often entailing chromaticism. A good deal of what occurs is contrapuntal, although not canonic or fugal, but rather after principles akin to isorhythmic construction. . . . Formally, the music is homophonic along classical precepts, developing as it does in that fashion.[15]

When the same orchestra repeated the work in 1986, critic Allen Young remarked on Lockwood's vivacious style.

> Lockwood's symphony is a lean, lively work which avoids matters lofty and sober. It is intoxicated with sounds that command, tease, and illuminate. The third movement, "Vivace," [races] out of the stable. Jazzy riffs for clarinet and trombone and a cadenza for kettle drums enliven this section which slows only to gather steam for a conclusion full of snap and vigor, like its composer.[16]

Young's remarks not only capture the spirit of the composition, they are also a comment on the energy with which
Lockwood has pursued composition in his retirement.

Lockwood's high regard for another artist and friend was the
catalyst for the last work of the middle period. *Panegyric for
String Orchestra and Horn* (1978-79), a single-movement work,
was composed in honor of Boulder author Donald Sutherland.
Lockwood described his music which is appropriately somber,
but free of overt sentimentality, in these words.

> *Panegyric,* a gathering of persons, of strong friends, a
> unanimous laudation—more that than a formal eulogistic
> speech—was begun a few months before Donald Sutherland's
> death and finished a few months after. The solo instrument is
> alternately in and out of the string texture even as Sutherland's
> thought and expression entered and affected the thought and
> expression of others.
>
> There is a passage, a section, that refers to Elysium by way of
> the Schiller-Beethoven subject fairly respectably disguised, for
> Sutherland was not one to indulge in the obvious. Besides, his
> preference was Mozart. In these and all other aspects the
> listener is, however, on his own and need not bother himself
> over particulars.[17]

Sutherland and Lockwood had collaborated on several works
during the composer's years at the University of Denver,
including the opera *Requiem for a Rich Young Man* (1964)
and the extended solo song *The Dialogue of Abraham and
Isaac* (1972). Sutherland also introduced Lockwood to Rubén

Example 10.18, "Noble" horn theme, *Panegyric for String Orchestra and Horn*, MSC, pp. 2-3, mm. 1-19.

Example 10.18, continued.

Darío's poem "To Margarita Debayle." Lockwood used
Sutherland's English translation of Darío's poem in a 1977 solo
song of the same name. Through their shared efforts, com-

poser and librettist/lyricist created a strong artistic, as well as personal bond, which is reflected in Lockwood's words.

Panegyric is based on a noble horn theme; its opening, A-E-A upward fanfare is anticipated, then suggested in the string accompaniment (Example 10.18). At first, the strings incorporate the pattern in two-part counterpoint, then the five parts become more independent of each other. In the contrasting section, a solo violin spins a fifteen-bar-long melodic line while the rest of the ensemble, including horn, surround it with chords in a low register. The stately first theme returns, although it has been altered to stress sixteenth notes and major seventh intervals.

In the second section of the work the horn plays a beautiful tonal melody in D major. Muted strings offer only short statements for support until halfway through the forty-two-bar section, when their roles expand to full, dissonant, harmonic accompaniment. The pensive horn solo serves as a bridge to the third section, "Allegro," in which the primary horn theme returns. After various quartal and octatonic passages, a "con grazia" section introduces the disguised "Hymn to Joy," embellished by tritone appoggiaturas. Both thematic ideas from the first section, the noble theme and the horn solo, make another appearance, the latter bringing the piece to a quiet close.

Late Period Works

With its sparse instrumentation and pared-down thematic materials, *Prayers and Fanfares* is characteristic of many of Lockwood's later compositions. The nine-minute piece in fugal style is scored for brasses, a full complement of percussion instruments, and strings. To begin, a lyrical, rhythmically homogeneous subject is stated by a solo violin. Each repetition of the exposition is separated by highly contrasting passages, one taking the form of more dissonant, free counterpoint, and the other, a quartal trumpet fanfare, embellished by strings. Composed in 1980, *Prayers and Fanfares* has not yet been performed.

In *Concerto for Two Harps and Orchestra* (1981), Lockwood returned to traditional structures: a sonata, a passacaglia, and a rondo with variations. The concerto is not, however, a wholly traditional work; his thematic material is generated from a tone row interspersed with a passage of half steps (underlined below) linked by augmented seconds or their enharmonic equivalents (indicated below by breaks in underlining). The opening, twelve-tone row, played by the oboe, is interrupted after pitch nine by such a pattern (Table 10.1).

TABLE 10.1

←Opening pitches, score order→

g♯ a f e♭ d b c♯ g f♯ e♭ d f e c♯ c e♭ d b b♭ c♯
Row, pitches 1-9→   ↑Half steps linked by augmented seconds

Perhaps this procedure was designed to make the primary thematic set more memorable for the listener. Lockwood also took extra pains to make the sonata form of the first movement clear to the conductor, with section headings such as "A-1," "Subsidiary Section B," and "Development Section" notated in the score.[18]

The ground bass of the "Passacaglia," the second movement, also alternates half steps and augmented seconds. Two "Digressions," the second of which features tremolo marimba chords, interrupt the inevitable repetitiveness inherent in this Baroque structure. Horns state the "Source" of the "Rondo-Variations" third movement, another quartally-inspired fanfare. This theme is treated to nine variations, several of which are separated by Ivesian, non-tonal interludes. In the first of these interludes, the quartal theme becomes a fugue subject.

Lockwood's care in score preparation extended beyond the marking of structural sections for the conductor, to preparations of the solo parts. There, he carefully indicated harp pedal changes, a chore which is often left to the performer. The harp writing itself features bitonality—the two solo parts are often written in different key signatures—harmonics, "glassy" arpeggios, and oriental pentatonic sections. Unique orchestral devices include a "sizzle" cymbal and passages for the string section marked "Bartók pizzicato."[19]

The work was commissioned by and dedicated to mother and daughter harpists Suzann Davids and Deborah Kay Davids-Wylde. The two women performed the piece with the Orquesta Sinfonica Nacional Costa Rica in San Jose in September of 1983, making the *Concerto for Two Harps and Orchestra* Lockwood's second concerto to be premiered outside of the United States.

Choreographic Suite for String Orchestra (1986), as yet lacking a premiere, is abstract in concept as well as in music. In the choreographic suggestions contained in the score, Lockwood included the admonition that "its music deals in anachronism and incongruity," a phenomenon which, he felt, should be reflected in the dance. Its five movements range from a "Canonic fugue" to a "Nocturnal, barcarolic" song to a "Scherzo" which purports "Pure neo-eighteenth century" style, complete with a Mannheim "rocket" theme of sorts (Example 10.19).

One of Lockwood's gems occurs in the fifth movement, "Celebration," which offers the anachronistic and unexplained subtitle, "David and the Ark." Here he treats the listener to one of his most innovative, exuberant passages: an often bichordal

Example 10.19, "Rocket" theme, *Choreographic Suite for String Orchestra*, MSC, mvt. III, p. 15, mm. 1-12.

Example 10.20, "Hyfrydol" rendition, *Choreographic Suite for String Orchestra,* MSC, mvt. V, p. 32, mm. 3-7.

rendition of the hymn tune "Hyfrydol" in compound quadruple meter (Example 10.20). The last movement alone makes this piece worthy of performance, but the other movements are well-wrought enough to balance it admirably.

Another multi-disciplinary project dating from the same year, a collaborative piece which was conceived with a performance imminent, is *Return of the Spirits.*[20] Lockwood's music, scored for synthesizers, acoustic flute, and percussion, was composed in response to a story outline before Denver choreographer William Thompson created the movement. The setting is Colorado's historic Mesa Verde, an ancient home of cliff-dwelling Anasasi Indians. The work was commissioned by Denver's KRMA television and first broadcast in 1986.

The program of the work deals with the "Dark" and "Light" spirits which Native Americans have historically credited with influencing human behavior. Faithful to his subject, Lockwood endeavored to make the piece idiomatic in the sense that the instrumentation and tonal patterns such as the cross-cultural "sol-mi" motive are representative of Native American music. Each of the three main characters, the spirits and the human, has a corresponding leitmotif which is transformed in response to the action.

The score indicates only traditional elements of music; final programming of the computers was achieved in collaboration with technicians Chris Hewitt and Gannon Kashiwa of Evergreen, Colorado. Lockwood felt that he lost some control of the final product, a state of affairs which probably plagues all composers involved with the highly-edited medium of television. His ambivalence is evident in these words, "The composer was not consulted regarding title. My concept of the entire project was based on an idea more existential and the music so conceived, so the title is basically inappropriate."[21] The composer's intention was to create an abstract art work which reflected a broader conceptual realm than was presented in the final product. This striving to suggest, rather than to represent, an ineffable artistic quality became more important in his later works.

Lockwood was very much at home when another art form was incorporated in his music, whether it was text, movement, or drama. In those cases, his penchant for rapid thematic shifts was well justified, and fairly often motivated, by the visual or textual aspect. He shares his later interest in works for dance with a compatriot, William Schuman, who created several works for modern dancer Martha Graham. With respect to composing for the dance, Schuman stated, "Just about the best way for an American composer to have his music most often heard [is] to have his music seen."[22]

Lockwood's three most recently completed works feature wind instruments. *Lenten Sequence, Interval, and Ascent,* composed in 1989, is scored for symphonic winds, harpsichord, and percussion. Its pervasive style is full and melodious, particularly in movement one, "Swedish melody," and movement three, "Chorale." In the latter, he borrowed a tune by seventeenth-century hymnodist Johann Schop for musical material. At about fifteen minutes in duration, Lockwood's sonorous work is a fitting addition to the rapidly expanding repertoire of the modern wind band.

Metaphors (1991) was commissioned and programmed by the Colorado Wind Ensemble to commemorate its tenth anniversary. The twelve-minute piece reflects Lockwood's many musical tastes: the "Lento moderato" features a lyrical, ascending motive; the "Andante fluendo" is based on a gentle duet between various upper wind instruments; the "Scherzoso" exploits chromatic and octatonic materials; and the "Allegro" is a sectional form in which the tritone and the octatonic scale serve as sources.

Finally, Lockwood explored a new method for generating a composition in *Pi March* (1992). Pitch material for the central section of this sprightly wind band piece is generated from the decimal value of pi, the Greek symbol designating the ratio of the circumference of a circle to its diameter. As comic relief from the mathematical gravity of the work, Lockwood gives the members of the ensemble the opportunity to shout, "Tah-rah-rah-boom-de-ay," just before its close. *Pi March* is just over—perhaps even fourteen seconds over—three minutes in duration.

*   *   *   *   *

Because they span his compositional career, the instrumental ensemble pieces represent a microcosm of Lockwood's greater creative development. Works with a decidedly academic orientation sprang from the Oberlin and New York years, a very fruitful period in his career. In his middle period, the works became more dense with ideas and instrumentation as he searched for a more individual style. Denver, whether as the site of an academic post, or the chosen area for retirement, proved to be as positive an environment for instrumental composition as it was for opera. Many of the works composed after 1980 exhibit the refined economy and focused purpose of a composer who has experimented with various styles and has settled on a most effective few.

However, even in his more laconic third period, Lockwood's music still exhibits the freshness and asymmetry apparent in his earliest works. His instrumental works are never conventional in any sense, because he refuses to adhere to any one style long enough to allow it to take root. This tendency is indirectly addressed by his former student, Peter Mennin: "For an American composer melodies will have unpredictable contours. The American mentality does not fit into neat categories."[23] Judging by this characterization, Lockwood has once again proven himself to be a typically non-conformist native composer.

Chapter Eleven

Opera and Non-Operatic Theater Music[1]

Overview—Operas

Two periods in Normand Lockwood's academic career seem inextricably linked to particular genres of his compositions. Most of his string quartets were composed in the short span of years from 1930 to 1945. Similarly, his operas illuminate a later part of his career. With the exception of *The Scarecrow* (1945), Lockwood's operatic works were completed between 1961 and 1964, when his faculty responsibilities at the University of Denver were divided equally between the Music and Drama Departments. Included in this concentrated operatic period are *Early Dawn* (1961), *The Wizards of Balizar* (1962), *No More from Thrones* (1962), *The Hanging Judge* (1964), and *Requiem for a Rich Young Man* (1964).

After 1964 Lockwood wrote incidental music for twenty-three dramatic productions at the University of Denver, accompanying works such as Arthur Miller's *The Crucible*, Eugene O'Neill's *The Emporer Jones*, W. H. Auden's *For the Time Being*, and *Medea* of Euripides. Only for Donald Sutherland's

My Sister, My Spouse (1972) has the musical score survived; that score will be addressed in this chapter.

Although none of Lockwood's operas have been published, all of them have been performed. It seems to be a foregone conclusion that composers have both performers and location in mind when generating an opera, but this situation is unique in comparison to Lockwood's other compositions. In all of the other genres, some pieces were composed "for the shelf." However, as Gilbert Chase has expressed it, "Opera is meant to be both seen and heard,"[2] and Lockwood's operas support that point.

Lockwood applied his lyrical vocal style, already seen in the choral and solo works, quite successfully in the medium of opera. Motivically-dense orchestrations and colorful instrumentations, rich in wind timbres, also make Lockwood's operas distinctive. His fondness for descriptive, programmatic writing in all genres is equally present, as well the episodic structures seen in the oratorios. These episodes progress from one to another with few complete breaks, creating a relatively continuous form. Occasionally, a passage emerges from this unbroken current of music and might even be considered a "set piece." However, Lockwood avoids the traditionally pervasive numbers format associated with opera. His musical units flow into one another with few obvious seams.

With regard to the other elements of opera, Lockwood steers a course that visits both progressive and traditional arenas of twentieth-century American opera. He shares Gian-Carlo Menotti's preference for the beautiful presentation of the human voice. Although his is not strictly a "bel canto" style, even his most dissonant lines are constructed with a concern for lyricism, as well as proper word stress. Disjunct, angular writing is used most often as a tool by which a certain word is highlighted. The most accented syllable of an emotionally charged line often leaps out of the linear structure and is succeeded by a large melodic interval of some kind, particularly a tritone if the mood calls for it.

Lockwood is eclectic, representing a middle ground between the conservatism of Carlisle Floyd and the progressiveness of Roger Sessions. Unlike Douglas Moore he does not attempt to maintain a consistent musical language germane to a specific opera, such as the folk style used in Moore's *The Ballad of Baby Doe* (1956). On the contrary, Lockwood's sound is consistently diverse. Associative styles such as jazz are used in much the same way as angularity, to emphasize a word or idea. Devices, ranging from octatonic scales and their derivative diminished harmonies, to bichords and tritones, are other fabrics of his musical collage, used for color and accent. The operas are often unified by the schematic repetition of these devices.

Lockwood shares with another compatriot, Marc Blitzstein, a theatrical flair, a fascination with social commentary, and a high ratio of dissonance to consonance. A further parallel between the two composers exists in the use of spoken dialogue in Blitzstein's *Regina* (1948-49) and in Lockwood's first few operas. Still, Lockwood's product is wholly his own, and these characteristics serve only to place him among a wide assortment of native opera composers.

Locating suitable librettos has presented a consistent challenge for Lockwood, one that has probably plagued composers for centuries. He was drawn to worthy plays or ideas; however, his gifted collaborators sometimes knew little about the literary demands of the libretto. In the case of *The Scarecrow*, too much text keeps the opera from reaching its fullest effective potential. In his first attempt in the medium, Lockwood was joined by his first wife in attempting to pare down Percy MacKaye's play to workable operatic proportions. Their product was only partially successful. Some of his collaborations with Denver author Russell Porter exhibit a similar disadvantage. Porter's literary gifts were not naturally suited to

the specially focused, and even repetitive, dramatic requirements of an opera.

In contrast, *Requiem for a Rich Young Man*, with a libretto
by Donald Sutherland, represents a favorable balance of text
and music. The scope is small in that work; the story itself is
limited to a few ideas, presented by characters who, because of
the satirical nature of the play, appear more as caricatures than
as people. These parameters were well suited to Lockwood's
distinctive operatic gifts.

All of Lockwood's six operas are, however, important works
of art, and they represent his tremendous range of expression.
Through his music, characters such as Percy MacKaye's
scarecrow or Russell Porter's murderous, preacher-turned-
colonel Shannon are depicted in a grippingly realistic way. The
vocal writing shows Lockwood's considerable understanding of
the voice, and his well-crafted, piquant orchestrations consistently enhance the works. His seamless structure gives a sense
of the drama's unfolding: ever progressing, yet tethered here
and there to points of orientation by recurring motives. These
operas warrant repeated performances, but with the exception
of one, their premiere runs have defined the boundaries of their
productions. *Requiem for a Rich Young Man* is the exception,
being performed in several major cities as recently as 1985.

The Scarecrow

In the choice of literary inspiration for his first opera, Lockwood drew upon the creative works of two of his countrymen.
Percy MacKaye (1875-1956) had found inspiration for his play
The Scarecrow: Or Glass of Truth (1908), in Nathaniel Hawthorne's "Feathertop" (1846, *Mosses from an Old Manse*),
although MacKaye insisted that his play was more than a mere
dramatization of its original source.

The scarecrow Feathertop of Hawthorne is the imaginative epitome or symbol of human charlatanism. . . . Thus the "Moralized Legend"[3] reveals itself as a satire upon a restricted artificial phase of society. . . . As such, it runs its brief course . . . to its appropriate *denouement*—the disintegration of its hero.

Hawthorne ends his narrative with an undeveloped aspect of his theme, which constitutes the starting-point of the conception of my play: the aspect, namely, of the essential *tragedy of the ludicrous.*[4]

MacKaye's tragedy was born out of the final speech of Feathertop's creator, Mother Rigby.

Poor Feathertop! I could easily give him another chance and send him forth again tomorrow. But no! *His feelings are too tender—his sensibilities too deep.*[5]

The scarecrow's vulnerability, his consuming desire to become human after masquerading as such, is the element of the drama that fired MacKaye's imagination. Whereas Feathertop is seen "as the emblem of a superficial fop," the playwright's scarecrow, Ravensbane, is presented as "the emblem of human bathos."[6]

The resultant play was set in late seventeenth-century Massachusetts. A macabre couple, the witch-like Goody Rickby and Dickon, "a Yankee improvisation of the Prince of Darkness,"[7] together create a scarecrow made of flails, beets, bellows, and a rotted jack-o-lantern. In order to avenge the abandonment of Goody by Justice Gilead Merton twenty-two years earlier, the ghoulish pair give the scarecrow life and a comely human figure. Lord Ravensbane, as he is named, will take the place of the child of Merton and Goody, who died soon after Merton's departure. Justice will be served when Merton's innocent niece, Rachel, is won by Goody's surrogate son, Ravensbane.

Contrary to their plan, Ravensbane returns the love of Rachel and desperately wishes to become mortal. His identity is betrayed by the Glass of Truth, a magic mirror which Rachel had previously bought from Goody to test the sincerity of her former love, Richard. The jealous and righteously skeptical Richard forces Rachel and Ravensbane to look at their reflections in the mirror, where Rachel sees only a scarecrow in place of her lover's image. Ravensbane eventually confesses to her, as her love outweighs Dickon's threats. As he dies, his image in the mirror becomes a normal one instead of that of a scarecrow; his honesty has apparently absolved him of guilt.

Lockwood's opera was commissioned in 1944 by the Alice M. Ditson Fund of Columbia University and presented there in 1945, under the baton of Otto Luening.[8] Lasting about two hours, the three-act work has been performed on only one occasion, the premiere, which Lockwood remembers as "flabby."[9] As a result of World War II, well-trained male singers were almost impossible to find, so the abilities of the premiere cast left much to be desired.

The opera's libretto was begun by the composer, but as deadlines encroached, the task was shared by journalist Dorothy Sanders Lockwood, the composer's first wife. The Lockwoods followed the MacKaye original closely, making few substantial cuts in the dramatic dialogue, retaining the six primary characters, and adding a chorus. Their greatest editorial freedom occurs with the occasional substitution of rhymed for unrhymed text. Lockwood's orchestra comprises a woodwind section of single players on a part, two each of trumpets and French horns, one trombone, timpani, percussion, piano, three first violins, two second violins, two violas, two cellos, and a single string bass. This chamber ensemble is utilized in a traditional manner, supporting the recitatives and most arias with strings only. Brasses make emphatic statements when appropriate, while woodwinds add color with instrumental combinations such as bassoon and viola in the song of the crows (Example 11.1). Here also, Lockwood depicted Goody's childlike rhyme somewhat programmatically, with uncomplicated music.

Example 11.1, Colorful instrumentation and childlike rhyme, *The Scarecrow,* MPVC, I, i, p. 3, mm. 6-11.

Stylistically, the opera resembles many of Lockwood's works from mid-century. Octatonic scales and quartal, quintal, chromatic, modal, and bichordal writing are used to punctuate and accent MacKaye's story. In contrast, some sections are simple and unadorned, as in Rachel's love song from Act I (Example 11.2). These moments of simplicity contribute welcome areas of focus to the opera as a whole.

Example 11.2, Static vocal line and sustained chords, "Rachel's Love Song," *The Scarecrow,* MPVC, I, i, p. 27, mm. 1-12.

Example 11.3, Eighteenth-century instrumental style, *The Scarecrow,* MPVC, II, i, p. 1, mm. 1-10.

To call forth the spirit of the time and place, several instrumental interludes and introductions are presented in sixteenth- and eighth-note rhythmic patterns which call to mind the late eighteenth-century instrumental genres (Example 11.3). Gilbert and Sullivan's choruses are suggested in the echoing crowd responses of the party scene, especially in repetitions of the words "rarity" and "sincerity."

The "diabolus in musica," the tritone, is used in the motto representing the satanic Dickon; other examples of text painting abound. The most programmatic element of the opera is an instrumental refrain to Ravensbane's strophic aria: the sound of crows, announced by an ominous octatonic flourish (Example 11.4). Less overt, but still suggestive, are musical allusions to personality traits such as the taunting chant sung by Dickon to Merton. Juvenile rhymes (e.g., Merton, curtain, certain) and a melodic pattern on sol-mi-la-sol-mi, the universal children's tune, subliminally support the childlike attitude represented by the chant.

Example 11.4, Octatonic scale and programmatic sound of crows, *The Scarecrow*, MPVC, II, i, p. 13, mm. 8-9 and p. 14, mm. 1-2.

In setting Dickon's tutoring session with Ravensbane, Lockwood created a clever musical structure which not only illustrates, but also enhances the drama. In order to make a good impression on the nobility he wishes to deceive, Dickon guides his apprentice's speech toward proper syntax and emphasis (Example 11.5). The composer's skill in text setting and subtle sense of humor are evident in this section of the opera. Here Lockwood created a melodic and rhythmic representation of Dickon's subtle syntactical modifications of Ravensbane's speech.

Example 11.5, Dickon's tutoring session, *The Scarecrow*, MPVC, I, iii, p. 3, mm. 14-15; p. 4, mm. 1-5.

In *The Scarecrow* the youthful Lockwood shares with the audience most, if not all, of the tricks of his compositional trade. Such eclecticism diminishes as his career progresses, fortunately so because, as in the first opera, the profusion of ideas and methods occasionally weakens the dramatic impact. Reviewer Mark A. Schubart of the *New York Times* found fault with Lockwood's dramatic pace, as well.

> If the performance of *The Scarecrow* was not a totally pleasing experiment, it was at least an experiment; and in these days of extreme conservatism in the field of opera, it was a refreshing change.
>
> In his setting of the text, Mr. Lockwood has to resort all too often to the spoken word in order to speed up the action. The few moments of repose, mostly allotted to Rachel, the young girl, are thus Mr. Lockwood's most successful ones, while the spoken lines, accompanied by background music, are his least rewarding.[10]

Schubart also noted the quality of the orchestrations, stating

> Mr. Lockwood is no amateur, however, and what shortcomings his opera has are by no means those of an untrained or insensitive hand. The orchestration seems competent, the prosody is above reproach, and the vocal writing lies well for the voices and is eminently singable.[11]

The strongest moments in the opera are when Lockwood allows himself to indulge the intense feeling inherent in the plot. One such occasion is the love duet between Rachel and Ravensbane. Beautiful as this music is, it represents the sort of conservatism that Schubart criticized in others and that Lockwood himself tried to avoid. The opening words sustain a single pitch, accompanied by parallel seventh chords reminiscent of Ravel's music. Perhaps it was such a passage that

Lockwood had in mind when he said of *The Scarecrow,* "Oh, it is such a sweet work, it wouldn't offend anybody."[12]

Those tender moments are interspersed throughout a manifold fabric of musical materials. The overall mood of the opera is one of bleakness, created by the repeated use of octatonic and chromatic materials and the tritone. Such an atmosphere befits the Faustian nature of MacKaye's play, focusing ironically as it does on the vindication of the deserted and deceived. In part, these pointedly gloomy surroundings create a perfect backdrop to intensify the jewel-like impression made by the lyrical passages. In any case, Lockwood's first attempt at opera remains consistent with his daring juxtaposition of diverse musical materials seen in the oratorios and extended works for solo voice.

Early Dawn

Lockwood's second opera ushered in his productive period at the University of Denver, but because it was begun before his faculty appointment there, *Early Dawn* is not wholly a Denver opera. Lockwood spent the 1960-61 academic year in Honolulu as visiting faculty at the University of Hawaii. The process of creating *Early Dawn* is thus documented in frequent, fascinating letters between Lockwood and librettist R. Russell Porter, who was already a theater faculty member at the University of Denver.[13]

A commemoration of the Civil War Centennial at the University of Denver was the occasion for the commissioning and performance of the *Early Dawn* opera, based on Porter's 1957 concert reading by the same name. The opera version opened on August 7, 1961, and played for six consecutive evenings. Thomas Scherman, conductor of the Little Orchestra of New York City, was engaged for the work, which he described as "one of the most challenging things I have ever

done."[14]   Reviewers were enthusiastic in their praise, as was
Robert W. Dumm of the *Christian Science Monitor.*

> Mr. Lockwood has in this score, as on many other occasions,
> proven himself a sensitive craftsman. His lyrical sense takes off
> from the sound of the words themselves, intensifying their
> dramatic inflections.
>   His orchestra is large, well-padded with French horns and
> strings that cushion the seethe and surge of his dissonance.
> Above all, it is his songfulness, full-hearted American folk song,
> that catches the ear and tugs at our feelings. The musical idiom,
> like the story it supports, is as homespun as calico and just as
> tough.[15]

In comparison to *The Scarecrow, Early Dawn* is a more
mature work, well-suited to Porter's image-laden and poetic
libretto. It resembles the earlier work in length and number of
acts, however. The orchestra is also essentially the same, except
for the addition of bass clarinet and tuba in *Early Dawn.* The
story focuses on a family at the opening of the Civil War, the
members of which are sharply etched dramatically and musically. Jeb and Mary are the parents, and with his strong sense of
family, Jeb serves as the sympathetic foil to Mary, an antago-
nistic prophet of doom.   Their troubled daughter Miriam
embodies both parental qualities, being torn between her love
for Jeff, the adopted son and a transplanted Southerner, and
her abolitionist feelings. Joel, the natural son, allies himself
with his adopted brother from the South, even defying the town
and his childhood companions. Finally, the runaway slave is
presented as a man of dignity and, even in his extremely disad-
vantaged position, is never pictured as a pathetic object. The
Editor, serving the same function as the Narrator in Thornton
Wilder's *Our Town,* sets the time and place, but also comments on the world outside the war, often against the backdrop

of a Debussyian modal chorus or orchestra. The recurring image of Spring is juxtaposed ironically with the nation at war.

Just as Jeff and Miriam announce their wedding plans, with the approval of the family, the "Rebels" fire the first shots on Fort Sumter, signaling the beginning of the war. Remembering his relatives, Jeff decides not to join the fight. Miriam is appalled; she has just observed the wounds of the beaten slave and heard how his family was murdered. Mary declares that justice is being served by the war, while her husband Jeb and son Joel focus instead on the bonds of family and the price of war.

Eventually Miriam betrays Jeff's plans to avoid enlisting, the townspeople arrest him on a false charge and, in a kangaroo court, sentence him to hang. Too late Miriam realizes that her love was stronger than her hate. Jeb and Joel attempt to save Jeff, but the townspeople are carried away by a fevered patriotism, and he is hanged. Jeb is killed trying to save the life of his adopted son. As stated in the program of the opera's premiere,

> Though *Early Dawn* uses an episode of the first day of the Civil War as a framework, the opera deals with conflicts that are more far-reaching, more universal than the events of the story. It deals rather with the bewildering dilemma of mankind who, faced with the necessity of action, is torn not so much between the forces of good and evil as between the philosophies of righteousness and love.[16]

Questioning of such philosophies also accompanied the civil issues concerning many American citizens in the early 1960s, a factor which made the opera timely in its appeal.

Lockwood's score matches the high quality of the libretto. A cohesiveness that was missing in *The Scarecrow* is aided by the increased use of recurring motives. Besides the octatonic scale, his staple materials include two other patterns: the first is a melodic line harmonized in major thirds, descending by the minor third or its equivalent (Example 11.6); the second is a quartal obbligato over various seventh, major/minor, and bichordal sonorities (Example 11.7). Modally-inspired passages and tritones also add frequent reference points.

The composer's tone rows are not developed in a serial fashion, but simply provide a framework for non-tonal passages. These dodecaphonic sections, along with those based on the octatonic scale, are appropriate to the tensions in the drama and are used most often to underscore the recitatives.

The "Spring" chorus, appearing near the beginning of Act I and later in Act III, features ninth chords in parallel motion and whole-tone constructions which resonate in the sensuous, "plein air" style of Debussy (Example 11.8). The natural subjects of spring, dawn, and night, referenced as they are at the beginning of each act, are yet another integrating factor.[17] Act I opens with the Editor's speech: "The wheel has turned: the earth, so the books say, tilts toward the sun."[18] Here the music is poignantly soaring, over a pulsating B-C-E cluster and occasional octatonic figurations. Dawn is figuratively depicted at the beginning of Act II: "The earth once more has rolled eastward. The shadow thins. A gray day nudges the night before it."[19] The biting chill of an early dawn is suggested in the close-position bichords which underpin the "telegraph code" motive from Act I. Day's advance over night comes in the form of ascending octaves in first a whole-tone, and then an octatonic scale pattern.

Night is the temporal aspect summoned when the Editor, now aided by the chorus, opens Act III: "Night comes. . . . The houses stand in the valley, desolate, like ghosts of sunken ships long since forgotten."[20] The octatonic pattern from Act II reappears, but now is played "pesante" by the low instruments of the orchestra, under quartal and quintal sonorities in the woodwinds and violins (Example 11.9).

Example 11.6, Parallel third motive, *Early Dawn*, MPVC, I, p. 129, mm. 5-8.

Example 11.7, Quartal obbligato motive, *Early Dawn*, MPVC, I, p. 4, mm. 11-14.

Example 11.8, Whole-tone and ninth-chord material, *Early Dawn*, MPVC, I, p. 9, mm. 1-4.

Example 11.9, "Pesante" octatonic octaves, *Early Dawn*, MPVC, III, p. 2, mm. 1-9.

Lockwood's extended use of spoken dialogue, prompted by an overabundance of text, has the unfortunate side effect of forcing the listener in and out of the sense of suspended reality associated with the opera genre. Other twentieth-century Americans struggled with the same issue, whether or not they attempted to solve it by resorting to the spoken word. Marc Blitzstein used dialogue in *Regina*, seeing it as an advantage in the achievement of his aim. He considers his work "opera comique,"[21] and therefore is free to use speech or song. Perhaps his description of his own work as "play in terms of music" may be applied to Lockwood's operas, although the latter admittedly used dialogue as an expedient method of setting large amounts of text, while Blitzstein saw it as an artistic device.[22]

Early Dawn is constructed so that the first act ends with Miriam's rejection of her betrothed, Jeff, as war is declared. Consequently, Lockwood is limited to the first act for gentle, "untroubled" lyricism, and he places his memorable arias there. Mary's strophic aria, perhaps the inspiration for critic Dumm's description "as homespun as calico, and just as tough," is one such lyrical moment, although it is not wholly devoid of a dark side. Its compound meter, minor tonality, and melodic thirds create a lyrical framework for Mary's advice to her son; however, this simplistic music is juxtaposed ironically with her harsh, rather fatalistic textual message (Example 11.10). Lockwood's insight into the warmongering matriarch of the family is evident here.

The impassioned lament of the runaway slave, "Why you wait so long?", is another memorable moment. When told that his neighbors are now fighting for his freedom, the character responds with the text:

Dear Jesus, Why so long?
Last week I got a wife and child,
This week I got none.[23]

Example 11.10, Mary's folklike ensemble, *Early Dawn*, MPVC, I, p. 114, mm. 1-8.

The slave's aria, prepared by an anguished octatonic prelude, features the minor mode, phrase irregularity, and melodic simplicity of black American folk idioms (Example 11.11).

Example 11.11, Slave's folk lament, *Early Dawn*, MPVC, I, p. 121, mm. 1-12.

These elements of the spiritual develop quickly into the more dissonant language of the opera, including a bitter major/minor chord to underscore the word "pain" (Example 11.12). Later in

Example 11.12, Dissonant materials in slave's lament, *Early Dawn*, MPVC, I, p. 123, mm. 1-5.

the aria, as the slave vows to go to war himself, the tonality
changes to G-sharp major/minor and a dialogue develops in
which the tortured Miriam supplies the tritone. Emotional
content intensifies as the opera progresses, matching the moun-
ting tension of Act II and tragic events of Act III.

Early Dawn gave Lockwood an opportunity to apply his
interpretive gifts to a first-rate drama, and he was equal to the
task. In comparison to *The Scarecrow*, the latter product is
more artful than craftful. When devices are used, they depict
abstract   emotions   and   concepts   instead   of   concrete
phenomena. As seen in the case of the slave's lament, changes
of emotive or dramatic direction are more developmental than
abrupt: more logical and motivated than surprising.   The
unifying motives are subtle enough to form an integrated web,
instead of disruptively uncomfortable bindings. In the words
of *The Denver Post* critic Max Price, "*Early Dawn* [is] an
important new American opera."[24]   Although it is no longer
new, Lockwood's second opera is an important contribution to
the native art form.

The Wizards of Balizar

The third Lockwood/Porter effort was aimed at a new
audience. *The Wizards of Balizar*, subtitled "A Comic Fantasy," borrows many elements from popular musical theater,
while retaining the artistry that Lockwood had found to be
successful in his earlier operatic creations. With a chamber
orchestra of thirteen players, including flute, oboe, clarinet,
bassoon, trumpet, horn, strings, and percussion, Lockwood
paints a suitably fantastic backdrop for Porter's fanciful story.
The cast of this one hour, forty-five minute work is small, with
only six leads and a miniature chorus. It opened on August 1,
1962, at the University of Denver's Little Theater.

The story is related by Abdullah, a teller of tales in the mythical city of Arabic inspiration, Balizar. His fabrication is inspired by a real object: a street sign advertising the services of Ismad the tailor. In Abdullah's story, Ismad, although happy to be a tailor, is persuaded by his dissatisfied and greedy wife to become a wizard. Although his pursuit of the goal is diligent, roses are the only results of the incantations pronounced by the tailor and his nephew/apprentice, Maki.

Just as Ismad decides to resume tailoring, which he recognizes as his true calling, Kamal appears. He is the King's treasurer, and demands the services of Ismad, whose sign had been changed to "Ismad the Wizard . . . Necromancy While You Wait!!!" The King's favorite ruby has been stolen, and Ismad is given the choice of recovering the stone or being hanged. Maki, the apprentice, eventually saves the day by forcing a confession of guilt from Kamal's wife, who had greedily stolen the gem. Ismad again takes up his true calling, the wife grants her husband the right to his chosen profession, and the narrator/storyteller Abdullah returns, posing the question, "Tell me, was the tale I told you true?"

The same busy, colorful street scene opens and closes the work. Cries from vendors interspersed with exotic augmented second intervals, Phrygian scales, bichords, and open fifth intervals create a realistic setting. Instrumental interludes alternate singing and an abundance of spoken dialogue; operatic suspension of reality does not rely on continuous music in this fairy tale. Sustained chords often provide a background for the action, sometimes creating clusters as new tones are added and sustained. Clever puns—"so it seems," contrasted with "sew its seams"—insure the work's appeal to children.

Ismad's joyful "I'm Glad I am a Tailor" (Example 11.13) is melodically tonal, but major/minor chords add just the spice needed to separate it from musical theater works of the period such as Lerner and Loewe's *Camelot.* The rousing, consonant

"Let's Give it a Whirl," written in the same spirit as "I Ain't Down Yet" of Meredith Willson's *The Unsinkable Molly Brown*, is sung by the child apprentice, Maki. The jazzy chorus

Example 11.13, Tonal melody with major/minor chords, *The Wizards of Balizar*, MPVC, p. 34, mm. 11-12, and p. 35, mm. 1-4.

"There Ought to Be a Rule" is reminiscent of George and Ira Gershwin's musical comedies, seasoned with a dash of Gilbert and Sullivan's comic patter (Examples 11.14 and 11.15).

Example 11.14, Jazz writing in *The Wizards of Balizar*, MPVC, p. 110, mm. 1-7.

If the creators of *The Wizards of Balizar* intended to avoid the genre of musical comedy, the credit for doing so resides wholly with Lockwood. Most aspects of the libretto, even the

Tevye-like Ismad, forever at odds with his wife, might suggest lighter music.[25] But Lockwood's repeated use of complex devices such as octatonic and whole-tone scales, bichordal, quartal, and major/minor chords forces the listener to approach this work with more sophisticated ears.

Example 11.15, Street patter in *The Wizards of Balizar*, MPVC, p. 115, mm. 1-4.

One single genre does not capture the style of *The Wizards of Balizar*. Musical theater in which art music is combined with comedy has only recently become common, as in the later works of Stephen Sondheim. In the year of its creation, Lockwood's third theater piece resembled opera more than any other genre. By today's standards, however, the spoken dialogue, in combination with various comedic tools, points more toward the musical play. Since the composer never refers to it as an opera, *The Wizards of Balizar* is perhaps best categorized as the "Comic Fantasy" of its subtitle.

No More from Thrones

An unfortunate missing link in the extant Lockwood scores is *No More from Thrones*, a work with a Biblical setting, to which only the libretto remains. According to Lockwood, the music was lost shortly after its only performance, the annual Christmas Vespers at the University of Denver in 1962. Russell Porter wrote the libretto for the hour-long musical play and directed the production.

Lockwood summarized the music before its premiere.

> *No More from Thrones* is in no sense an opera. . . . It is a musical play, a play with music. . . . Only one of the leading characters on the stage, and three lesser characters, do any singing at all. . . . These four are all baritones.
>
> There is a mixed choir in the pit with the orchestra . . . the choir does not participate in the stage action. . . . It functions somewhat as a Greek chorus, also it participates with the orchestra as though it were simply a part of it.
>
> [The nineteen-piece orchestra does not call for violins; only violas, cellos, and basses.] This is to assure a darkness of shade as the play hardly calls for brightness of light.[26]

Thought-provoking in its irony, Porter's libretto is cast in the ancient, rhythmic cadences of Shakespeare. On the night when the sky is filled with a holy light and heavenly hosts sing of peace to all people, Petronius' wife and unborn child are lost in childbirth, just as her brother is murdered by a family friend. In his final speech the anguished Petronius cries out

> What hapless kingdom comes to earth?
> Does God rejoice that suffering and death
> Now come to birth?
> Not God Himself can know what He has done,
> For God . . . for God has never lost a son. [27]

Dark orchestral sounds and a pervasive baritone quality are surely suited to this uniquely somber look at the nativity, foreshadowing as it does the eventual death of God's son. Porter shows a great dramatic capability in a very limited structure and yet credits Lockwood's music in a note to the composer on the libretto: "To Norm—without whose music this piece gets pretty slim—in more ways than one."[28]

The Hanging Judge[29]

The fifth Lockwood-Porter collaboration was commissioned by the University of Denver for its centennial celebration, and presented on March 6 and 7, 1964. The story, one about a minister-turned-military colonel, was modeled on an actual figure in Colorado history, but Porter insisted on a diplomatic disclaimer in the opera's premiere program.[30]

> *The Hanging Judge* is not a historical opera. The events therein depicted are the purest fiction. Without doubt, the neophyte in Colorado history, confronted with any work in which the principal character is first seen as a minister, trades

his frock coat for a military uniform and engineers an Indian massacre, will immediately smile knowingly and exclaim, "Ah, Colonel Chivington and the Sand Creek Massacre." In the case of this opera, however, he will be wrong.[31]

A strong moral message, that even godly intentions may be perverted by a lust for power, is set forth by composer and playwright with equal efficacy. Each of the three acts introduces the audience to a new phase in the progressive demise of the protagonist, Shannon. In the first act, he stands firmly opposed to the violence of his parishioners. He begins to perceive himself as their Joshua, their leader in battle, only toward the close of the act. As the second act opens, he has become the merciless judge who eventually banishes his own friend from the town. Shannon's destruction is completed in the final act, when he not only leads a bloody raid against a peaceful Indian settlement, but also murders four chiefs in cold blood and strangles a prostitute who had earlier befriended him.

The Hanging Judge relentlessly chronicles the downfall of its tragedian in a solemn atmosphere. Shannon is a baritone, supporting his dark nature with his vocal range. Shannon's wife Elizabeth, and the town prostitute, Rheba, are the only female characters. Their music contrasts with the strident and tense idiom of the remaining music of the opera in opposing ways: Elizabeth is characterized by peacefully soothing, somewhat static melodic lines (Example 11.16). The prostitute, on the other hand, communicates most often in the language and music of her habitat, the saloon or barroom (Example 11.17). These characters are therefore memorable for the musical contrast they represent.

The composer introduced variety in many ways. The war tune "When Johnny Comes Marching Home" is parodied in the first act. The hymn tune "Ein' feste Burg" forms the foundation for the church meeting at the end of the act. Music characterized by open fifths, heavy downbeats, and modal harmony provides a backdrop for the massacre in Act III.

Example 11.16, Elizabeth's static recitative, *The Hanging Judge*, MPVC, I, p. 90, mm. 10-11 and p. 91, mm. 1-4.

Example 11.17, Vernacular style in prostitute's aria, *The Hanging Judge*, MPVC, I, p. 78, mm. 2-5.

These examples add momentary sparks of color, but are not used as unifying devices.

Lockwood's common thread is, instead, the outwardly expanding, ominous chromatic motive which opens the work (Example 11.18). Each act begins with this motive, and Shannon sings it on several occasions. It is modified in Acts II and III into a "lust for power" motive, associated with Shannon's increasingly zealous passions (Example 11.19). Other devices, such as bichordal harmony, are even more pervasive and stringent than in the earlier operas, appearing prominently when Shannon realizes that he has lost the respect of the town (Example 11.20). Sweeping octatonic scales serve not only as

Example 11.18, Outwardly expanding chromatic motive, *The Hanging Judge*, MPVC, I, p. 2, mm. 1-15.

Example 11.19, Transformation of chromatic motive, *The Hanging Judge*, MPVC, II, p. 59, mm. 4-6.

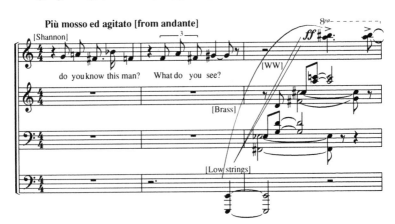

Example 11.20, Bichordal harmony in *The Hanging Judge*, MPVC, III, p. 39, mm. 1-6.

instrumental transitions and musical points of exclamation, but also as source material for vocal lines.

The Hanging Judge is as voluminous as other Porter librettos, but is written entirely in prose, a fact that created problems for the composer. The continuous, non-repetitive nature of the text prevented Lockwood from writing set pieces, which require repetition and development. With an over-abundance of words to set, the time element may have become a deterrent to the composition of arias and ensembles. Lockwood also avoided spoken dialogue, which would have exhausted great amounts of text in a minimum of time. The end result of these textual considerations is an opera written almost wholly in recitative style, lasting two and one half hours.

Several reviewers, including Dennis Riley of Denver's *Rocky Mountain News*, complained about the text.

> The fitting of such a libretto to music would seem a nearly hopeless task. The blame for many of the score's unsuccessful passages may be clearly laid upon the text, which for the most part does not lend itself to musical interpretation.[32]

However, others saw the positive qualities beyond the difficulties. "Though judicious pruning would intensify impact and allow greater dynamic pace, a stern score and stark frontier drama have been skillfully blended."[33]

Since it differs so strikingly from their previous collaborations, *The Hanging Judge* may be seen as an experimental work for Lockwood and Porter. At this point, the composer and librettist had worked together enough to be comfortable with each other. They had collaborated on a "dramatic portrait" (*Land of Promise*, 1960), a more traditional opera, a children's musical play, and a shorter musico-dramatic piece. Pure tragedy, in the form of *The Hanging Judge*, presented challenges for the librettist, but problems for the composer. Still, it exhibits one of Lockwood's finest qualities: his willingness to take a chance for the sake of art. Additionally, *The Hanging Judge* shows his most sophisticated transformation of a motive (e.g., the expanding chromatic motive) to reflect the drama. His abandonment of spoken dialogue may also be seen as an improvement over the earlier operas. For a serious composer, and especially one with Lockwood's artistic curiosity, *The Hanging Judge* may be seen as a qualified success.

Requiem for a Rich Young Man

Lockwood's first collaborative effort with Donald Sutherland, then faculty member in the Classics Department at the University of Colorado at Boulder, was generated by a commission from the National Opera Association in preparation for its 1964 annual convention in Denver. In the opening night program, composer and playwright summarized the mood of *Requiem for a Rich Young Man.*

> Though superficially a short, reckless farce on the order of a "zarzuela," [it] is thoroughly serious in depth, even didactic. It teaches how an adequate amount of capital can be a sovereign remedy, not only against bereavement, but also against the disorders and frustrations of animal passion itself.[34]

Sutherland's libretto opens as Gladys's husband Hubert has died. The widow is sharing her post-funereal grief with Hubert's brother Terence. They await the arrival of Gladys' sister Olivia and her husband William, from the crematorium. Sutherland's humor is sometimes broad to the point of absurdity, as seen in Gladys' recurring vision: "I can see now that plunging, hurtling car, Hubert torn to pieces three, each of them propelled afar!"[35] At other times, the author uses a more subtle style, as in Terence's speech: "But we're together in our grief for husband and for brother, so jointly we may find relief consoling one another." To emphasize the sexual innuendo, Lockwood underscores the moment with a blues melody and the dotted eighth, sixteenth-note pattern associated with a "bump and grind" dance (Example 11.21). Gladys shares confessions of love and lust with not one, but both brothers-in-law, then dedicates herself to one specific aspect of the dear departed's memory: "I shall clip with feelings fond the coupons of each sacred bond."[36]

Example 11.21, Vernacular style in *Requiem for a Rich Young Man*, MPVC, p. 5, mm. 1-6.

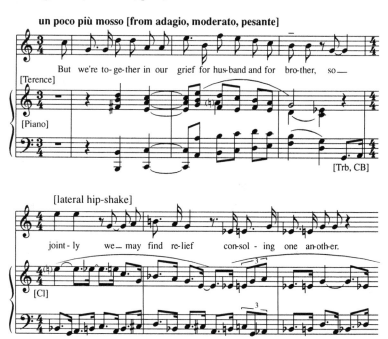

Forces for this twenty-five minute work are small: a cast of four, no chorus, one set, and a nine-piece orchestra consisting of flute, oboe, clarinet, piano, trumpet, trombone, percussion, cello, and bass. The dimensions of the opera were suggested in a letter dated April 15, 1964, to Lockwood from Genevieve McGiffert, then director of the University of Denver Opera Workshop.[37] She also suggested that the characterizations and vocal ranges should not overly tax the student performers who would eventually star in the work, but Lockwood, as always, composed for the sake of the music.[38] McGiffert's direction of the final product drew critical approval, as well as Lockwood's respect.

The composer managed to fit a surprisingly large amount of musical material into this brief work. Direct illuminations of the text occur, as in Terrence's speech mentioned earlier, and Lockwood's use of the Dies Irae sequence, but these are not overly distracting. Even Lockwood's impish quotation from Wagner's *Tristan und Isolde* (labeled "isoldevole" in the score), happens so quickly as to be missed by all but the most perceptive of listeners (Example 11.22). With tongue placed firmly in cheek, Lockwood inserts the quotation after Gladys's loving remembrance of her departed husband's teeth.

Example 11.22, Wagner quotation in *Requiem for a Rich Young Man*, MPVC, p. 25, mm. 3-7.

Motivically, the opera hinges upon an accompanimental idea in compound meter, based on the octatonic scale. Stated by the woodwind section of this small orchestra, it recalls the crisp, colorful wind writing of Stravinsky's *L'Histoire du Soldat*. When it accompanies a quick "pas de deux" between Gladys and Terence, Lockwood adds other timbral strata: Latin-influenced castanets (Example 11.23) and, later, a "walking" bass line played pizzicato. The effect is delightfully diverse and polyrhythmic. Perhaps it was just such a section which led critic Allen Young to describe the music as "pointed and clean in texture."[39]

Example 11.23, Octatonic motive in *Requiem for a Rich Young Man*, MPVC, p. 3, mm. 1-7.

The vocal lines are largely musical translations of dramatic speech patterns. Stressed words usually correspond with large intervallic leaps (Example 11.24). The few set pieces are memorable for their more conjunct structure (Example 11.25),

Example 11.24, Leaps corresponding with word stress, *Requiem for a Rich Young Man*, MPVC, p. 6, mm. 2-7.

contrasting as they do with the angular and unpredictable recitative-like sections. However, in spite of Lockwood's vocal artistry, the instrumental component is the most striking.

Example 11.25, Conjunct "set" piece, *Requiem for a Rich Young Man*, MPVC, p. 33, mm. 7-9; p. 34, mm. 1-4.

Wayne Johnson's observation is true only in part: "The music is the servant of the words, supporting a witty sally here and

emphasizing an ironic twist there."[40]   The instrumental portions are quite capable of standing alone as compositions.

Unlike the other Lockwood operas, *Requiem for a Rich
Young Man* has been recognized and performed beyond its
premiere presentation. It was recorded in Denver on KOA-TV,
and has been presented in a wide variety of settings: at the
University of Houston in 1967, Carnegie-Mellon University
and Northwestern University in 1974, and by small opera
companies in Denver and New York as recently as 1985.[41] Its
satire and jaded quality give it a charm which has been very
attractive to sophisticated audiences and viewers, as evidenced
by a 1974 review: "In this pungent libretto by Donald
Sutherland, Lockwood has found a marvelous way of applying
musical wit, and its satirical spark has if anything increased
over the years."[42]

Non-Operatic Theater Music

My Sister, My Spouse

In the second Lockwood/Sutherland collaboration, the
composer provided incidental music for *My Sister, My Spouse*,
a three-act Biblical comedy. The verse drama was premiered
October 26, 1972 at The Changing Scene, a small theater in
Denver. For the performance, the University of Denver faculty
members recorded the instrumental music, scored for seven
players including flute, oboe, clarinet, trumpet, and trombone,
piano, and percussion. Lockwood's score was composed in
nine segments, including three choral numbers, one solo vocal
piece, and five instrumental interludes. The music represents
approximately one-sixth of the total work; however, the play
provided creative material for another musical work.
Lockwood later excerpted a non-comic portion of the text, *The*

Dialogue of Abraham and Isaac, and set it for solo voice and piano.

Although the music for *My Sister, My Spouse* is less serious than that of an opera, Lockwood manages to fill it with elements of his recognizable style. In "Doing the Gaza Strip" (Sarah Before the Throne of Egypt), he quotes Brahms's popular lullaby, "The Beautiful Blue Danube" of Strauss, and "Good Night Ladies." In the chantey "Hey! for a Stiff Wind," a suggestive piano figuration evokes the sea, "where extravagant visions baroquely cavort."[43] Finally in the Philistine National Anthem, he mischievously sets the text "Hail, Philistia" on the opening strains of Handel's "Hallelujah Chorus." Such musical jokes are appropriately matched to a play full of witticisms, one of which was cited in a review. "'Sir, don't excite yourself,' one of the angels cautions when God is on the verge of rage over a small matter. 'You know your weakness for catastrophe.'"[44] Critical praise of Lockwood's music ranged from "entertaining" to "deeply imagined."[45]

*   *   *   *   *

After his opera *The Scarecrow* (1945), Lockwood did not return to the genre for sixteen years. When he came to the University of Denver in 1961, he was jointly hired by the Music and Theater Departments, presumably in order to create a full-time appointment there. Although the generation of this post may have been purely for contractual reasons, it brought about Lockwood's abrupt return to the medium he had abandoned after his first opus. In the Denver environment, he could devote a fair amount of time to the production of new American opera. This work was seemingly un-monitored; at the very least he was given free creative reign, as well as access to facilities and personnel for performances.

Even the involvement of student performers did not daunt
this operatic pioneer. He wrote the music which seemed appropriate to him, without adaptations or scaled-down characters, regardless of the maturity of the performing forces.
Because his works are of such a sophisticated literary and
musical substance, they serve as a tribute, both to the forward-
looking philosophy of the institution, and to its composer-in-
residence during that period.

An interesting epilogue to Lockwood's concentrated operatic
period is found in a 1976 interview for a Denver newspaper. In
Marjorie Barrett's article,

> Lockwood admits he has become disenchanted with opera.
> "You can't get anything off the ground here," he commented.
> "People don't pay any attention to what's going on. We have
> marvelous talent here . . . the musicians and the singers."
>
> "When Denverites think of producing opera," he continued,
> "they think in romantic terms. They hire third rate Metro-
> politan singers in place of first class Denver singers. I have seen
> it happen. I wish I had the imagination to do something about
> it. It is a dreadful concept, if you can dignify the treatment of
> singers with such a term. I don't understand why we think
> something imported is so much better."[46]

In these words, Lockwood addressed a problem which has been
a continuing frustration for many native composers in this
century. Perhaps in the future, our fascination with foreign
opera will be replaced by an interest in native works, just as our
former fascination with European musical education has
yielded to that of our own institutions. When and if that takes
place, Lockwood's operas will be waiting in the wings.

PART III

CATALOG OF MUSIC

This catalog of Normand Lockwood's music is based primarily on a list of the holdings of the Normand Lockwood Archive (NLA) at the Music Library, University of Colorado, Boulder. Completed by Kay Norton in 1990, the list was appended to her 1990 dissertation entitled "Normand Lockwood, 1930-1980: Fifty Years of American Composition." Prior to that date, the formidable task of sorting the manuscripts and papers comprising the collection was accomplished by Normand and Vona Lockwood. A partial list of Lockwood's works, begun by Susan L. Porter in 1970, also provided valuable help in the generation of the present catalog. Finally, the staffs of the American Composers Alliance and Broadcast Music, Inc. supplied archival information that was incorporated herein.

The majority of Lockwood's extant manuscripts may be found in the Normand Lockwood Archive; the Boston Public Library and the Penrose Library at the University of Denver also hold original works in their collections.

The works are listed alphabetically within eleven divisions.

Each entry includes, if applicable,

1. Catalog number

2. Appraisal marks (used separately or in combination):
   *—historically significant or much performed works,
   **—works worthy of inclusion in today's repertoires,
   S—works suitable for performance by gifted student or amateur performers, and
   P—works suitable for performance by professional or highly skilled amateur performers

3. Title in italics or in quotation marks, the latter designating component parts of larger works

4. Date of composition and publisher or accessing agent, if any

5. Performing forces

6. Duration in minutes (′) or hours plus minutes

7. Location in the NLA for unpublished works

8. Best format of NLA holdings for unpublished works (see keys to abbreviations)

9. Date of premiere

10. Source of the text and/or tune

11. Dedication

12. Movement titles for multi-movement works

Key to Musical Format Abbreviations

AH--manuscript "in another hand"
CAH--copy of manuscript "in another hand"
IRREG--boxes of irregular dimensions, NLA
MPC--photocopy of parts in manuscript
MPVC--photocopy of piano-vocal reduction in manuscript
MS--score in manuscript
MSC--photocopy of manuscript
MSP--parts in manuscript
MSPC--photocopy of parts in manuscript
MT--score on transparency
MTP--parts on transparency
NB--"new boxes," cataloged since 1990, NLA
NEG--photonegative of score
OV--oversized boxes, NLA
PV--vocal score with piano reduction
PVC--copy of piano-vocal score

Other Abbreviated Terms

AGO--American Guild of Organists
Arr.--arranged
BPL--Boston Public Library
Comm.--commissioned
Ded.--dedicated
ISCM--International Society for Contemporary Music
Narr.--Narrator
NLA--Normand Lockwood Archive, Music Library, University of
    Colorado, Boulder
Opt.--optional
Orig.--originally
PL--Penrose Library, the University of Denver
Rev.--revised
RSV--Revised Standard Version of the Bible

Instrument Abbreviations

A--alto voice
Accord--accordion
A cl--alto clarinet
B--bass
B cl--bass clarinet
Bar--baritone voice
bsn--bassoon
CA cl--contra-alto clarinet
cb--string bass
CB cl--contra-bass clarinet
C bsn--contrabassoon
cel--celeste
Children--children's choir
cl--clarinet
cor--cornet
cymb--cymbal
E♭ cl--E-flat clarinet
E hn--English horn
eu--euphonium
fl--flute

HD--handbells
hn--horn
hp--harp
harps--harpsichord
M--male
Mez--mezzo soprano
ob--oboe
perc--percussion
S--soprano voice
SQ--string quartet
stgs--strings
sax--saxophone
T--tenor voice
trb--trombone
tri--triangle
trpt--trumpet
V--voice
vcl--cello
vla--viola
vln--violin

Publisher Abbreviations

AG--Augsburg
AM--Arrow Music
AMP--Associated Music
    Publishers
BH--Boosey and Hawkes
BR--Broude Brothers
CFI--Carl Fischer
CFP--C. F. Peters
CS--Costello Music
CSI--Choral Services, Inc.
GMP--Golden Music Press
GS--G. Schirmer
GX--Galaxy Music Corp.
HB--Handy Brothers
HL--Hal Leonard
HMP--Hargail Music Press
HWG--H. W. Gray
JN--Jenson Music
KP--Kenwood Press, Ltd.
LJ--La Jolla Music
ML--Malcolm Music
MM--Mills Music

MMU--Merion Music
MPI--Music Press, Inc.
MR--Mercury Music
MY--Merrymount
NAK--Neil A. Kjos
OD--Oliver Ditson
OP--O. Pagani
RM--Rongwen Music
SM--Southern Music Co.
SP--Shawnee Press
SPAM--Society for the
    Publication of American
    Music
TP--Theodore Presser
TR--Tromba Publications
WCC--Westminster Choir
    College
WM--Wilshorn Music
WP--Westwood Press
WT--Witmark
ZO--Zondervan

CHORAL WORKS

1   **   s,p   *Acclamations of the Mass* (1967). SATB a cappella.
5´. NLA 1. MSC, MSC. Montview Boulevard
Presbyterian Church, Denver, 17 September 1967.

2   **   s,p   *Affirmation* (1982). SATB, fl/picc, perc, organ, cb. 8´.
NLA 1. MT, MTP--fl/picc, perc, cb. Community
Church of Honolulu, 19 February 1984. Text:
Statement of Faith, United Church of Christ.
1. Faith, 2. Statements, 3. Covenant.

3   s   *All My Heart Rejoices* (1956, AMP). SATB/piano.
1.5´. Text: Paul Gerhardt.

4   **   s,p   *Alleluia, Christ Is Risen* (1974, BR.) (Orig. *Christ Is
Born*, 1951). SATB a cappella. 4.5´. To Ward
Bedford.

5   **   s   *Alleluia (Hearts and Voices)* (1956, SM). SATB a
cappella. 4´. To Rolf Espeseth and the Texas
Lutheran Choir, Sequin, TX.

6   *Almighty King* (Laramie, 1959). SATB/organ. 3-4´.
NLA 1. MSC. "Sopra Moscow" hymn tune.

7   s,p   *America! O Democratic Nation* (1942, MM). SATB a
cappella. 3´.

8   s   *Apple Orchards* (1952, SP). Mixed or treble
voices/piano. 4´. Text: Walt Whitman.

9   *Arise, Shine* (1966). SATB. 2′. NLA 1. MSC, MPVC.
                  Text: Isaiah 60: 1-3. To Dr. Roger Dexter Fee and
                  the University of Denver A Cappella Choir.

10   **   s   *As a Hart* (1956, SM). SATB a cappella. 3′. Text:
                  Psalm 42.

11   *At the River*, arr. by NL (1980, ACA). SATB/organ.
                  3.5′. Text and tune by Rev. Robert Lowry. To Rev.
                  Frederica Mitchell.

12   **   s,p *A Babe Lies in the Cradle* (1956, AMP). SATB/piano.
                  2.5′. Text: German Carol (1649).

13   *Ballad of Father Dyer*, excerpt from *Land of Promise*
                  (1959-60). SATB, Solo Bar., Narr. 3.5′. NLA 1. MT.

14   *A Ballad of the North and South* (1959, AMP).
                  SATB, Band or Piano, Narr. Band: 2/picc-2-E♭
                  cl-3-A cl-B cl-2-2 A sx-T sax-Bar sax; 4-3/2-3-2-2;
                  cb, perc. 25′. NLA 1. MSC; AMP ed. of bass,
                  snare, C and B-flat treble inst.; AMP ed. of PV.
                  Northwestern University Summer Band and
                  Chorus, 19 July 1962.

15   **   s,p *Because I Could Not stop for Death* (1980, JN).
                  SATB a cappella. 4′. Text: Emily Dickinson. To
                  Angie.

16   *Benediction* (May 21, 1952). SATB. 1.5′. NLA 1.
                  MT.
                  Text: Book of Common Prayer.

17   *Benedictus* (1939, GS). SATB divisi. 4´. MSC.
            Dedicated to Dr. John Finley Williamson and the
            Westminster Choir.

18 ** s,p *The Birth of Moses* (1949, MMU). SSA/piano. 8´.
            Text: Exodus.

19   *Break Thou the Bread of Life*, arr. by NL (1956, SM).
            SATB. 4´. Text Mary A. Lathburg, tune Sherwin.

20   *The Bully Boat is Coming*, arr. by NL (1940).
            TTBarB. 3´. NLA 1. MSC. To G. Wallace
            Woodworth and the Harvard Glee Club. Text and
            tune, Halliard chantey.

21   *By'm By* (1950, TP). SATB a cappella. 4´. To Dolly.

22 ** s,p *Call to Faith* (1982). SATB, HD, SQ. 10´. NLA 2.
            MSC. Moravian Music Foundation, Winston-Salem,
            NC, 8 Oct. 1982.

23   *Carol: And Lo, the Star* (n. d., ACA). SATB 4´.
            Text: Matthew 2: 9-11. To the Adult Choir of Our
            Savior's Lutheran Church, Denver, Michael B.
            McBride, Organist-Choirmaster.

24 *,** s,p *Carol Fantasy* (1949, AMP 1952). SATB/Orchestra: 2
            ob, 2 trpt, timp, stgs. 24´. Westminster Choir, George
            Lynn, conductor, Jersey City, NJ Philharmonic
            Symphony, 14 Dec. 1949.

25   *Carol Fantasy* (1962 AMP, rescored). SATB/Band:
            2/picc-2-E hn-E♭ cl-3-A cl-B cl-CB cl-2-2 A sax-T sax-
            Bar sax; 4-3/3-3-bar/eu-1; cb, timp, cel, perc. 24´.

26   *Carol: Today Christ is Born, Noel!* (n. d.). SMezAT
            a cappella. 4´. NLA 2. MS.

27   *,** s,p *Children of God* Oratorio (1956). SATB divisi,
            Children, SATBarB Soli, Orch: 2-E hn-2 B cl-1; 4-2-2-
            1; timp, perc, stgs. 1 hr 49´. NLA OV 11. MSC, PVC,
            MTP. Octavos (CSI) 3-5´ each: "Return to the Lord,"
            "See What Love," "Sermon on the Mount"--text in
            Eng. and Chinese, "Service Music," including 3: 1.
            "Seek the Lord and Live, 2. "The Mouth of the Lord
            has Spoken," 3. "Let the Peoples Praise Thee." Berea
            College Choir and Cincinnati Symphony dir. by Thor
            Johnson, 4-5 Jan. 1957. Biblical Text: Clara Chassell
            Cooper, 1955.

28   **   s,p *Choreographic Cantata* (1968, AG 1970).
            SATB/organ, perc. 25´. 1968 National AGO
            Convention, Comm. Reuter Org. Co. Chorales trans.
            by Harold Heiberg.
            1. Sound the Cymbal, 2. In the Midst of Life,
            3. Beside the Streams of Babylon, 4. Up, Up, My
            Heart, 5. Abide with Us.

29   *A Christmas Anthem: In the Beginning was the Word*
            (1959 ACA). SATB/Organ. 4´. Text: St. John I.

30   *A Christmas Cantata: Masters, In This Hall* (1933).
            SATB divisi. 5´. NLA 2. MSC. Text: William Morris.
            "In remembrance of Deborah's first Christmas, 1928,
            aged 5 days."

31   s   *Christmas Garland* (1937). SATB. 15´. NLA 2. MS-
            AH. Text: from *The Bibelot* of Thomas B. Mosher.
            To Deborah.

32   *Christmas Hymn* (1948, WCC). M or F voices, 3 parts. 2´. Text: Delight Williamson Holt. To Debby, Angy, Heidi.

33   s,p *Christmas in Olde England* (1991). A Miracle (semistaged enactment) for Children SSA, Mez, fl, ob, cl, bsn. 15´. NLA 38. MSC. Text Wm. Morris, "Masters, In this Hall."

34 *,** s,p *The Closing Doxology* (1950, BR). SATB/Band: 3-2-4-3 sax-1; 4-4-2-bar-3; timp, perc, stgs. 10´. BR PV, 1952. For Westminster Choir College Band.

35 ** p *A Cloud of Witnesses* (1960, HWG). SATB/organ, S Solo. 10´. For the 50th Anniversary of the Cleveland Chapter, AGO.

36   "Come with us, O Blessed Jesus" from NL's *Jesus the King* (1959, CSI). SSAA. 3´. Text: John Henry Hopkins, Jr. Tune "Jesu, Joy," Johann Schop, 1642. Arranged for Jean Reeve.

37   *Come Ye Disconsolate*, arr. by NL (1956, SM). SATB, Organ, S Solo. 30´. Text: Thomas Moore and Thomas Hastings. Tune Webbe.

38   *Cradle-Song* (1939, SP 1953). SATBar. 4.5´. Text: Adelaide Crapsey.

39 *,** s,p *David Mourneth for Absalom* (1937, rev. 1988, NAK). SATB divisi. 4´. To Robert Moleson.

40 ** s,p *Darest Thou Now, O Soul* (1959, ACA). 3 SATB choirs/piano. 8´. The George Lynn Singers,

Colorado State University Choir, and The University of Denver Choir, 17 May 1959. Text: Walt Whitman.

41 *,** s,p Dirge for Two Veterans (1936, WT). 3 editions: SATB a cappella, TTBB a cappella, SATB a cappella, S solo. 5′. Text: Whitman. For Leonard de Paur and the Infantry Chorus.

42   *Dixie Land*, arr. by NL (1963, GMP). SATBarB. 4′. To Alvin C. Voran and the Centenary College Choir. Text and tune Dan Emmet.

43 ** s,p *Donne's Last Sermon* (1978; KP 1992). SATB/Organ. 20′. NLA 4. Comm. by the Classic Chorale of Denver. Text: John Donne.
1. Sombre, 2. Adagio moderato, 3. Stesso tempo, 4. Dead march, 5. Adagio moderato.

44   *Down in the Valley,* arr. by NL (1956, MMU). SATB a cappella. 3′. Text and tune "My Little Mohee," folk.

45   *The Earth is the Lord's* (1950, TP). SATB a cappella. 3′. Composed for the 1950 Talbott Festival of the Westminster Choir College. Text Psalm 24. To Mother.

46   *The Earth has Yielded its Fruit* (1981). SATB. 4′. NLA 3. MS. To Robert E. Kreutz and the Choir, St. Bernadette Catholic Church, Lakewood, CO. Text: Psalm 67, adapted.

47   *An Eating Song* (1943). M Quartet. 3′. NLA 3. MT. Text: Francis de N. Schroeser.

Electra, see *Three Odes from the Electra* (Choral).

48 *,** s,p *Elegy for a Hero* Cantata (early 1950s, SP 1962).
SSAATTBarBarBB a cappella. 25´. Text: "Memories
of President Lincoln," Whitman. To Dr. Wilfred C.
Bain and the Indiana University Singers.
1. When Lilacs Last in the Dooryard Bloom'd, 2.
Everreturning Spring, 3. In a swamp in secluded
recesses, 4. Oh captain, my captain, 5. This dust was
once the man, 6. Come lovely and soothing death, 7.
Praised be the fathomless universe.

49 *Erie Canal*, arr. by NL (1956, TP). SATB a cappella.
3´. Text and tune, folk.

50 *Evening Hymn* (1952, SP). SATB, Organ opt. 7´.

51 *Eventide* (1980, GS). SATB a cappella. 4´.

Exhortation, see *Three Choruses for Peace*.

52 ** s,p *Farewell, Vain World*, arr. by NL (1953, HWG).
SSAATTBB a cappella. 2.5´. Text and tune, folk.

53 *For a Child's Room* (1949, WCC). SATB a cappella,
S solo. 2´. To Jim.

54 *Four Choral Responses to the Words of Christ* (1939,
OD). SATB divisi a cappella. 6´. To Mlle Nadia
Boulanger.
1. Tell the Vision to No Man, 2. Why Callest Thou
Me Good? 3. Suffer Little Children, 4. Arise, and be
not afraid

55 **   s   *Four Songs* (1938, NAK). SSAATBar a cappella. 6´.
                 To Arthur and Marguerite Quimby.
                 1. Forever be my Song of Songs, 2. Be not
                 Disconsolate, 3. Omen, 4. Tinmouth Town

56 **   s,p *Four Songs of Sappho* (1979). Women's
                 Voices/piano, fl, tamb, Choreo. 6´. NLA OV7. MSC.
                 1. Epithalamium, 2. Linus-song, 3. The Cretan
                 Women, 4. Hesperos

57   *Fragments from Sappho* (1933) SSAA a cappella. 5´.
                 NLA 3. MS (incomplete), CAH. For Jacob A.
                 Evanson--and his "Hetaerae."
                 1. I Loved Thee Once, Atthis, Long Ago, 2. Raise
                 High the Roof Beam, 3. The Moon has Set, 4.
                 Delicate Adonis is Dying

58   *Fragments from Sappho* (1939) SATB/organ, brass:
                 4-3-3-1; timp, vcl, cb. 4´. NLA 3. MS, PV.
                 1. Hesperus, 2. Midnight, 3. The Cretan Woman, 4.
                 Linus-Song, 5. Verse before an Ode, 6. Quotation
                 from Aristotle

59   *Francis Thompson's "The Making of Viola"* (1934,
                 Keene Valley). Women's 3-part. 4´. NLA 3. MS.

60   *Frankie and Johnnie* (1935). SSAATTB a cappella.
                 5´. NLA 38. MSC. Text and tune, folk.

61   *Friendless Blues*, arr. by NL (1951, HB). SATTBarB.
                 3´. Text and tune, W. C. Handy.

62 ** s,p *Funeral Service* (1988). Vocal Quartet (SATB), 5 fl, 2 trpt, hn, trb, tuba, celebrant. 30´. NLA 34. MSC. Texts: Psalms, John 14, E. Dickinson, e. e. cummings, P. B. Shelley.
I. Bell tolling, Introduction, Celebrant Talk 1, Psalm 23 (voices/insts);
II. Celebrant Talk 2, Psalm 13 (voices/insts), Tenor recitative, Psalm 124 (voices/insts);
III. Celebrant Talk 3, "Because I Could Not Stop for Death" (S, A/insts), "if i have made, my lady . . ." (T/insts), Introduction and Hymn (voices/insts)
IV. Celebrant Talk 4, After-Song "Music, When Soft Voices Die" (S, A, B/insts)

63 ** s,p *The Gettysburg Address, 1863* (1977, SP). SATB, fl, ob, perc. 5´. To the Littleton High School Choir of Littleton, CO, Donald L. Arnold, Director.

64 *Gifts of the First Christmas* (1935, ACA). SA divisi/piano. 8´. Text: E. Merrill Root.

65 ** s,p *Give Me the Splendid, Silent Sun* (1937, ACA). SATB divisi. 10´. To Jacob H. Evanson and the Summer Chorus of Columbia University.

66 *Give the King Thy Justice* (1957, CSI). SATB/organ or piano. 2´.

67 *Glorify the Lord with Me* (1981). SATB, tamb, b drum. 3´. NLA 3. MS. Text: Psalm 34, adapted. To Robert E. Kreutz and the Choir, St. Bernadette Catholic Church, Lakewood CO.

68 "God of All Wisdom: A University Anthem," excerpt from *Land of Promise* (1959-1960, ACA). SATB. 3´.

Opening Convocation, University of Denver, 15 Jan. 1964.

69 ** s,p *The Gospel According to Matthew: Chapter One, Genealogy and Birth* (1986). Men's Voices/piano. 7´. NLA 3. MT. Text: Matthew 1: 2-24. To the ASU Statesmen, Z. Randall Strooke, conductor.

70   *Grace* (1950s). SATB a cappella. 1´. NLA 3. MSC. To the Trinity University Choir.

71   *Hail to Thee, Glad Day!* (1956, SM). SATB/Organ. 5´. Text: from 16th-century hymn "Salve Festa Dies." To Donald Willing and the Trinity University Choir, San Antonio, TX.

72   *He Who Walks Blamelessly* (1981). SA or TB or both, stgs, fender bass or piano or organ. 2 muted trpt opt. 1.5´. NLA 3. MS. Text: Psalm 15, adapted. To Robert E. Kreutz and the Choir, St. Bernadette Catholic Church, Lakewood, CO.

73 ** s,p *The Heavens Are Telling* (1959, rev. 1974, ACA). SATB/Organ. 10´. NLA 3. MS. Text: Psalm 19. Comm. by, ded. to the First Presbyterian Church, Nashville, TN, Henry Fusner, Organist and Choirmaster.

74   *Here 'Mongst Ass and Oxen Mild*, arr. by NL (1956, AMP). SATB/piano. 3´. Tune, French carol.

75 ** s,p *The Holy Birth* (1958, CSI). SATB, S T soli, piano. 10´.
         Intro., 1a. The Angel Gabriel was sent from God, 1b. I know a rose-tree, 2. The angel came to her, 2a. He

will be great, 3. Blessed is she, 3a. My Soul doth
Magnify the Lord, 4. A decree went out from Caesar
Augustus, 4a. Come, thou long-expected Jesus, 5.
There were shepherds in the field, 5a. What sign be
this? 5b. "Fear not," said he, 6. Glory to God in the
highest, 7. How Far Is It to Bethlehem? 7a. Pitying
love for fallen man, 7b. Fervent praise will I to thee,
8a. It had been revealed to Simeon, 8b. A great and
mighty wonder.

76 ** s,p *Hosanna* (1939, GS). SATB a cappella. 5´. NLA 4.
Dedicated to Dr. John Finley Williamson and the
Westminster Choir.

77 *How Far Is It To Bethlehem?* (1946, HMP). SATB a
cappella. 5´. The Millikin Conservatory, Decatur, IL,
14 Feb. 1943. To My Children.

78 *How Long, O Lord? Alleluia! Amen.* (1960s). TTBB.
7´. NLA 4. MT. Text: Psalm 13. Comm. by Wayne
State University. Ded. to the Men's Glee Club.

79 *How Long Wilt Thou Forget Me, O Lord* (1950s).
Dramatic Soprano, SATB/organ. 5´. NLA 4. MT.
Text: Psalm 13.

80 *Hymn of Paradise* (1953, SP). SATB. 5´. NLA 4.
MSC. Text: from Canto 27, *The Divine Comedy* of
Dante Alighieri.

81 ** s,p *I Hear America Singing* (1953, SP). SATB/piano. 8´.
Text: Walt Whitman. To the choir of Hood College
and the Glee Club of Franklin and Marshall College.

82   *I Heard the Voice of Jesus* (1954, SP). SATB/organ
                opt. 5′. Text: Horatius Bonar.

83   *I See tho' My Eyes are Closed*, arr. by NL (1951,
                HB). SATB. 4′. Text and tune, Lazarus A. Aaronson.
                Dedicated to W. C. Handy.

84   *I Will Give Thanks with all my Heart* (1966, AG).
                SATB a cappella. 4′. Text: Psalm 9. Dedicated to
                Olaf C. Christiansen.

85 **   s,p *If You Pour Out Your Soul* (1976, LJ). SATB. 7′.
                Text: Isaiah 58: 10, 11, 14. To Rolf E. Hoven and the
                Berea College Choir.

86 **   s,p *I'm Goin' Home*, arr. by NL (1952, SP). SATB a
                cappella. 4′. Text and tune, folk. To Heidi.

87 **   s,p *Inscriptions from the Catacombs* (1930s, rev. AG
                1965). SATB divisi, a cappella. 14′. Concordia
                Choir, Moorhead, MN, 1957 season.
                1. Vivas in Deo, 2. Cum Sanctis, 3. Vivas inter
                Sanctos, 4. Accersitus ab Angelis, 5. Dulcis Anima, 6.
                Sophorina, Sophorina Dulcis, Vivas in Deo.

                In the Beginning was the Word, see *A Christmas
                Anthem.*

88 **   s,p *In Thee Do I Take Refuge* (1970, ACA). SATB, fl,
                ob, cl, cel, tri, gong, cymb, snare, bass, chimes. 9.5′.
                Lamont School of Music, University of Denver, 2
                March 1971. Text: Psalm 7. To the University Choir,
                DU, Dr. Roger Dexter Fee, director.

89   *Jesus! Name of Wondrous Love!* (1959, ACA).
        SATB/organ opt. 3′. NLA 4. MS. Text: adapted,
        hymn of W. W. How, 1954. To Edward Anderson
        and the Colorado State University Choir.

90   *Jesus, O Precious Name* (1955, SMC). SATB/organ
        or piano. 4′. Text: adapted, Anna Hoppe.

91   *Jesus the King* (1958, ZO 1959) S and T soli, SATB/
        piano or organ. 30′. Text: Scriptures and Hymns. To
        the Reverend Gerald E. Graham.

92   *Joseph, Dearest Joseph* (1956, AMP). SATB/piano.
        3′. Text: German Carol. See also *Five Christmas
        Songs.*

93   *Joyful, Joyful, We Adore Thee* (1956, MY). SATB/
        organ. 3.5′. Text: Henry Van Dyke.

94   *The King Shall Come* (1956, MY). SATB/piano or
        organ. 4′. Text: from Greek.

95   *The Lamb that was Sacrificed*, arr. by NL (1950, TP).
        SATB/organ. 4′. Tune after J. S. Bach. For the 1950
        Talbott Festival of the Westminster Choir College,
        Princeton, NJ.

96 **   s,p *Land of Promise: A Dramatic Portrait of Rocky
        Mountain Methodism Presented by the University of
        Denver in Cooperation with the General Conference
        and the Rocky Mountain Conference Centennial
        Committee: An Outline of the History of Methodism
        (1540-1960) and of Rocky Mountain Methodism
        (1959-1960).* SATB, Orch, Narr., and Bar solo. 2 hrs.
        NLA 5. PVC only. The Rocky Mountain Quadrien-

nial Methodist Conference, Auditorium Theater, Denver, 30 April 1960. Libretto by Russell Porter. Concert performance version, 12 Jan. 1964. W/excerpts "Ballad of Father Dyer" and "God of all Wisdom."

"Laud," see *Three Choruses for Peace.*

"Laudate Dominum," see *Psalmus CL.*

97   *Le Secret Humain* (n. d.). SATB. 6´. NLA 5. NEG.

98   *Let Nothing Disturb Thee* (1955, SMC, KP 1992). SATB/organ, S Solo. 4´. Text: St. Teresa, Trans. H. W. Longfellow.

99   *Let the Heavens Rejoice* (1937). Double SATB. 3.5´. NLA 5. MS--AH. Text: Psalm 96.

"Let the Peoples Praise Thee," see *Children of God.*

100 *,** p   *Life Triumphant* (1975, ACA). SATB, 2 fl, 2 trpt, 2 hn, 2 trb. 22´. Ann Arbor Festival Chorus, 26 June 1976. Texts: Moravian and Whitman. Dedicated to Thor Johnson.
I. Prelude, Friedberg, Requiem, II. My comrade! Ground, Gaudeamus pariter, III. What is the grass? Interlude, Fanfare, Sing hallelujah.

101 *,** s,p   *Light Out of Darkness* (1957, ACA). SATB, Bar solo, Orch: 3-2-E hn-2-B cl-2-C bsn; 4-3-2-1; timp, perc, stgs. 30´. Buffalo Philharmonic Orchestra, Buffalo Schola Cantorum, dir. by Josef Krips, 18 Feb., 1958.

1a. God the Father has Delivered us from the Dominion of Darkness, 1b. For in Him all the Fullness of God was Pleased to Dwell, 2a. We are Afflicted in Every Way, 2b. I Love the Lord, 3a. The Word of the Cross is Folly to Those Who are Perishing, 3b. Make a Joyful Noise unto the Lord, 4a. Why Dost Thou Stand Afar Off, O Lord? 4b. There is no God, 5a. We Look Not to the Things that are Seen, 5b. The Lord is My Rock, 5c. Alleluia.

102   *London Town* (n. d.). Male Chorus or Quartet. 4´. NLA 5. MT. Text: by John Masefield.

103   *The Lord is My Shepherd* (1956, MR). 2-part mixed choir/organ. 4´. Text: Psalm 23.

104   *Lord, Thou hast been our Dwelling Place* (1977, LJ). SATB, organ opt. 4´. Text: Psalm 90.

105   *The Lord's Prayer*, arr. by NL (1954, SP). SATBarB a cappella. 4´. Tune, G. F. Handel's *Largo*.

106   *Love Divine* Anthem (1980s). SATB/organ. 5´. NLA 5. MT.

107 **   s,p *Love Divine* Cantata (1957, ACA). SATB, S and A Solos, Children, organ, 2 trpt, stgs. 25´. Text: Deuteronomy, Psalms I & II. Sources "Hyfrydol" and Charles Wesley's "Love Divine." Comm. Gloria Dei Lutheran Church (St. Paul, MN), Plymouth Congregational Church (Des Moines, IA), and Westminster Presbyterian Church (Buffalo, NY).

108 **   s,p   *Magnificat* (1958, ACA). S solo, SATB divisi, orch: 3/picc-3-3-1; 2-2-1-1; timp, stgs. 20´. Boston Conservatory Christmas Concert, 18 Dec. n. d. 1. My Heart Extols the Lord, 2. For the Almighty has Done Wonders for Me, 3. He has done Mighty Deeds, 4. Glory Be to the Father.

109 **   s,p   *Make a Joyful Noise Unto the Lord* from *Light Out of Darkness* (1957, rev. 1988). SATB, organ, 2 trpt, 2 trb, cb. 5´. NLA 38. MT, MTP. To St. Andrew Presbyterian Church, Boulder, Kay Norton, Music Director.

110   *Mary Wore Three Links of Chain*, arr. by NL (1954, HWG), SATB a cappella. 3´. Text and tune, folk.

111 **   s   *Mass for Children and Orchestra* (1976-77, ACA). Child. choir, orch: 3/picc-2-2-B cl-2; 2-2-1-B trb-0; perc, harp, stgs. 30´. Children's Chorale of Denver, Duain Wolfe, dir., May 1977. Dedicated to the Children's Chorale, Denver, CO, Duain Wolfe, conductor.

112 **   s   *Mass for the Christmas Eve Midnight Service* (1969). SATB, S A T B Soli, organ, harps. 15´. NLA 5 & 6. MT. St. Thomas's Episcopal Church, Denver, 1969. To Robert C. Johnson, Organist and Choir Director, St. Thomas's Episcopal Church, Denver.

        Masters, In this Hall, see *A Christmas Cantata.*

113 **   s,p   *Monotone* (1937, NAK) SATB a cappella. 3´. Text: Carl Sandburg.

114　　　　　*Moralities* (early 1930s). TTBB a cappella. 4´. NLA
　　　　　　6. MS. Text: R. E. Brown.

　　　　　　"The Mouth of the Lord has Spoken," see *Children of
　　　　　　God.*

115　　　　　*Music Lesson and Soft-Shoe Alleluia* (n. d.). SATB a
　　　　　　cappella. 4´. NLA 6. MS. To the University of
　　　　　　Denver Chorale. Robert Penn, conductor.

116　　　　　*My Tommy's Gone Away,* arr. by NL (n. d.).
　　　　　　TTBarB. 4´. NLA 6. MSC. Text and tune, folk. To
G.　　　　　Wallace Woodworth and the Harvard Glee Club.

117　　　　　*No Title* (early 1930s). SSAA. 2´. NLA NB1. MS.

118　　　　　*O Come, Let Us Sing to the Lord* (n. d.). SATB, fl,
　　　　　　ob, SQ. 4´. NLA 6. MT. Text: Psalm 95. To Roger
　　　　　　Dexter Fee and the University of Denver A Cappella
　　　　　　Choir.

119　　　　　*O for a Shout of Sacred Joy* (1949, Princeton). SATB.
　　　　　　4´. NLA 6. MSC. Text: Psalm 47 from the *Psalms
　　　　　　and Hymns of the Reformed Dutch Church in
　　　　　　America* (New York, 1818).

120　　　　　*O Lord, How Manifold are Thy Works* (1951). SATB
　　　　　　a cappella. 3´. NLA 6. MSC. Text: Psalm 104: 24.
　　　　　　To M/M James Claude Thomson.

121　　　　　*O Lord, the Measure of our Prayers* (1952, SP).
　　　　　　SATB divisi/organ opt. 2´. Text: Julia Ward Howe.
　　　　　　To Robert and Dorothy Lee.

122   *O Lord, What is Man?* (c. 1970). SATB, S Bar Soli,
            orch: 1-1-1-1; 2-1-0-0; tamb, chimes, stgs. 30´. NLA
            34. MT, PV. Text: selected from Psalm 8, Prayer
            Book, Judah Halim, Lamentations, Isaiah 58, *High
            Holidays Prayer Book*, Deuteronomy 6.

123   *O Our Father, Who Art in Heaven* (1938, GX). SATB
            a cappella. 4´. Text: Dante. To Jacob A. Evanson and
            Teachers College Summer Chorus of Columbia
            University.

124 ** s,p *O Thou Who Clothest the Lily* (1974, AG). SATB a
            cappella. 1´. Text: Richard Euringer. To Dr. Rolf E.
            Hovey and the Berea College Choir.

125 ** s,p *Old Hundredth Cantata* (1958, ACA). SATB,
            children, orch: 2/1-1-EH-2-B cl-1; 2-2-3-1; timp, perc,
            hp, stgs. 25´. Based on "Old Hundredth" (Geneva
            Psalter), Psalms. Comm. by 6 Des Moines, IA, area
            churches.

126   *Open My Eyes, That I May See* (1954, SP). SATB a
            cappella. 4´. Text: Charles H. Scott.

127 *,** s,p *Out of the Cradle Endlessly Rocking* (1938, GS).
            SATB a cappella. 12´. 1938 World's Fair. Text:
            Whitman.

128   *Outlanders, Whence Come Ye Last?* (n. d.). Two
            Quartets of Equal Women's voices, One quartet of
            equal Men's voices. 5´. NLA 6. MS. Text: by William
            Morris. To Deborah.

129   *Pacific Lament* (1948, ACA). SATB. 4.5´. Text:
            Charles Olson. In memory of William Hickey, a

member of the crew of the U.S.S. "Growler," lost at
sea in February, 1944.

130   *The Passion after the Seven Last Words* (1941, ACA).
Minister, Chapel Choir/organ. 30´. To Arthur Leslie
Jacobs.

131   *Pastoral* (mid-1960s). TTBB a cappella. 5´. NLA 6.
MSC. Text: Psalm 23.

132   *Pater, Dimitte Illis* (1950, ACA) excerpted, arr. w/
orch. from *The Passion after the Seven Last Words*.
SATB, Speaker, fl, ob, B-flat cl, bsn, timp, stgs. 5´.

133   *Patriotic Overture* (1945, ACA). SATB, Orch: 2/2-2-
4-1; 4-4-4-2; timp, bells, perc, stgs. 12´. Text:
Whitman. Tunes "America" and "The Star-Spangled
Banner." Comm. by Brevard Music Camp.

134   *Praeludium*, arr. by NL (1951). SATBarB divisi. 4´.
NLA 6. MT. Tune, J. S. Bach. To Hugh Porter.

135 *,** s,p *Prairie* (1952, RM). SATB, Orch: 2/picc-2 E hn-2 B
cl-2; 4-3-2-1; timp, perc, stgs. 30´. Ann Arbor May
Festival, Univ. of MI, 30 April-3 May 1953. Text:
Carl Sandburg.
1. I was Born on the Prairie, 2. Here the Water Went
Down, 3. After the Sunburn of the Day, 4. The
Overland Passenger Train, 5. I am Dust of Men, 6.
Towns on the Soo Line, 7. I am the Prairie, Mother of
Men, 8. Look at Six Eggs, 9. Any New Songs?, 10. O
Prairie Mother.

136 **   p   *Praise to the Lord, the Almighty, the King of
Creation* (1958, CFP). SATB, opt. accomp. 6´.

Dedicated to Sigma Alpha Iota's American Music
Awards Series.

137   *Prelude-Introit-Hymn (Vigiles et Sancti)* (1985, ACA)
            SATB/organ. 5′. Text: Cologne Gesangbuch 1623.

138 **   p *Prelude to Western Star*, selections arr. by Ludwig
            Lenel (1961, BH). TTBB/piano. 7′. Text: Stephen
            Vincent Benet.
            1. Americans, 2. Lend Me Your Music.
            See *Prelude to Western Star* (Solo Song.)

            Psalm, see *Three Choruses for Peace.*

139   *Psalm VIII* (n. d.). SATB. 7′. NLA 7. MSC.
            Text: King James Bible. To Norman D. Rian.

140   *Psalm 30* (1979, rev. 1980). SATB/Organ.
            5′. NLA 7. MT.

141 **   s,p *Psalm 114 (An Exhortation to Fear God in His
            Power)* (1940, GS). SATB, Orch: 3-1-2-3; 4-2-2-1;
            timp, perc, hp, stgs. 6′.

142 **   s,p *Psalms 117, 63, 134* (1938, NAK). SATB a cappella.
            8′. To Olaf and Ellen Christiansen.

143   *Psalm 123* (1939, AM). SATB a cappella. 2′. To Paul
            MacCollin and the Morningside College Choir.

144   *Psalmus CL (Laudate Dominum)* (1930s). 2 SATB
            choirs. 5′. NLA 7. MS. To Ellis E. Snyder and the
            Chapel Choir.

145   *Quodlibet* (1970s). SATB, Guitar or Piano, Triangle. 3´. NLA 7. MS.

146 **   s,p   *Rejoice in the Lord* (1968, WP). SATB, 2 hn, 2 trb, timp. 8´. Text: Psalm 33. To the Classic Chorale, Gerald L. Lepinski, Director.

147 **   p   *Remember Now Thy Creator* (1965, AG). SATB a cappella. 2´. Text: Ecclesiastes 12:1.

     "Return to the Lord," see *Children of God.*

148   *Righteous Joseph* (1953). MezTTBarB/piano. 5´. NLA 38. MSC. Text: Cornish.

149   *Round--He that Buys Land Buys Stones* (1949). SATB. 3´. NLA 34. MT.

150 **   p   *Sabbath Eve Service* (c. 1960). SATB/Organ; rev. (c. 1960) for SATB, Organ, Orch: 2/1-1-2-1; 2-2-2-0; timp, perc, stgs. 30´. NLA OV6. MT. Comm. Rabbi Lederman, Denver.
     1. L'cho dodi, 2. Bar'chu, 3. Sh'ma yisroël, 4. Mi shomocho, 5. V'shomru, 6. Yism'chu, 7. May the Words, 8. Va-anachnu, 9. On that day.

151   *Sea Fever* (n. d.). Male Chorus or Quartet. 3´. NLA 8. MT. Text: John Masefield.

152 **   p   *Second Group of Psalms* (1940, ACA). SSAATTB. 12´. Texts: Psalms 133, 1, and 8. Written for Pittsburgh Bach Choir.

     "See What Love" see *Children of God.*

"Seek the Lord and Live," see *Children of God.*

"Sermon on the Mount," see *Children of God.*

"Service Music," see *Children of God.*

153   *The Seven Churches* (1959). SATB. Music lost. Text:
             the Book of Revelations.

154 **   s,p *Shine, Perishing Republic* (1967, ACA). SATB,
             organ, 3 trpts, trb, 3 perc, 2 vla. 10.5´. Middlebury
             College, VT, October 1968.

155   *Shout for Joy*, arr. by NL (1951, SP). TTBB.
             4´. Text and tune, folk. Text and tune, folk. To the
             University of Denver Men's Glee Club, Gordon de
             Broder, director.

156 **   s   *Shout the Glad Tidings, A Christmas Anthem for
             Choir and Harp* (1982). SATB/hp. 3´. NLA 8. MT.
             Text: William Augustus Macklenberg, 1826. To the
             choir of Community Church, Honolulu.

157 **   s,p *Silent Night*, arr. by NL (1951). MezTTBarB. 3´.
             NLA 38. MSC. Tune F. Gruber.

158   *Sing Unto the Lord a New Song* (1952, ML).
             SATBarB, a cappella. 2.5´.

159 **   s,p *Six Songs of Adelaide Crapsey* (1939). Women's
             Voices. 10´. NLA 8. MT. To Helena Johanna
             Strassburger.
             1. I Make My Shroud, 2.Pierrot, For Aubrey
             Beardsley's Picture "Pierrot is dying," 3. Anguish,

4. The Grand Canyon, 5. Shadow, 6. To Walter Savage Landor.

160   *The Snow Lay on the Ground* (1956, AMP). SATB/piano. 4´.

161   *Soe Wee May Sing* (1950, SP). SSATB, opt. accomp. 2.5´. Text: *Bay Psalm Book.*

162   *Steal Away*, arr. by NL (1981, HWG). SATB a cappella. 3´. Text and tune folk. To George Lynn.

163   *The Story of St. Nicholas* (1952). 4 male voices, S solo, orch. 12´. Music lost.

164   *Sweet and Low* (1937, GX). SSAATTBB a cappella. 3´. Text: Alfred, Lord Tennyson. To Jacob A. Evanson.

165   *A Table Grace: In Mem'ry of . . .* (n. d.). SATB. 2´. NLA 8. MS.

166   *Tenting on the Old Camp Ground*, arr. by NL (1950, HWG). SATB/piano. 3´. Text and tune, Walter Kittredge. To Howard Boatright.

167   *This Moment* (1971, WP). SATB a cappella. 3´. Text: Whitman. To Warren Taylor.

168   *Thou Hallowed Chosen Morn* (1956, MR). SATB a cappella. 3´. Text: St. John of Damascus.

169 **   s   *Thought of Him I Love* (1982). Child., Narrator-Bar, Chamber Orch: fl, ob, b flat cl, hn, trpt, piano, perc, stgs. 20´. NLA 34. MT. Texts: Whitman "Memories

of President Lincoln" and Lincoln "Gettysburg Address." To the Colorado Children's Chorale and Duain Wolfe.
1. When Lilacs last in the Dooryard Bloom'd, 2. O Captain, My Captain I, 3. How shall I Warble, 4. O Captain, My Captain II, 5. Hush'd be the Camps Today, 6. Over the Breast of Spring, 7. It is for Us, the Living.

170   *Three Capri Songs for Girls' Voices* (n. d.). SA divisi, a cappella. 4´. NLA 8. MS. To My Mother.
1. Song of an Old Fisherman, 2. Tarantella, 3. Ninarella.

171   *Three Choruses for Peace* (1938, CFI). SATB a cappella. 5´. To Dr. Ernest Hatch Wilkins.
1. Exhortation, 2. Psalm, 3. Laud.

172   *Three Negro Songs*, arr. by NL (1936). SATB a cappella. 6´. NLA 8. MS. Texts and tunes, folk.
1. When de Good ol' Gabriel, 2. De Camptown Ladies, 3. When I was a Little Baby.

173   *Three Odes from the Elektra* (1930s). Women's Voices. 6´. NLA 8. MS. Danced and sung (simultaneously) in performance in Finney Chapel, Oberlin College, under the direction of Margery Schneider in the 1930s. Text after Sophocles.

174   *To Thee We Turn*, arr. by NL (1951, TP). TTBB a cappella. 4´. Tune after J. S. Bach and George Lynn.

175   *Two Table Graces* (c. 1972). SATB. 3´. NLA 8. MSC. Text: Richard Euringer, trans. Mignon McMenarry

1. To the Trinity University Choir, 2. To Dr. Rolf E. Hovey and the Berea College Choir

176 ** s,p *We are of God* (1987). MezATB Soli. 6´. NLA 8. MT. Text: First epistle of John. To Roy and Barbara Carey.

177 *When de Good Ol' Gabriel*, arr. by NL (n. d.). 3´. TTBar Bar BB a cappella. MT. Text and tune, folk. To My Mother.

178 *While Shepherds Watched,* arr. by NL (1955, SM). SATB/organ or piano. 3´. Text N. Tate, tune Old English.

KEYBOARD WORKS

179   *Adagio* (c. 1925, Paris). Piano. 2´. NLA NB1. MS.

180 **   s,p *Alternations* (1975, ACA) Piano. 16.5´. University of
             Colorado, 8 March 1976. Composed for Paul and
             Phyliss Parmelee.
             1. Schumannesque I, 2. Black Keys I, 3.
             Schumannesque II, 4. Black Keys II, 5. Flag Day, 6.
             Interlude, 7. Flag Day II, 8. Interlude II, 9.
             Restatement.

181   *American Heritage.* (1930s). Piano, to accompany
             dance. Music Lost. For Margery Dorian.

182   *Andante* (c. 1913). Piano. 1´. NLA 31. MS by Albert
             Lockwood.

183 **   s,p *Canonic Toccata* (1979, ACA). 2 Organs. 3.5´.
             Annual Meeting, Denver, AGO, 19 May 1980. To
             Phyllis S. Tremmel and Austin C. Lovelace.

184   *Capriccio* (Jan. 1922). Piano. 3´. NLA NB1. MS.

185   *Capriccio* (Apr. 1922). Piano. 3´. NLA NB1. MS.

186   *A Childhood Recollection: "Lunch at the Putnam
             Camp"* (1991). 3´. NLA 38. MS. For Festschrift
             honoring William K. Kearns by the Sonneck Society,
             1992.

187 *,** s,p *Concerto for Organ and Brasses* (1951, AMP). Organ,
             2 trpt, 2 trb. 15´. E. Power Biggs, organ, Arthur
             Fiedler, cond. on Contemporary American Festival of

the Air (CBS Radio) 27 April 1952. Comm. by CBS.
Ded. to E. Power Biggs.
1. Andante con moto deciso, 2. Larghetto, 3. Allegro.

188 **   s,p   *Concerto for Organ and Chamber Orchestra* (1973).
Organ, 1 picc, 2 fl, 2 ob, 2 trpt, 2 hn, timp, chimes,
stgs. 15´. NLA OV 9. MT, MSP. Comm. by
Cleveland Museum of Art. Cleveland Museum of
Art, 24 April 1974.
1. Sinfonia, 2. Ciacona, 3. Tema con variazioni, 4.
Rondo capriccioso.

189   *Dichromatic Variations* (1935, ACA). Piano. 14´.

190 **   s,p   *Duo Sopra Pedale* (1976, ACA) Organ. 3´.

191 **   s,p   *Eight Details and a Summary* (1982, ACA). Piano.
20´. Brian Marks and The Ariel Ensemble, 17 Nov.
1982. To Theodore L. Lichtmann.

192   *Eight Dances* (1921). Piano. 5´. NLA NB1. MS.
1. Andante, 2. Tranquillo, 3. Animato, 4. Tempo di
Mazurka, 5. Allegretto, 6. Sostenuto, 7. Vivace, 8. A
L'Hongroise. Orch. version by Samuel Pierson
Lockwood, NL's father. 2/picc-2-2-2; 2-2-2-1; timp,
perc, stgs. NLA NB1. MS.

193 **   s,p   *Eight Preludes for Organ* (1979-80, AG). 12´.
See also *Twenty-Five Preludes for Organ.*

194 **   s,p   *Encores* (1968). Piano, also called *Five Encores.*
5´. NLA 20. MT. University of Denver, 26 June 1968.
1. Rowena, for Anna, 2. The Phoebe, for Carolyn,

3. Locrian Fragment, for David, 4. Sonata Breve, for
Bernard, 5. Round, for Bernard and Carolyn--2
pianos: "Ite missa est."

195   *Etude* (1924). Piano. 2´. NLA NB1. MS.

196 **   s   *Etude* (1991). Piano. 2´. NLA 38. MSC.

197 **   s,p *Fantasia* (1971, ACA). Piano. 10´. To David A.
             Karp.
             1. Improvisazione, 2. Introduzione con soggietto, 3.
             Fughetta, 4. Invocation, 5. Coda.

198 **   s,p *Fantasy on Jesus My Joy*, after "Jesu, Meine Freude"
             (1972, ACA). Organ. 10´. Western Michigan
             University, Alexander Boggs Ryan, 5 March 1972.
             Dedicated by Alexander Boggs Ryan.
             1. Introduction and Chorale, 2. Scherzo: allegretto, 3.
             Cavatina, 4. Scherzo: allegro assai, 5. Ground,
             Canon, Chorale.

199 **   s,p *Farfalle* (1991). Piano. 3´. NLA 38. MSC.

200 **   s,p *Festive Service for the Organ* (1976, ACA). 10´.
             (Concert version). Denver AGO, 21 Nov. 1976.
             Comm. by Denver AGO.
             1. Prelude: The Heavens are Telling, 2. Introit: St.
             Gertrude, 3. Litany, 4. Fanfare, 5. Offertory, 6.
             Benediction, 7. Postlude, 8. Exit: St. Gertrude.

             Five Encores, see *Encores.*

201 **   s,p *Fugue Sonata* (1969). Piano. 8´. NLA 20. MT.
             Composed for *Summertree*, a play by Ron Cowen.
             Bonfils Theater, Nov. 1969. To Kevin Kennedy.

202 **   s,p   *Hamburg* (1960s). Two pianos. 4´. NLA 21. MT. Based on Hymn tune, "Hamburg." To Markowski and Cedrone, Duo-Pianists.

203   *Improvisation* (early 1920s). Piano. 2´. NLA NB1. MS.

204 *   *Lento* (Sept. 1924, London). 4´. NLA NB1. MS. "First movement to a sonata."

205   *The Little Dustman*, transcribed by NL from J. Brahms. (1922). 2´. NLA NB1. MS.

206 **   s   *Little Suite for Piano (Five Out of Appalachia)* (1990). Piano. 4´. NLA 38.

207 **   s   *Lyric Arabesque* (1956, MMU). Piano. 3´.

208   *Lyric Poem* (early 1920s). Piano. 2´. NLA NB1. MS.

209 **   s,p   *Lyric Poem* (1977, ACA). Two Pianos. 5´. Derived from NL's *Out of May's Shows Selected* (SP, see Choral Music) and *Lyric Poem* (1948) for vcl and piano.

210   *The Ninety and Nine: A Piano Arrangement Written for Dance* (1937). 8´. NLA 20. MS. To Margery Schneider.

211 *   *Normand's Improvisation* (1912). Piano. 1´. NLA NB1. MS-AH.

212   *O Lord of Heaven* (n. d.). Organ w/opt. choir. 5´. NLA 6. MT. Text: Christopher Wordsworth (*Episcopal Hymnal*, #305). To Cecilia Mulrenin.

213   *Pensieroso* (1925, Rome). Piano. 5′. NLA NB1. MS.

                Piano Concerto see Instrumental Ensemble music.

214   *Piano Piece* (c. 1950). 5′. NLA 20. MSC.

215 **   s   *Pieces of Eight* (1985, ACA). Piano. 19′. To Julia
                Carey.
                1. Piano Song, 2. Monstrous Hailstones, 3. Whiskers
                the Cat, 4. Harp Song, 5. Offbeat March, 6. Daddy's
                Song, 7. Mother's Song, 8. Name that Tune, 8b.
                Name that Tune.

216   *Postlude for Albertine* (1982, ACA). Organ. 3′.
                Includes "Old Hundredth" Hymn tune.

217   *Prelude* (Jan. 1923). Piano. 3′. NLA NB1. MS.

218   *Prelude* (May 1923). Piano. 2′. NLA NB1. MS.

219   *Prelude* (1924). Piano. 1′. NLA NB1. MS.

220   *Prelude* (1925, Paris). Piano. 1′. NLA NB1. MS.

221 **   p   *Processional Voluntary* (1965, KP 1992). Organ. 10′.
                US Air Force Academy, Colorado Springs, by Phyllis
                Selby Tremmel, 1 Aug. 1965.

222 **   s,p   *Quiet Design* (1953, ACA). Organ. 4.5′. Marilyn
                Mason, Columbia University, 11 Aug. 1953.

223 **   p   *Second Concerto for Organ and Brasses* (1977).
                Organ, 3 trp, 2 trb. 15′. NLA OV 9. MT, MTP. For
                Marilyn Mason.
                1. Partita, 2. Canzona, 3. Ricercare Scherzoso.

224   *Series and Variations* (1974). Piano. 3´. NLA 21.
        MT.

225   *Six Piano Pieces* (1943). 8´. NLA 21. MSC.

226 ** s   *Six Short Pieces for the Small Hand* (c. 1961). Piano.
        6´. NLA 21. MT. To Diane Watanabe.
        1. Adagio-Casually, 2. Allegro, 3. Lento, 4. Lento-
        tempo of "The Humoresque," 5. Allegro molto, 6.
        Adagio molto-maestoso, funebre

227   *Sonata* (1923). Piano. 8´. NLA NB1. MS. 1.
        Cantabile sostenuto, 2. Prelude-Andante, 3. Andante
        semplice.

228   *Sonata* (April 1927, Paris). Piano. 20´. NLA 21. MS.
        1. Allegro molto e con brio, 2. Andante lentamente, 3.
        Scherzo: Allegro Vivace.

229 ** s   *Sonata* (1935, ACA). Piano. 15´.
        1. Singing, then lively and energetic, 2. Gay, but with
        a folk-like melancholy, 3. Fast.

230 ** s,p *Sonata for the Organ* (1960, ACA). 13´. Dedicated to
        Phyllis Selby Tremmel.
        1. Allegro, 2. Adagio assai, 3. Allegro.

231 ** s,p *Sonata for Two Pianos* (1965, ACA). 15´. James
        Duncan and Kent Holliday, Southern CO State
        College, 2 Apr. 1966. Comm. by Southern Colorado
        State College. Ded. to James Duncan and Kent
        Holliday.
        1. Allegro, 2. Adagio, 3. Moderato leggiero, 4.
        Allegro scherzoso.

232   *Sonatina* (1935, ACA). Piano. 12´. Arthur Dann,
               Oberlin Conserv., Cleveland Museum of Art, 16
               February 1940.
               1. Andante semplicemente ma non senza espressione,
               2. Adagio con gran' tranquillita, 3. Allegro.

233 **   s,p *Stopping on a Walk to Rest* (1963, KP). Organ. 3´.
               University of Denver, Senior Recital of Judy
               Hunnicutt, 8 May 1963. Ded. to Judy Hunnicutt.

234 *   *Suite* (1925, Paris). Piano. 5´. NLA NB1. MS. By
               "Brother Ben for Sister Hen," from NL to his sister
               Albertine on her birthday.

235 *   *Three Voice Invention* (1923). Piano, counterpoint
               exercise for Otto Jacob Stahl. 1´. NLA NB1. MS.
               Comments in pencil by Stahl.

236 **   s,p *Toccata* (1975). Organ. 4´. NLA 21. MT. State
               University of NY, Courtland, Robert Roulos, 21 Feb.
               1971. Ded. to Robert Roulos.

237 **   s,p *Twenty-Five Organ Preludes* (December 1979 to
               January 1980, ACA). 2-5´ each. See also *Eight
               Preludes for Organ*, AG (1981), incl. 1, 4, 5, 6, 9, 15,
               18, 20. Various dedications.
               1. Stille Nacht, 2. National Anthem, 1st Version, 3.
               National Anthem, 2nd Version, 4. Très gai, 5. Come,
               Thou Almighty King, 6. Praise, My Soul (Lauda
               Anima), 7. Love Divine (Hyfrydol), 8. Veni
               Emmanuel, 9. Lauda Sion, 10. Come with Us (Jesu,
               Joy), 11. Victimae Paschali, 12. He Leadeth Me, 13.
               Mit Freuden Zart, 14. Sleepers, wake, 15. Dear Lord
               and Father, 16. Ostande nobis, 17. L'homme armé,
               18. L'homme armé, 19. By'm By, 20. Vigiles et sancti,

　　　　　　21. When Jesus Wept, 22. Guidatti, 23. Veni Sancti
　　　　　　Spiritus, 24. Jesus, Jesus, Rest Your Head, 25. Kyrie
　　　　　　Eleison.

238　　　　*Untitled* (1921). Piano. 3′. NLA NB1. MS.

239　　　　*Valse Prelude* (1923). Piano. 3′. NLA NB1. MS.

240 **　　s,p　*World Without End. Amen.* (1985). Organ. 2′. NLA
　　　　　　28. MT. Dedicated to Roy Carey.

CHAMBER WORKS
(see also YOUNG PEOPLE'S RECORDS)

241 **   s,p   *Adaptations* (1984, ACA). 8´. Trumpet/piano.
Southern Methodist University, 25 September 1984.
To Richard S. Parks. See *Alternations* for piano.

242 **   s,p   *Atános* (1986, rev. 1988). Two Flutes. 6´. NLA 22.
MSC.
1. Vivace, 2. Adagio moderato, 3. Allegro, 4. Allegro
moderato.

243 **   s   *Church at Ripton* (1949). 2 fl, ob, hn, 2 vlns, vla, bass.
3.5´. NLA 24. MT, MTP. 2 September 1949, Fourth
Annual Middlebury College Composers Conference.

December Cradle Song, see *A Little Waltz*.

December Quodlibet, see *A Little Waltz*.

244   *Boll Weevil Song* (1942). Fl, ob, cl, hn, bsn. 2´. NLA
22. MSP. To Dolly. Includes quotations from Carl
Sandburg, *The American Song Bag*. Text and tune,
folk.

245   *By'm By. Fragment of a Spiritual* (1942). Fl, ob, cl,
hn, bsn. 1´. NLA 22. MSP. To Dolly. Includes
quotations from Carl Sandburg, *The American Song
Bag*. Text and tune H. T. Burleigh.

246 *,**   s,p   *Clarinet Quintet* (1959, ACA). Cl/SQ. 25´. Cleveland
Art Museum, 1 June 1960. Comm. by the Cleveland
Chamber Music Society in memory of Dr. Norman L.
Hoerr.

1. Introduzione et fuga, 2. Rondo scherzoso, 3. Canzona, 4. Andante con moto (variazioni).

Concerto for Organ and Brasses, see Keyboard Works.

247   *Diversion* (1941). WW quint. 3ʹ. MS, MSP. BPL.

248 **   s,p   *Diversion* (1950). Rev. for cl, 2 vln, vcl. 12ʹ. NLA 23. MT, MTP. Carnegie Hall, University of Maine tour, 13 May 1951.
1. Adagio, 2. Slow blues, 3. Slow rubato.

249   *Duo: A Little Wedding Present to R & R* (1984, ACA). Trpt, fl. 4ʹ. Southern Methodist University, 25 September 1984. To Richard and Rosemary Parks.

250 **   s,p   *Eidólons* (1989, ACA). C Trpt/picc trpt, 3 B-flat trpts, 2 fluegelhorns. 8ʹ.

251 **   s   *Eight Trumpet Duets* (1969, TR), also called *Little Suite for Two Trumpets.* 2 B-flat trpts. 10ʹ. NLA 22. MT. Adams State College, Alamosa, CO, National Trumpet Symposium, 10 Jan. 1970. To Gil and Susan Garcia.
1. Unison, 2. Dialogue, 3. Two Mosquitos, 4. Mirror, 5. Con spirito, 6. Solenne, 7. Chorale ("Ein' feste Burg"), 8. March.

252 **   s   *Five Pieces for Oboe* (1968, ACA). Unaccomp. ob. 5ʹ. To David Ledet.
1. Lento commodo, 2. Scherzoso, 3. Lirico, 4. Waltzer, 5. Adagio.

253 *,** s,p *Flute and Guitar* (1980, ACA). 12´. Carnegie Hall,
              NY. 11 Oct. 1980. To Susanella Noble and Charles
              Wolzein.
              1. Tripartito, 2. A Little Waltz, 3. December
              Quodlibet, 4. December Cradle Song--also called
              Christmas Cradle Song or Christmas Lullaby.

254   *Flute Piece for Otto* (1940s). Fl/piano. 3´. NLA 24.
              MS. Bard College, Otto Luening, fl, 10 December
              (1940s). For Otto Luening.

255 **   s   *Four Excursions for Four Basses* (1976, ACA). 4 cb.
              20´. Alaska String Bass Workshop, 19 June 1976. To
              my friend Lea T. Ball.
              1. An outing, 2. A Strolling in the Cemetery, 3. On a
              holiday, 4. Of an evening.

256 **   s   *Fun Piece* (1967, ACA). WW Quint. 5´. NLA 23.
              "Scherzo in polite circles."

              Funeral Service, see Choral Music.

              I Have Painted Elijah, see Solo Songs.

257 *,** s,p *Immortal Image* (1965). Instrumental arr. preceding
              When Lilacs Last . . . KRMA-TV. (Denver)
              documentary, 100th anniversary of the Assassination
              of Abraham Lincoln. Hn, 2 trpt, B trb, perc. 30´.
              NLA 31. MT, MTP. April 1965, KRMA-TV,
              Denver.

              Irish Songs, see Solo Songs.

              Kissinger in Egypt, see *Revery*.

258   *Le Chateau Overture* (1948, ACA). Fl, picc, ob, hn, stgs. 2´.

259 **   s,p *L'Homme Arme* (1955, ACA). Trpt/piano. 8´. The Institute of Contemporary Music, Hartt College, Hartford, CT, 20 Nov. 1955.
1. Andante con moto, 2. Adagio molto, 3. Allegro.

260   *Limericks and Coda* (1984). Trpt/piano. 3´. NLA 24. MT.

261   *Litany* (1938). Fl, ob, cl, hn, bsn, piano. 4´. NLA 23. MS. To George Waln and the Oberlin Woodwind Ensemble.

A Little Waltz, see *Flute and Guitar.*

Love's Secret, see Solo Songs.

262   *Lyric Poem* (Middlebury 1948, rev. Denver, 1977). Vcl/piano. 6´. NLA 21. MT, MTP. To George Finckel.

Memories of President Lincoln, see Solo Songs.

263 **   p *Mosaic* (1970, ACA). Accord./fl. 5´. University of Denver, 19 Nov. 1970. To Patrica Demillo and Patrick Bigler.

264   *Native Quarter, Tunis* (c. 1944). 2 fl, ob. 4´. NLA 23. MS. Dedicated to Bernard Rogers, Norman Corwin, and the Ditson Fund Committee. "Incidental Music for The Bedroom Scene from Hampton and Saliva."

O Lord, Our Lord, see Solo Songs.

265 **   s,p   *Once Upon a Silent Night* (1986, ACA). 5 fl. 7´.
                   1. Earthlings, 2. Angels, 3. Chorales and Recitatives.
266 **   s,p   *Pastures* (1943, ACA). Harp. 9´.

267 *,** s,p   *Piano Quintet* (1939, ACA). Piano/SQ. 40´. Yaddo
                   Festivals, Saratoga Springs, NY, 7 September 1940.
                   1. Adagio, 2. Adagio con gran' tranquillita, 3. Allegro
                   molto e vivace.

268 *   *A Prelude* (1925, Rome). Winds: fl/picc, ob, E hn, cl,
                   B cl, bsn, C bsn. 5´. NLA NB1. MS.

269 **   s,p   *Quartet in Three Movements* (1970, ACA). 4 vcl. 15´.
                   University of Denver, 15 March 1970.
                   1. Adagio, 2. Allegro, 3. Fugue.

270 **   s,p   *Revery* (1970s, HL). Cl/piano. 2´. NLA 25. MS. To
                   Ramon Kireilis. Orig. called *Kissinger in Egypt*. 2´.

                   Second Concerto for Organ and Brasses, see
                   Keyboard Works.

271 **   s,p   *A Sequence of Preambles* (1987). Fl. 3´. NLA 38.
                   MSC.

272 **   p   *Short Story for Horn and Piano* (1974, rev. 1987,
                   ACA). 6´. To David Kaslow.

                   (sitting in a tree--), see Solo Songs.

273 **   s,p   *Sonata Fantasia* (1964, OP). Accordion. 25´. Comm.
                   by the American Accordion Association. 1 mvt
                   printed in *Accordion Horizons,* 2, no. 4 (Summer
                   1966). To Robert Davine.

           1. Contemplativo, 2. Allegro giocoso, 3. Adagio
serioso.

274   *Sonata for Three Cellos* (1934). Music lost.

275 ** s,p *Sonata in Two Movements and Coda* (1969, ACA).
Fl/piano. 10´. University of Denver, 2 May 1968.
1. Lento, 2. Scherzoso.

276 ** s,p *Sonatina for Oboe and Piano* (1960s). 15´. NLA 25.
MT, MTP.

277 ** s,p *Suite for Accordion, Clarinet, and Bassoon* (1982,
ACA). 10´.
1. Fragments, 2. Dialogue I, 3. Scherzo, 4. Ricercare.

278 ** s,p *Suite for Solo Cello* (1933, rev. 1979). 15´. NLA 24.
MS 1933, MT 1979. The University of Denver
Camerata, 23 March 1979.
1. Rubato, 2. Grazioso, 3. Decisivo, 4. Lento,
5. Decisivo.

        Ten Songs from James Joyce's "Chamber Music," see
Solo Songs.

279 ** s,p *Three* (1964, ACA). Fl, ob, cl. 6´. Sandra Wahl's
Senior Recital, 12 May 1964.
1. Flowing lightly, 2. Adagio, 3. Scherzando.

280   *Three Canons for Flute and Clarinet* (1941). 6´. NLA
23. MSC.

281   *Three Chinese Tunes* (late 1930s). Ob or fl, or both in
unison, cl, hn, bsn. 6´. NLA 23. MS, MSP.
1. Verse Tune, 2. Folk Song, 3. Lute Tune.

282 **   s,p   *Three Chorale Voluntaries* (1980, WM). Trpt/organ.
                 8´. Rocky Mountain Contemporary Music Festival,
                 30 March 1982. To Richard Parks.
                 1. Es ist genug, 2. Aus meines herzens Grunde, 3. Ein'
                 feste Burg.

283   *Three Numbers for Woodwind Quartet* (1936, ACA).
                 Fl, ob, cl, bsn. 6´. To George E. Waln.
                 1. Dance, 2. Sing, 3. Play.

284 **   p   *Trio* (1984, ACA). Vln, vcl, piano. 25´. Colorado
                 New Music Series, "A Tribute to NL," Foote Music
                 Hall, Denver, 1 Dec. 1985.
                 1. Lento moderato, 2. Lento, 3. Duettino fra gli archi.

                 Tripartito, see *Flute and Guitar.*

285 **   s,p   *Trio for Flute, Viola, and Harp* (1941, rev. 1978). 20´.
                 Comm. and Ded. to Elizabeth Sprague Coolidge.
                 NLA Box 38. MT, MTP.
                 1. Grazioso, 2. Arioso, 3. Giocoso, 4. Comodo.

286   *Untitled.* (Skull and Crossbones drawn in place of
                 title). (pre-1920). Piano, bells, dish pan, voice, egg
                 beater, triangle. 2´. NLA NB1. MS.

287 **   s,p   *Valley Suite* (1976, ACA). Vln/piano. 15´.
                 1. Scenes and Sounds, 2. Cemetery Hill, 3.
                 Raymond's Tune (and a few others), 4. The Brook in
                 Summer

288   *Wedding Music* (1979, ACA). Vln, vlc. 9´. To Duane
                 and Patty Heller for their wedding.

1. Vorspiel, 2. Epithalamium en forme d'une sarabande, 3. Background Music, 4. Recessional-Sapphic Ode.

289   *Wir Christenleut* (1980). Fl, trpt, cl, bsn. 2´. NLA 24. MSC. Cantus firmus by Caspar Fuger, 1592. For Dick (Richard S. Parks) from Norm.

STRING QUARTETS

290   *Adagio* (1930s). 5′. NLA OV 6. MS.

291   *Andante* (Very Early 1930s). 5′. NLA 31. MSP-AH.

292   *Adagio Intristito* and *Grazioso Teneramente* (1935). 5′ each. NLA OV 6.

293 **   s,p   *Informal Music Number One* (1940, ACA). 15′. To the Walden String Quartet.
1. Serenade, 2. Variations, 3. Song, 4. Allegro moderato.

294 **   s,p   *Informal Music Number Two* (1941, ACA). 15′. ISCM, Budapest String Quartet, 3 Aug. 1942.

295 **   s,p   *Nine U. S. American Folk Songs* (1941, ACA). 30′. To Martha and Melville Smith.
1. He's Gone Away, 2. The Midnight Train, 3. Liza in the Summertime, 4. The Lone Prairie, 5. I Got a Gal at the Head of the Holler, 6. Tie-Shuffling Chant, 7. John Riley, 8. Li'l Boy Name David, 9. John Henry.

296 **   s,p   *Overture for String Quartet* (1987, ACA). 4.5′. St. Mark's Church, Denver, Simpatica String Quartet, 3 May 1987. Comm. by and ded. to the Simpatica String Quartet.

297 **   s,p   *Quartetto Breve (in Two Movements and Coda)* (1990). 6′. NLA 38. MSC. To Kay Norton.
1. Flessivoso, 2. Allegro molto, 3. Coda.

298 **   s,p   *Serenades* (1945, MPI), also called *Five Serenades*, also called *Six Serenades.* 10′. Lexington Ave. Young

Men's and Young Women's Hebrew Assoc., New
York City, 13 Jan. 1953. To my friends the Walden
String Quartet.
1. Easy-going, 2. A Little Slower, 3. Fast, 4. Slow, 5.
Fast, 6. Slow.

299   *String Quartet: Andantino* (1922). 1´. NLA NB1.
MS.

300   *String Quartet in C Major* (very early 1930s). 15´.
NLA 26. MS. To the Walden String Quartet.
1. Adagio molto tranquillo, 2. Allegro leggerissimo, 3.
Andante poco larghetto, 4. Allegro grazioso e
semplicemente.

301   *String Quartet in E Minor* (very early 1930s). 15´.
NLA 27. MS--AH.
1. Grave, moderato, 2. Presto leggiero, 3. Larghetto,
4. Allegro poco moderato, ma molto energico.

302   *String Quartet in C Minor* (1933, ACA). 30´.
1. Molto adagio e sostenuto, 2. Allegro e molto
marcato ed animato.

303   *String Quartet in D Minor, Number One* (1937). 20´.
NLA OV 6. MS, MSP.
1. Allegro molto, 2. Allegretto con moto, 3. Adagio
sostenuto.

304 *,** s,p *String Quartet Number Three* also called *Third String
Quartet*, also called *String Quartet in D Minor,
Number Two* (1938, GS 1945, SPAM ed.; ACA). 20´.
To the Walden String Quartet.
1. Allegro moderato ma ben decisivo, 2. Andante, 3.
Adagio, 4. Allegro molto.

305 *,** s,p *String Quartet Number Six* (1937, ACA). 15´. Mar
                2-30, 1947, 4th American Music Festival, National
                Gallery of Art, Wash., D. C., Gordon String Quartet,
                2-30 Mar. 1947.
                1. Slow, sustained, 2. Singing, folk-like, 3. Fast; light
                with digressions.

306 **   s,p *String Quartet Number Seven* (1938, ACA). 15´.
                Music Education Club, Chicago Public Schools,
                Walden String Quartet, 23 March 1948.
                1. Slow, 2. Fast, moderato e simplice.

307 **   s,p *String Quartet 1992* (1992). 20. NLA 38. MSC.
                1. Lento, 2. Allegro moderato leggermente, 3. Adagio,
                4. Minuetto and Trio, 5. Andante cantando con
                movimento, 6. Coda.

SOLO SONGS
(Cross-referenced titles in quotation marks represent significant single works from larger sets)

"Adventure," see *Six Songs.*

308   *All My Heart Rejoices* (1953). S/piano. 1.5´. NLA 16. MS. Text: Paulus Gerhardt, 1656.

"Americans," see *Prelude to Western Star.*

"Anguish," see *Five Cinquains.*

"Apple Orchards I and II," see *Four Songs--A Cycle.*

"Arbutus," see *Five Cinquains.*

"Because I Could Not Stop for Death," see *Three Verses of Emily Dickinson.*

309   *Cars Go Fast* (n. d.). V/piano. 1.5´. NLA 16. MT. Text: *The Golden Flute*, an Anthology of Poetry for Young Children, by Hubbard and Babbitt. For Rudy from Granddaddy.

310 ** s,p *Catskill Eagle* (1986, ACA). Mez/piano. 2´. NLA 16. MSC. Text: *Moby Dick*, Herman Melville.

311   *Cicada* (1949). V/piano. 2´. Score lost. Text by Dorothy S. Lockwood.

"Climbing in Autumn..." see *Four Poems of Liu Chang-Ch'ing.*

312   *De Profundis* (late 1960s or 70s). S/piano. 4´. NLA
              16. MSC. Text: Psalm 130.

313 ** p   *The Dialogue of Abraham and Isaac* (1965, ACA).
              V/piano. 15´. NLA 16. MSC. Colorado Women's
              College, Arthur Schoep and James Moon, 26 Apr.
              1965. Text: from the play, *My Sister, My Spouse* by
              Donald Sutherland. To Arthur Schoep.

              "Dirge," see *Six Songs*.

314   *Drop, Drop Slow Tears* (1945, AMP, rev. 1992)
              V/piano. 2´. NLA 16. Text: Phineas Fletcher, 1633.

              "Drowsily Come the Sheep," see *Slumber Song*.

              "Dust of Snow," see *The Pasture*.

315 ** s,p   *Duh midnaht train an' de fo'day train* (1984, ACA).
              4´. Text: folk source. To Barbara Hill Moore.

              "Elysium," see *Three Verses of Emily Dickinson*.

              "Evening," see *Six Miscellaneous Songs*.

316 ** p   *Fallen is Babylon the Great! Hallelujah!* (1955, ACA).
              Mez/piano. 17´. University of Denver, Truly B.
              Nelson, 9 May 1966. Text: Revelation 18, 19, RSV.
              For Truly Barr Nelson.

              "A Farewell to a Buddhist Monk," see *Four Poems of
              Liu Chang-Ch'ing*.

317   *Five Christmas Songs* (c. 1953). V/piano. 1-2´ each.
              NLA 16. MSC.

1. The Snow Lay on the Ground AMP, 1955, 2.
Joseph, Dearest Joseph" AMP, 1955, 3. Here 'Mongst
Ass and Oxen Mild, 4. A Babe Lies in the Cradle, 5.
All My Heart Rejoices.

318 **   s,p   *Five Cinquains of Adelaide Crapsey* (1942). S/piano.
15′. NLA 16. MSC. To Helena Strassburger. 1.
Triad, 2. Trapped, 3. Anquish, 4. Arbutus, 5. The
Grand Canyon.

319 **   s,p   *Five Inspirational Songs* also called *Five Inspirational
Lines* (1967). V/piano. 10′. NLA 16. MSC. University
of Denver, Hortense Zuckerman and David Karp.
Dedicated to Hortense Zuckerman.
1. Man's Heart, text St. Augustine, 2. He Who
Desires, text Dostoevsky, 3. Let Us Have Trust, text
Mozart, 4. I Believe, text Schopenhauer, 5. O Lead
My Spirit, text Beethoven.

"Flower-Gathering," see *The Pasture.*

"Flower of the Clove!" see *Rosemary Leaves!*

"Flower of the Flax!" see *Rosemary Leaves!*

320 **   s,p   *Four Poems of Liu Chang-Ch'ing* (1984) Contralto,
fl/piano. 5′. NLA 16. MT. Text: 8th century, trans.
Witter Bynner after Dr. Kiang Kang-Hu's *Oral
Anglicizing of T'ang Poets.* To Barbara Carey.
1. On parting with the Buddhist Pilgrim Ling-Ch'e,
2. On hearing a Lute-Player, 3. A Farewell to a
Buddhist Monk, 4. Climbing in Autumn for a View
from the Temple on the Terrace of General Wu.

321 ** s,p *Four Songs--A Cycle* (1977, ACA). S, vln, organ. 12'.
Cathedral of the Incarnation, Nashville, TN, Mary
Ann Kirk, May 1979. Text: Walt Whitman. To Mary
Anne Kirk.
1. Apple Orchards I, 2. Winter's Foil, 3. Halcyon
Days, 4. Apple Orchards II.

Funeral Service, see Choral Music.

322 ** s,p *The Gardner* (1955). S/piano. 3'. NLA OV 7. MT.
Text: Wm. Wordsworth's "To Lady Beaumont." To
Bernice.

"The Grand Canyon," see *Five Cinquains*.

323   *The Golden Lady: Lines to Go with a Picture* (1954
and 1955, RM). S/piano. 4'. Text: Dorothy
Lockwood. To Daisy Heard.

"Halcyon Days," see *Four Songs--A Cycle*.

324   *Handsome Sir Gilbert* (n. d.). V/piano. 5'. NLA 16.
MSC. Music for the play *Becket*, by Jean Anouilh,
produced at the University of Denver, 1972.

"He Who Desires," see *Inspirational Lines*.

"He Who Remains," see *Inspirational Lines*.

325   *He Who Remains Cheerful* (1967). S/piano. 5'. NLA
16. MSC. Text: Ralph Waldo Trine.

326   *The Hound of Heaven* (1937, GX). T/orch. 1 hour.
Withdrawn.

327 ** s,p *I Asked the Heaven of Stars: Night Song at Amalfi*
(n. d.). S/piano. Incomplete. NLA 17. Text: Sara
Teasdale. To My Mother.

"I Believe," see *Inspirational Lines.*

328 ** s,p *I Have Painted Elijah* (1943, ACA). S/piano. Opt.
inst. fl, B-flat cl, vln I and II, vla, vcl, bass. 2´. Text:
Erik Axel Harlfeldt, trans. Ellen Johnson.

329 ** s,p *I Know Starlight* (1952, ACA). S/piano. Orch: 2 fl,
ob, cl, bsn, 2 hns, timp, stgs. 1970. 2.5´. MSC
S/piano, MSC S/orch. Text: spritual. To Helen
Boatwright.

"I Make My Song," see *Prelude to Western Star.*

330 ** s,p *Indian Woman Down in the Marketplace* (1984).
S/piano. 5´. NLA 17. Text: Joaquin Pasos, trans.
Leland H. Chambers. To Phyllis Bryn-Julson.

331 ** s,p *Ingalill* (1941). S/piano. 4´. NLA 17. MSC. Trans.
Ellen Johnson.

Inspirational Lines, see *Five Inspirational Songs.*

332 ** s,p *Irish Songs* (c. 1950). T, fl, vcl, harp. 30´. NLA 17.
MT. For Christopher Lynch, CBS recording.
1. A Little Bit of Heaven, 2. The Palatine's Daughter,
3. The Young May Moon, 4. A Ballynure Ballad,
5. The Minstrel Boy, 6. The Garden Where the
Praties Grow, 7. The Rose of Tralee, 8. You'd Better
Ask Me, 9. When Irish Eyes Are Smiling.

"Lend Me Your Music," see *Prelude to Western Star.*

"Let Us Have Trust," see *Inspirational Lines.*

333 **   s,p   *Letter to Mother* (Mother's Day, 1955, SMC).
V/piano. 3´.

"A Little Shoe," see *Three Songs.*

The Lord is My Shepherd, see *Pastoral: The Lord . . .*

"Love's Comparings," see *True Gift.*

334   *Love's Secret* (1943, ACA). V/piano. Opt. inst: fl, cl,
vln I and II, vla, vcl, bass, piano. 2.5´. Text: William
Blake. To Norma Farber.

"Man's Heart," see *Inspirational Lines.*

"Margarita Debayle," see *To Margarita Debayle.*

335 **   s,p   *Mary, Who Stood in Sorrow* (1950, ACA). S/orch:
2/picc-1-1-1; 2-1-1-0; timp, perc, harp, stgs or piano.
Reduct., piano. 10´. MSC, red. Text: Sarah Moore.

336 **   s,p   *Medea Redux* (1992). Mez/orch: 2-2-2-B Cl-2-CBsn-A
sax; 4-3-3-1; timp, perc, stgs. 30´. NLA OV 10. MSC.
Text derived from Euripides, trans. Simon Goldfield.
To Marcia Ragonetti.
1. Medea soliloquizes, 2. Medea viz-à-viz Creon,
Jason, Women of Corinth, the Children, 3. Delphic
Hymn A and B, 4. Hymn to the Sun.

337   *Mein Haus* (1922). V/piano. 2´. NLA NB1. MS. Text
by Angelina Lockwood, NL's mother.

338 *,** s,p *Memories of President Lincoln: When Lilacs Last in the Dooryard Bloom'd* (1920s, Paris). T, 2 fl. 3.5´. NLA 17. MS. Signed Charles Caxton, NL's pseudonym. Paris, ISCM, 1920s.

"Messenger Nightingale," see *True Gift.*

"The Monk in the Garden" ("He Comes from Mass Early in the Morning"), see *Six Songs* with text by Adelaide Crapsey.

"The Moon," see *Six Miscellaneous Songs.*

"Moon-Shadows," see *Six Songs.*

"The Murmur of a Bee," see *Three Verses of Emily Dickinson.*

"My Love for Him," see *Six Miscellaneous Songs.*

339 *No Title* (Poem by Mrs. Shelley). (c. 1925, Rome or Paris). V/piano. 3´. MS either by copyist or by another composer. NLA NB1. MS.

340 ** s,p *Now and Then* (1943) V/piano. 5´. NLA 17. MSC. Text: Ellen Johnson.

"O, Lady, Let the Sad Tears Fall," see *Six Songs* with text by Adelaide Crapsey.

"O Lead My Spirit," see *Inspirational Lines.*

341 ** s,p *O Lord, Our Lord* (1960). T and Strgs. 6´. NLA 17. MSC, MPC. Text: Psalm 8. To my esteemed friends in the Music Department, Univ. of Hawaii.

342 **   s,p   *Observance: When Israel Went Forth From Egypt* (1985, ACA). Mez/organ. 4´. Text: Psalm 114, RSV.

           "Old Slee," see *Three Songs.*

           "On Hearing a Lute-Player," see *Four Poems of Liu Chang-Ch'ing.*

           "On Parting with the Buddhist Pilgrim...," see *Four Poems of Liu Chang-Ch'ing.*

343 *,** s,p   *Out of May's Shows Selected* (1939). V/piano. 3´. NLA 38. MSC.

344   *Out of May's Shows Selected* (rev. 1945). V/piano. 3´. NLA 38. MSC.

345 **   s,p   *Pastoral: The Lord is My Shepherd* (1955, ACA). S/organ. 3´. Text: Psalm 23. To Helen Boatwright.

346 **   s,p   *The Pasture* (1941). V/piano. 10´. NLA 17. MSC. Text: Robert Frost. To Helena Strassburger. 1. The Pasture, 2. Spring Pools, 3. Dust of Snow, 4. Flower-Gathering.

347   *Patapan* (1941, BH). T/piano. 2´.

348 **   s,p   *Prayer of David: Hear a Just Cause, O Lord: A Passacaglia* (1985, ACA). Mez/organ. 5´. Text: Psalm 17: 1-7 (RSV).

349 **   p   *Prelude to Western Star* (1951, rev. 1983, ACA). S/piano, rev. Bar/piano. 25´. University of Denver, Joel Eide, 7 Aug. 1983. Text: Stephen Vincent Benet. Comm. by Cathalene Parker.

1. Americans, 2. The Stranger, 3. Star in the West,
4. I make my Song, 5. Lend me your music.

350 ** s,p *Psalm 23* (1948, ACA). S/orch: 2-1-2-1; 2-2-0-1; timp,
stgs. 5.5'. Young Men's and Young Women's
Hebrew Association, New York, 23 March 1948.
Text: Eliot, Weld, and Mather, *Bay Psalm Book.* To
the memory of Godfrey Turner, 1913-1948. Comm.
by the Piano Ensemble Society.

351 *The Psychedelic Experience* (1960s). S/Bsn. 7'. NLA
18. MSC. Text: F. W. Hanley, M. D. To my friend
Wayne Winslow.

352 ** s,p *The Red Cow is Dead* (1942). S/piano. 6'. NLA 18.
MSC. Text: E. B. White. To Janet Fairbanks.

353 *Reluctance* (1976). S/piano. 4'. NLA 18. MS. Text:
Robert Frost. To Nancy Klingman.

"Remembered Scenes," see *True Gift.*

354 ** s,p *River Magic* (1945, MPI). V/piano. 3'. Text: Eva
Byron. To Helen Boatwright.

355 * *Robeson Arrangements* (1940s). Recording. Music
lost. IRREG 2.
1. Ah Still Suits Me (Gershwin), 2. It Ain't
Necessarily So (Gershwin), 3. Ol' Man River
(Gershwin), 4. Sylvia (An Sylvia, Schubert).

"Roma Aeterna," see *Six Songs.*

356 ** s,p *Rondeau: The First Day of the Month of May* (1985).

Mez, A, w/ opt. fl obbl. 2´. NLA 18. MT. Text: from
"Six Rondeaux" by Charles d'Orleans, trans. by
Donald Sutherland. To Barbara Carey.

357 **   s,p   *Rosemary Leaves!* (1938, rev. 1941). V/piano.
NLA 18. MSC. Incomplete. Text: A. Mary F.
Robinson.
1. Rosemary Leaves! 2. Flower of the Clove!
3. Flower of the flax!

358   *Set Me as a Seal Upon Thine Heart* (1987).
Mez/organ. 5´. NLA 18. MT. Text: Song of
Solomon. To Roy and Barbara Carey.

359 **   s,p   *She Dwelt among the Untrodden Ways* (1939, rev.
1941). V/piano. See Also *Six Miscellaneous Songs.* 4´.
NLA 18. MSC. Text: Wm. Wordsworth.

360 **   s,p   *She Dwelt among the Untrodden Ways* (1955, AMP).
V/piano. 4´. Text: Wm. Wordsworth. For Isabelle
Taylor.

361 **   s,p   *(sitting in a tree--)* (1943, ACA). V/piano or v/fl, 2 vln,
vla, vcl, bass, piano. 1.5´.

362 **   s,p   *Six Miscellaneous Songs* (1956). V/piano or v/SQ.
14´.
1. Evening, text: Sappho, trans. John Addington
Symonds, 2. The Moon, text: Sappho, trans. J. A.
Symonds, 3. She Dwelt among the Untrodden Ways,
For Isabelle Taylor, Text: William Wordsworth,
4. The Spring Time, Text: from Shakespeare's "As
You Like It," 5. My Love for Him, For Mary Ann
Noonan, Text: Medieval Norman, trans. J. A.
Symonds, 6. The Thought of You, author unknown.

363 **   s,p   *Six Songs* (1938, rev. 1941, MPI). V/piano. 20 . Texts:
by Adelaide Crapsey.
1. Dirge, For Prudence Fish, 2. The Monk in the
Garden, For Prudence Fish, 3. Adventure, For
Marguerite Quimby, 4. Moon-Shadows, for Ruth
Lewin Foster, 5. Roma Aeterna, for Ruth Lewin
Foster, 6. Oh, Lady, Let the Sad Tears Fall, For
Marguerite Quimby.

364   *Slumber Song* (pre-1920s). V/piano. 5´. NLA NB1.
MS.

365   *Slumber Song: Drowsily Come the Sheep* (early
1930s, rev. 1945, rev. 1992). S/piano. 2.5´. NLA 18.
MS. Text: Louis V. Ledoux. Rev. for Jean and Louis,
Christmas, 1945.

366 **   s,p   *A Song of the Virgin Mother* (1955, rev. 1980s).
A/piano. 5´. NLA OV 1. Text: from Los Pastores de
Belen (Lope de Vegas, 16th cent.), trans Ezra Pound.
To Eleanor Pudil Anop.

367 **   s,p   *Sonnet* (1943). T/piano. 4´. NLA 19. MSC. Text: e. e.
cummings.

         Spring Pools, see *The Pasture.*

         "The Spring Time," see *Six Miscellaneous Songs.*

         "Star in the West," see *Prelude to Western Star.*

         "The Stranger," see *Prelude to Western Star.*

368   *Take Thy Tabor and Thy Flute* (1941). V/piano. 2´.
Music lost.

369 **   s,p   *Ten Songs from James Joyce's "Chamber Music"* (1939-40). Also *Three Songs from James Joyce's "Chamber Music."* S/SQ. 25´. The Town Hall, New York, Cathalene Parker, 28 Mar. 1948.
1. My dove, my beautiful one, 2. Lean out of the window, Golden Hair, 3. Oh, cool is the valley, 4. Silently she's combing, combing her long hair, 5. My love is in a light attire, 6. O Sweetheart, hear your lover's tale, 7. Strings in the earth and air, 8. When the shy star goes forth in heaven, 9. Oh, it was down by Danny Carney, 10. Sleep now, O sleep now, O you unquiet heart.

"The Thought of You," see *Six Miscellaneous Songs.*

370 **   s,p   *Three Songs* (1943). V/piano. 5´. NLA 19. MSC. Text: Jean Yourd.
1. Old Slee, 2. Whistle Rules, 3. A Little Shoe.

371 **   s,p   *Three Verses of Emily Dickinson* (1938). S/piano. 4.5´. NLA 19. MSC. To Warren and Adele Taylor.
1. The murmur of a bee, 2. Elysium, 3. Because I Could Not Stop for Death.

372   *Tight With Unwept Tears Your Face* (n. d.). V/piano. 1´. NLA 19. MSC. Text: Jean Yourd.

373 **   s,p   *To Margarita Debayle* (1977, ACA). S/piano. 12´. Text: Rubén Darío, trans. Donald Sutherland. For Phyllis Bryn-Julson.

"Trapped," see *Five Cinquains.*

"Triad," see *Five Cinquains.*

374 **   s,p   *True Gift* (1939, rev. 1941). V/piano. 5´. NLA 19.
MSC. Text: Pierre de Ronsard, trans. Curtis Hidden
Page.
1. True Gift, 2. Remembered Scenes, 3. Messenger
Nightingale, 4. Love's Comparings.

375   *Variation on a Popular Theme* (1943). V/piano or
V/cl, vln I and II, vla, vcl, bass. 3´. NLA 19. MS,
MSC. Text: Edward Fenton. Tune, "Don't Sit Under
the Apple Tree" by Lew Brown. To Janet Fairbank.

     We Are of God, see Choral Music.

376   *When Beauty Grows Too Great to Bear* (n. d.).
S/piano. 3´. NLA 19. MSC. Text: Sara Teasdale.

     When Israel Went Forth From Egypt, see
Observance.

377   *Whence Art Thou* (1983, AG). V/piano. 2´. NLA 38.
In *Christmas: The Annual of Christmas Literature
and Art*, Vol. 53, p. 39.

     "Whistle Rules," see *Three Songs*.

     "Winter's Foil," see *Four Songs--A Cycle*.

INSTRUMENTAL ENSEMBLE WORKS

A Year's Chronicle, see *Symphony: A Year's Chronicle*.

378   *Bernie's Animal Orchestra* (1950s). Piano/orch. Score lost. For Dorothy Frels and the San Antonio Symphony, for children.

379 *   *Brass Music for Their Majesties' Entry: At the Opening of the May Exhibit of the American Academy in Rome* (1929 or 1930). 3 trpt in C, 1 trpt in B-flat, 4 B-flat trb. 2´. NLA 22. MSC.

380 **   s,p   *Choreographic Suite for String Orchestra* (1986). 15´. NLA 31. MSC. Notes on choreography. 1. Canonic fugue, 2. Dorian Song, 3. Scherzo, 4. Chorale and Plainsong, 5. Celebration.

381   *Chorus Girl*, arr. by NL (1940s). Orch: 2-1-2-1; 2-3-2-0; timp, drum, stgs. NLA OV 10. MT. Text and tune, "Chicago" by Fred Fisher.

382 **   s,p   *Concertino for Trumpet and Concert Band* (1992, TR). Solo B♭ trpt-1/picc-1-E♭ cl-3-B cl-1-2 A sax-T sax-bar sax; 3-4-3-eu-1; timp, perc, cb. 10´. NLA OV 8. MSC. To Gerald Endsley.

383 **   s,p   *Concerto for Oboe* (1967). 2 hn, timp, perc, celeste, stgs. 20´. NLA 31. MSC. Orquesta de la Universidad Nacional Autonoma de Mexico, Mexico City, dir. by Eduardo Mata, 19 April 1968. To My Friend Richard Pointer. 1. Adagio moderato, 2. Molto adagio, 3. Scherzo.

Concerto for Organ and Chamber Orchestra, see
Keyboard Works.

384 **   p   *Concerto for Two Harps and Orchestra* (1981, ACA).
2 solo hp, 2/2 picc-1-1-1;2-1-1-0; perc, marimba,
celeste, stgs. 30´. Orquesta Sinfonica Nacional Costa
Rica, 9 and 11 September 1983. Composed for and
Dedicated to Suzann Davids and Deborah Kay
Davids-Wylde.
1. **Andante moderato**, 2. **Passacaglia**, 3. **Rondo-
variations.**

385 *   *Erie* (1936). Orch. Music lost.

386 **   s,p   *From an Opening to a Close* (1973, ACA). Band: 2-2-
2-B Cl-2; 2-2-2-1; perc; piano. 10´. To Maurice B.
Mitchess. Composed for the University of Denver
Wind Symphony: Leigh Burns, Conductor.
1. Opening and Dialogue, 2. Fanfare and March, 3.
Hymn and Close.

387   *Goin' to Town* (1950). Concert Band. 10´. Music
Lost.

The Hound of Heaven, see Solo Songs.

I Know Starlight, see Solo Songs.

388 **   s,p   *Lenten Sequence, Interval, Ascent* (1989, ACA).
Symphonic Winds: 3/picc-1-E♭ cl-3-CA cl-2; 4-3-3-
bar-E♭ tuba-2; harps, perc. 15´.
1. Swedish melody, 2. Prediction, 3. Chorale, 4.
Duetto accompagnato, 5. Tenebrae, 6. Interval and
Ascent.

389   *Marche Breve* (1946). Music Lost. Middlebury
               College Composer's Conference, Middlebury, VT.
               Ded. to Barbara and Alan Carter.

               Mary, Who Stood in Sorrow, see Solo Songs.

               Medea Redux, see Solo Songs.

390 **   s,p *Metaphors* (1991). Symphonic Winds and Perc.
               Picc/police whistle-2-2-3-B cl-A sax-2; 4-3-3-eu-1;
               timp, perc. Colorado Wind Ensemble, Martha E.
               Cox, dir., Wellshire Presb. Church, Denver, 16 Feb.
               1992.
               1. Lento moderato, 2. Andante fluendo, 3. Scherzoso,
               4. Allegro.

391 *   *Odysseus* (1929). Orch. Withdrawn. Chicago
               Symphony Orchestra, Frederick Stock, conductor.

392 **   s,p *Panegyric for String Orchestra and Horn* (1978-79,
               ACA). 15′. In Memory of Donald Sutherland.

393 **   s,p *Pi March* (1992). Wind ens: picc-2-2-E-♭ cl-4-B cl-2-2
               A sax-T sax-bar sax; 4-3-3-eu-E♭ tuba-1; timp, perc.
               3.5. NLA OV 10. MSC. To Gary W. Hill.

394 **   s,p *Piano Concerto* (1973, ACA). Piano, 1-1-1-1; 1-1-1-0;
               timp, stgs. 25′. Zita Carno of Los Angeles Symphony
               and Orchestra of Chamber music Center and
               Composers' Conference, Johnson, VT. 25 Aug. 1973.
               To David Karp.
               1. Allegro, 2. Adagio, 3. Scherzo.

395 **   s,p *Prayers and Fanfares* (1980). Brass 4-3-3-0; perc; cel;
               stgs. 10′. NLA 31. MS.

396 **   s,p *Return of the Spirits*, also called *Coming of the
               Spirits* (1986). 2 Synthesizers, fl, perc. 30´. NLA 31.
               MS. Filmed in Mesa Verde, CO, Oct. 1986 for
               KRMA-TV, Denver. Synth. programmer, Chris
               Hewitt; mixer, Gannon Kashiwa; choreographer,
               William Thompson; executive producer, Kaye S.
               Levine; producer, Jim Levy; director, Jon Husband.

397   *Sleeping Beauty* (n. d.). Chamber Orch: fl, cl, trpt, hn,
               stgs. 10´. NLA 37. MSC.
               1. Picture 1, 2. Picture 2, 3. Picture 3, 4. Picture 4, 5.
               Picture 5, 6. Picture 6, 7. Picture 7.

398 **   s,p *Symphonic Sequences* (1965, ACA). 3/3 picc-2-2-B cl-
               2; 2-2-2-0; hp, timp, perc, stgs. 15´. University of
               Denver, 19 April 1967. To the University of Denver
               Symphony Orchestra, Fred Hoeppner, conductor.
               1. Lento-allegro, 2. Andantino, 3. Allegro.

399 *   *Symphony* (1941). 1-1-2-2; 2-2-1-0; timp, stgs. 30´.
               NLA 29 & 30. MS, MSP. To: Adella Prentiss
               Hughes.
               1. Allegro con spirito, 2. Adagio cantabile, 3. Allegro
               deciso.

400 *   *Symphony: A Year's Chronicle* (1934). 1-1-2-2; 2-1-1-
               0; timp, perc, stgs. 30´. NLA OV 8. MS, MPC.
               Chicago Symphony Orchestra dir. by Frederick
               Stock, 4 Apr. 1935.
               1. Allegro, 2. Adagio molto sostenuto con
               espressione, 3. Maestoso largamente.

401 **   s,p *Symphony for Large Orchestra* (1979, ACA). 3/picc-
               2-E hn-E flat cl-2-1; 4-3-3-1; timp, perc, hp, stgs. 30´.
               Community Arts Symphony, Denver, 21 Nov. 1980.

                Commissioned by The Community Arts Symphony
of Denver, T. Gordon Parks, director.
1. Andante, 2. Interlude, 3. Vivace.

402 **   s,p *Symphony for String Orchestra* (1975, ACA). Stgs.
15´. Chamber Music Conference, Bennington
College, Bennington, VT, 20 Aug. 1975. Comm. by
Broadcast Music, Inc. for Chamber Music
Conference.

403 *   *Symphony in E* (1928-1929: "Begun in Traverse City
Spring 1928, Finished in Rome 1929"). 3-2-3-3; 6-0-2-
1; perc, stgs. 20´. NLA IRREG 1, MS.
1. Largo, 2. Molto largo, 3. Allegro molto con brio.

404   *Toccata for Brass and Percussion* (n. d.). 6´.
Recording only. NLA IRREG 2.

405   *Triptych to the Memory of W. R. B. Willcox.* Narr,
fl, 3 trpt, 3 trb, perc, timp. 8´. Music lost.

406   *Variations on a Gitlin Tune* (1949). Music lost.

407 **   s,p *Weekend Prelude* (1944, ACA). 3/picc-2-E Hn-2-B cl-
2 C Bsn; 4-3-3-1; timp, 2 perc, hp, stgs. 8´. American
Academy of Arts and Letters Program by Recipients
of Awards, 23 May 1947.

OPERATIC WORKS

408 *,** s,p   *Early Dawn* (1960-1961, ACA). 3 Acts. 2-2-2-2; 2-2-2-2; perc., stgs. 2.5 hrs. Libretto by R. Russell Porter. University of Denver, 7-12 Aug. 1961.

409 **   s,p   *The Hanging Judge*, also called *The Inevitable Hour* (1963-64, ACA). 3 Acts. 2-1-E Hn-2-2; 2-2-2-0; timp, perc, stgs. 2.5 hrs. Libretto by R. Russell Porter. 6 and 7 Mar. 1964.

410 **   s,p   *Requiem for a Rich Young Man* (1964, ACA). 1 Act. 1-1-1-0; 0-1-1-0; piano/celeste, perc, vcl, bass. 28´. Libretto by Donald Sutherland. University of Denver, 24 Nov. 1964. Comm. by the National Opera Association.

411 *,** s,p   *The Scarecrow* (1945, ACA). 2 Acts. 1-1-1-1; 2-2-1-0; timp, harp, stgs. 2 hrs. Story by Percy MacKaye, Libretto by Normand and Dorothy Lockwood. Comm. by the Alice M. Ditson Fund, Columbia University.

412 **   s,p   *The Wizards of Balizar: A Comic Fantasy* (1962, ACA). 1 act. 1-1-1-1; 1-1-1-1; perc, stgs. 1 hr, 45´. Libretto, R. Russell Porter. University of Denver, July 1962.

INCIDENTAL MUSIC FOR DRAMA

413   *The Bacchae* (1972). Music Lost. University of
        Denver, 1972. Euripides.

414   *Becket* (1972). Music Lost. University of Denver,
        1972. Jean Anouilh. See *Handsome Sir Gilbert.*

415   *The Crucible* (1973). Music Lost. University of
        Denver, 1973. Arthur Miller.

416   *The Devils* (1971). S, Bar, org, brass: 2-1-1-0; perc,
        harp, vcl. Music Lost. University of Denver Little
        Theater, 17 Nov. 1971. *The Devils of Loudon* by
        John Whiting.

417   *Dreamboat* (1952). Musical revue/operetta. Arr. &
        orchestrations, w/George Lynn. Penrose, MS. For
        Princeton University production.

        Electra, see *Three Odes from the Electra,* Choral
        Works.

418   *The Emporer Jones* (1970s). Timp only. Music Lost.
        University of Denver, 1970s. Eugene O'Neill.

419   *The Farce of the Worthy Master Pierre Patelin*
        (1966). Music Lost. University of Denver, 1966.
        Anonymous.

420   *For the Time Being* (1966, rev. 1971). Fl, ob, cl, perc,
        org, vln, vla, SATB, S and B soli, dancers, choral
        reading. 1 hour. Music Lost. Mountain View United
        Methodist Church, Boulder, 5 Dec. 1971, NL,
        conductor. W. H. Auden.

421   *The Ghost Sonata* (1970). Music Lost. University of
        Denver Theater, Jan.-Feb. 1970. Johann August
        Strindberg.

422   *The Glory of Her Crown* (1974). Music Lost.
        University of Denver, 1974. Hillary Powell.

423   *The Good Woman of Setzuan* (1966). Music Lost.
        University of Denver, 1966. Bertolt Brecht.

424   *Hippolytus* (1972). Fl, harp, hn, perc. Music Lost.
        University of Denver Theater Annex, 2-4 Mar. 1972.
        Euripides.

425   *Ikkaku Sennin* (1965). Music Lost. University of
        Denver, 1965. Japanese Noh play.

426   *Macbeth* (1974). Music Lost. University of Denver,
        1974. Shakespeare.

427   *The Mandrake* (1969). Music Lost. University of
        Denver, 1969. Machiavelli.

428   *Medea* (1969). Music Lost. University of Denver,
        1969. Euripides.

429   *My Sister, My Spouse* (1972). Incidental music for
        Donald Sutherland's Verse-Drama. 1-1-1-0; 0-1-1-0;
        perc, piano. 15´. NLA 15. MSC, MSP. University of
        Denver Wind Symphony and Madrigal Singers, Leigh
        Burns cond., Ronald Worstell as Abimelech. 2 Dec.
        1971. Musical portions only.
        1. Intro to the Prologue, 2. Doing the Gaza Strip, 3.
        Ladies' Song, 4. Hey! For a stiff wind, 5. Music in the
        Interlude, 6. Abemelech raised by guards and carried

off, 7. Battle Music and Victory March, 8. Philistine
National Anthem, 9. Song and Dance (Finale).

430   *No More From Thrones* (1962). A Play with Music.
           Music Lost. Libretto by R. Russell Porter. University
           of Denver, 6-8 Dec. 1962.

431   *The Queen and the Rebels* (1967). Music Lost.
           University of Denver, 1967. Ugo Betti.

432   *Sons of Coronado* (1959). SATB/string orch. Music
           lost. 7-8 Aug. 1959. Comm. by the Cultural Institute
           of Spain in America.

433   *Summertree* (1969). See Keyboard Works, *Fugue
           Sonata.* University of Denver, 1969. Ron Cowen.

434   *Tamburlaine the Great* (1965). Music Lost.
           University of Denver, 1965. Christopher Marlowe.

COLUMBIA WORKSHOP/STUDIO ONE (CBS Radio, 1940s)

435   *Moby Dick* (1946). Chamber (radio) orch. 2 1-hour
           segments. Music lost. Recording NB 3. Herman
           Melville.

436   *The Return of the Native* (1940s). Music lost.
           Recording NB 3. Thomas Hardy.

SAWYERS CORRELATED CLASSROOM MATERIALS
(Music by NL).

437	#3106 "Fun at the Zoo"
438	#3105 "Fun with Pets"
439	#3101 "Goldilocks and the Three Bears"
440	#3104 "The Sleeping Beauty"
441	#3103 "The Three Little Pigs"
442	#3102 "The Ugly Duckling"

YOUNG PEOPLE'S RECORDS, FRANSON CORPORATION

443 **	*Animal Supermarket* (1951). Fl, trpt, vln, vcl, cb, ATTB. 7´. Score lost.
444	*Hiawatha* (1952). 8´. Music Lost.
445 **	*Mickey Goes to School* (1952). SAT, narr, fl, cl, trb, perc, cb. 7´. Music lost.
446 **	*Riddle Songs* (Riddle Me This) (1951). T, fl, piano. 8´. Music lost.
447 **	*Travels of Babar* (1951). 1-1-1-1; 0-2-1-1; timp, 6 stgs, singers, narr. 15´. Music lost.

Chapter Notes

Chapter One--ANCESTRY AND PRE-EUROPEAN YEARS

1. Because he was born at home, a search in Manhattan for his birth certificate, originated by Normand Lockwood and dated 16 December 1955, was unsuccessful. His birth is verified in a separate document by the U. S. Department of Commerce, Bureau of the Census, by order 1K 5-202-764. Census of 1910, "taken April 15 in Ann Arbor, County Washtenaw, State Michigan, shows Normand Lockwood, age 4, enumerated in the family of Samuel P. and Angelina Lockwood. "The Bureau of the Census does not issue birth certificates, but this record is often accepted in the place of one." George H. Brown, Director, Bureau of the Census. Normand Lockwood Private Papers.

2. *Catalogue of the Officers and Graduates of Yale University in New Haven, CT: 1701-1924.* Information supplied by phone, 8 September 1989, by Judith Ann Schiff, Chief Researcher and Archivist, Manuscripts and Archives Section, Yale University Library.

3. Normand Lockwood, interview by Kay Norton in Denver, 3 March 1988.

4. Normand Lockwood, Denver, CO, letter to Kay Norton, Boulder, CO, 1 October 1989.

5. Charles Ives, as quoted in Henry and Sidney Cowell, *Charles Ives and His Music* (New York: Oxford University Press, 1955), 66.

6. Charles Ives, as quoted in John Kirkpatrick, ed. *Charles E. Ives: Memos* (New York: W. W. Norton and Co., 1972), 186-87.

7. *Bulletin of the University [of Michigan] School of Music* 17, no. 1 (June 1923): 90.

8. Albertine Lockwood Reynolds, Keene Valley, NY, letter to Kay Norton, Kansas City, MO, 14 July 1991.

9. Normand Lockwood, interview by Kay Norton in Denver, 2 June 1991.

10. Normand Lockwood, interview by Kay Norton in Denver, 4 September 1989.

11. Programs from Albert's 1894 recitals in Davos feature works by Beethoven, Hummel, Weber, Mendelssohn, Schubert, Chopin, Schumann, Henselt, and Liszt. Normand Lockwood Archive (NLA), Box NB1.

12. *Columbia University Alumni Register: 1754-1931.* (New York: Columbia University Press, 1932), 531.

13. *Columbia University, City of New York: Master's Essays, 1891-1917.* (New York: Columbia University Press, n.d.), 80.

14. W. S. B. Matthews, *The Ann Arbor News,* 9 November 1933, 1 and 13. Matthews does not provide the names of the other two pianists mentioned.

15. *The Michigan Alumnus,* T. Hawley Tapping, ed. 25 November 1933, 143.

16. Normand Lockwood, interview by Kay Norton in Denver, 9 August 1991.

17. Ibid.

18. "Catalogue of the University School of Music: 1917-1918," *Bulletin of the University [of Michigan] School of Music* 12, no. 1 (June 1918): 81, 83.

19. Dena J. Epstein, "Frederick Stock and American Music," *American Music* 10, no. 1 (Spring 1992): 20.

20. Samuel Pierson Lockwood, *Elementary Orchestration.* (Ann Arbor, MI: George Wahr, Publisher, 1926), 3.

21. Richard Crawford, "Music at Michigan: A Historical Perspective," chap. in *100 Years of Music at Michigan: 1880-1980* (Ann Arbor, MI: University of Michigan and Edwards Brothers, Inc., 1979), 23.

22. Matthews, 13.

23. Albertine Lockwood Reynolds, Keene Valley, NY, letter to Kay Norton, Kansas City, MO, 14 July 1991.

24. Envelope labeled "Normand's Programs," NLA, Box NB1.

25. Normand Lockwood, Denver, letter to Kay Norton, Boulder, CO, 1 October 1989.

26. Normand Lockwood, interview by Kay Norton in Denver, 2 June 1991.

27. NLA, Box NB1.

28. Normand Lockwood, Denver, letter to Kay Norton, Boulder, CO, 1 October 1989.

29. Ibid.

30. Albertine Lockwood Reynolds, Keene Valley, NY, letter to Kay Norton, Kansas City, MO, 14 July 1991. Emphasis original.

31. H. Wiley Hitchcock and Stanley Sadie, eds. *The New Grove Dictionary of American Music* (London: Macmillan, 1986), s.v. "Chamber Music After 1920," by Leonard Burkat and Gilbert Ross.

32. Normand Lockwood, interview by Kay Norton in Denver, 3 March 1988.

33. Normand Lockwood, *Three-Voice Invention.* NLA, Box NB 1.

34. Normand Lockwood, interview by Kay Norton in Denver, 2 June 1991.

35. Normand Lockwood, interview by Kay Norton in Denver, 4 September 1989.

36. Normand Lockwood, as quoted in Tony Max Davis, *A Study of Stylistic Characteristics in the Major Choral Works of Normand Lockwood* (D.M.A. thesis, University of Missouri-Kansas City, 1980), 7.

37. Normand Lockwood, interview by Susan L. Porter in Denver, 14 July 1980, NLA, Box 40.

38. Normand Lockwood, interview by Kay Norton in Denver, 4 September 1989.

Chapter Two--EUROPEAN YEARS

1. Normand Lockwood, interview by Kay Norton in Denver, 4 September 1989.

2. Normand Lockwood, interview by Susan L. Porter in Denver, 14 July 1980, NLA, Box 40.

3. Normand Lockwood, interview by Kay Norton in Denver, 4 September 1989.

4. Normand Lockwood, as quoted in Allen Young, "Children's Choir to Perform *A Child's Christmas in Wales*," *City Edition* [Denver], 12-19 December 1984, 31.

5. Elsa Respighi, *Ottorino Respighi: His Life Story Arranged by Elsa Respighi*, trans. by Gwyn Morris. (London: G. Ricordi & Co., 1962), 92.

6. Normand Lockwood, interview by Kay Norton in Denver, 4 September 1989.

7. Elsa Respighi, 93.

8. Normand Lockwood, as quoted in Davis, 7.

9. Normand Lockwood, as quoted in Allen Young, "Young and Old Bring Zest to Community Arts Concert," *Rocky Mountain News*, 2 February 1986, 6(E).

10. Normand Lockwood, interview by Kay Norton in Denver, 4 September 1989.

11. Normand Lockwood, Denver, letter to Kay Norton, Boulder, CO, 7 September 1989.

12. Leonie Rosenstiel, *Nadia Boulanger: A Life in Music.* (New York: W. W. Norton, 1982), 207-8.

13. Normand Lockwood, as quoted in Wes Blomster, "A Tribute to Lockwood, Who Earned It," *The Sunday Camera* [Boulder, CO], 24 November 1985, 1(D) and 4(D).

14. Normand Lockwood, *When Lilacs Last in the Dooryard Bloom'd*, NLA, Box 17.

15. Rosenstiel, 208.

16. Normand Lockwood, interview by Kay Norton in Denver, 4 September 1989.

17. Ibid.

18. Normand Lockwood, as quoted in Peggy Scott, "Composer-in-Residence Helps Unlock Student Musical Ability," *Southeast Missourian* [Cape Girardeau, MO], 19 March 1989, 7(A).

19. Nadia Boulanger, as quoted in Bruno Monsaingeon, *Mademoiselle: Conversations with Nadia Boulanger*, trans. by Robyn Marsack. (Manchester, Eng.: Carcanet Press, 1985, first published as *Mademoiselle: entretiens avec Nadia Boulanger*, Editions Van de Velde, 1981), 55.

20. Normand Lockwood, interview by Kay Norton in Denver, 4 September 1989.

21. Boulanger letters to Lockwood, NLA, Box 39.

22. Vona Lockwood, interview by Kay Norton in Denver, 4 September 1989.

23. Normand Lockwood, interview by Susan L. Porter in Denver, 14 July 1980, NLA, Box 40.

24. Normand Lockwood, as quoted in Allen Young, 1986.

Chapter Three--EARLY PROFESSIONAL YEARS

1. Normand Lockwood, interview by Kay Norton in Denver, 4 September 1989.

2. Willard Warch, *Our First 100 Years: A Brief History of the Oberlin College Conservatory of Music.* (Oberlin, OH: Oberlin College Conservatory of Music, 1967), 45-6.

3. Warch, 46.

4. Normand Lockwood Commemorative Album, Normand Lockwood Private Papers.

5. Peter Mennin, New York, NY, letter to Normand Lockwood, Denver, CO, 23 April 1971. Normand Lockwood Commemorative Album, Normand Lockwood Private Papers.

6. Paul Christiansen, Moorhead, MN, letter to Normand Lockwood, Denver, CO, April 1971. Normand Lockwood Commemorative Album, Normand Lockwood Private Papers.

7. William Hoskins, Jacksonville, FL, letter to Kay Norton, Kansas City, MO, 8 August 1991.

8. Ibid.

9. NLA, Solo Songs, Boxes 16-19.

10. Howard and Helen Boatwright, Syracuse, NY, letter to Normand Lockwood, Denver, CO, 22 April 1971. Normand Lockwood Commemorative Album, Normand Lockwood Private Papers.

11. Normand Lockwood, as quoted in Allen Young, "The Critics," *The Sentinel* [Cherry Creek/Denver, CO], 30 May 1974, 22.

12. Ludwig Lenel, Orefield, PA, letter to Kay Norton, Kansas City, MO, 12 July 1991.

13. Fred Steiner, New York, letter to Normand Lockwood, Oberlin, 6 July 1943, Normand Lockwood Private Papers.

14. Normand Lockwood, Denver, CO, letter to Kay Norton, Kansas City, MO, 16 August 1991.

15. Normand Lockwood, interview by Susan L. Porter in Denver, 14 July 1980, NLA Box 40.

16. Olaf C. Christiansen, Northfield, MN, letter to Normand Lockwood, Denver, CO, 23 April 1971. Normand Lockwood Commemorative Album, Normand Lockwood Private Papers.

17. Martha Smith, Cambridge, MA, letter to Normand Lockwood, Denver, CO, 24 April 1971. Normand Lockwood Commemorative Album, Normand Lockwood Private Papers.

18. Normand Lockwood, interview by Kay Norton in Denver, 9 August 1991.

19. "Oberlin's Prize-Winning Composer Highly Rated," *The Cleveland Plain Dealer,* 2 March 1935. Clipping, NLA, Box 40.

20. Ibid.

21. Carl Engel, *Modern Music* 12 (May-June 1935): 200-201.

22. Herbert Elwell, *Modern Music* 13 (4 May-June 1936): 48.

23. Peggy Glanville-Hicks, "De Paur Chorus," *The New York Herald Tribune,* 18 October 1954, 12.

24. NLA, Box 6.

25. Jean Riegger, New York, NY, letter to Normand Lockwood, Oberlin, OH, undated except for the year 1940. NLA Box 6.

26. Mabel Daniels, Boston, MA, letter to Normand Lockwood, Oberlin, OH, 15 March 1942. NLA Box 6.

27. Harold Taubman, "Sixth Music Period is Ended at Yaddo: Thirty-Eight Works by Thirty-Six Contemporary Composers are Played at Festival in Saratoga: Merit is Seen in Compositions by Normand Lockwood and David Diamond," *The New York Times,* 9 September 1940, 18 (L).

28. Ibid.

29. Normand Lockwood Personnel File, Oberlin College Archives. Photocopy from Roland Baumann, Archivist, Oberlin, OH to Kay Norton, Kansas City, MO, 15 July 1991.

30. Normand Lockwood, phone interview by Kay Norton, 19 July 1991.

31. Igor Stravinsky, *Stravinsky: Selected Correspondence, Vol. I*, ed. with commentary by Robert Craft (New York: Knopf, 1982), 266n-267n.

32. Normand Lockwood, Denver, CO, letter to Kay Norton, Kansas City, MO, 16 August 1991.

33. Sarah Moore, daughter of Lockwood's colleague and fellow composer Douglas Moore, wrote the text of *Mary, Who Stood in Sorrow.*

34. "Music Arrangers Present Concert," *New York Sun*, 29 September 1946, 14. Clipping, NLA Box 17.

35. Recordings of *Moby Dick*, a *Columbia Workshop* episode, are housed in two locations: at the Museum of Television and Radio, 1 East 57th Street, New York, NY 10022, and in the NLA, NB3.

36. Normand Lockwood, Denver, CO, letter to Karl Kroeger, Boulder, CO, 30 May 1991. NLA, Box NB3.

37. Lockwood did not serve in the war due to previous surgery and resultant back problems. Normand Lockwood, interview by Kay Norton in Denver, 22 September 1989.

38. NLA, Boxes IRREG 2 and 17.

39. H. Wiley Hitchcock and Stanley Sadie, eds. *The New Grove Dictionary of American Music* (London: Macmillan, 1986), s.v. "Awards," by Jane Gottlieb.

40. Otto Luening, *The Odyssey of an American Composer: The Autobiography of Otto Luening.* (New York: Charles Scribner's Sons, 1980), 455.

41. Pamphlet, Ditson Fund Award Winners, Normand Lockwood Private Papers.

42. Luening, 456.

43. Glenn Watkins, *Soundings: Music in the Twentieth Century.* (New York: Schirmer Books, a Division of Macmillan, 1988), 153.

44. As quoted in Luening, 456.

45. Holly Haswell, Archivist, Columbiana Collection, Columbia University, New York, NY, phone interview by Kay Norton, Kansas City, MO, 13 September 1991.

46. Emily Moore, New York, NY, undated letter to Normand Lockwood, Denver, CO. Normand Lockwood Commemorative Album, Normand Lockwood Private Papers.

47. Seth Kasten, Reference Librarian, Burke Library, Columbia University, New York, NY, letter to Kay Norton, Kansas City, MO, 16 July 1991.

48. Ibid.

49. Oliver Daniel, "New Recordings," *American Composers Alliance Bulletin* 4, no. 2 (1954): 15-16.

50. The recording was re-released by Varese Sarabande in 1978.

51. John Briggs, "Records: Works by Scriabin and Ives," *The New York Times*, 23 May 1954, 6(X).

52. Martin Bookspan, *The Jewish Advocate*[Boston], 3 June 1954.

Reprinted in *American Composers Alliance Bulletin* 4, no. 2 (1954): 15-16.

53. NLA, Box OV 9.

54. Austin C. Lovelace, Denver, CO, letter to Kay Norton, Kansas City, MO, 17 July 1991.

55. Program, Concert of Award Recipients' Music, National Institute of Arts and Letters, 1947. Normand Lockwood Private Papers.

56. Normand Lockwood, "Report of Committee on Programs," ACA, Normand Lockwood Private Papers.

57. Normand Lockwood, as quoted in Allen Young, 1984.

58. Oliver Daniel, Scarsdale, NY, letter to Normand Lockwood, Denver, 24 March 1979. Normand Lockwood Commemorative Album, Normand Lockwood Private Papers.

59. Normand Lockwood, phone interview by Kay Norton, 15 July 1991.

60. Oliver Daniel, "Lockwood," *American Composers Alliance Bulletin* 5, no. 1 (1955): 17.

61. Beveridge Webster, New York, letter to Normand Lockwood, Denver, 20 May 1979, Normand Lockwood Commemorative Album, Normand Lockwood Private Papers.

62. Roland Baumann, Archivist, Oberlin College Archives, Oberlin, OH, Photocopy to Kay Norton, Kansas City, MO, 15 July 1991.

63. Charles Harvey Schisler, "A History of Westminster Choir College, 1926-1973" (Ph.D. diss., Indiana University, 1976), 465ff.

64. Normand Lockwood, Denver, CO, letter to Kay Norton, Kansas City, MO, 3-5 October 1991.

65. *Bulletin of Yale University: School of Music for the Academic Year 1952-1953* (New Haven, CT: Yale University, 1952), 5.

66. Normand Lockwood, Denver, CO, letter to Kay Norton, Kansas City, MO, 3-5 October 1991.

67. Robert MacKinnon, Stanford, CA, letter to Normand Lockwood, Denver, CO, 20 April 1971. Normand Lockwood Commemorative Album, Normand Lockwood Private Papers.

68. Fred Waring Glee Club, tour program, NLA, Box 3.

69. Charles A. Sink, Ann Arbor, letter to Normand Lockwood, Denver, 26 April 1971. Normand Lockwood Commemorative Album, Normand Lockwood Private Papers.

70. J. Dorsey Callaghan, "Choral Work Enthralls Ann Arbor," *Detroit Free Press*, 4 May 1953, 33.

71. Harvey Taylor, "Acclaim Soprano at May Festival," *The Detroit Times*, 4 May 1953, 7.

72. Heidi Lockwood, interview by Kay Norton in Long Beach, CA, 5 August 1991.

73. Normand Lockwood, interview by Kay Norton in Denver, 9 August 1991.

74. Heidi Lockwood, interview by Kay Norton in Long Beach, CA, 5 August 1991.

75. *Musical America* 14 (January 1954): 23.

76. Robert Washburn, Potsdam, NY, letter to Kay Norton, Kansas City, MO, 15 July 1991.

Chapter Four--MID-CAREER

1. Normand Lockwood, interview by Kay Norton in Kansas City, MO, 16 September 1991.

2. George Lynn, "Normand Lockwood and Choral Music," *American Composers Alliance Bulletin* 6, no.4 (1957): 3.

3. Clara Chassell Cooper, Berea, KY, letter to Normand Lockwood, Denver, CO, 26 April 1971.

4. Johnson's *Children of God* score, bearing his performance markings, is included in NLA, Box OV 11.

5. Bill Lichtenwanger, "Thor Johnson: A Personal Memoir," essay in *A Celebration of American Music: Words and Music in Honor of H. Wiley Hitchcock*, ed. by Richard Crawford, R. Allen Lott, and Carol J. Oja. (Ann Arbor: University of Michigan Press, 1989), 101.

6. Published choruses from *Children of God* include "Return to the Lord," "See What Love," "Sermon on the Mount," and "Service Music," including three choruses: 1. "Seek the Lord and Live, 2. "The Mouth of the Lord has Spoken," 3. "Let the Peoples Praise Thee." NLA, Box 32.

7. Normand Lockwood, interview by Kay Norton in Denver, 5 May 1988.

8. Josef Krips, Buffalo, NY, letter to Normand Lockwood, Laramie, WY, 26 November 1958, NLA, Box OV 3. The oratorio was recorded in performance by Howell Recording Studio of Buffalo, J8-OP-5663. NLA, Box OV 3.

9. NLA, Box 34.

10. Normand Lockwood, interview by Kay Norton in Denver, 5 May 1988.

11. "Normand Lockwood: Principal Works and Biographical Note," *American Composers Alliance Bulletin* 6, no. 4 (1957): 5.

12. Dexter's article, "The Organization of a Co-operative Commissioning Program," details this interchange with Lockwood. *American Choral Review* 1, no. 4 (Fall 1958): 1.

13. John Dexter, Rochester, NY, letter to Normand Lockwood, Denver, CO, 26 April 1971.

14. William Wood, Albuquerque, NM, letter to Kay Norton, Kansas City, MO, 5 July 1991. Emphases original.

15. Normand Lockwood, publicity release for KVOD radio, Denver. Normand Lockwood Private Papers.

16. Daniel Moe, Oberlin, OH, phone interview by Kay Norton, 12 September 1991. Although the date of this meeting is uncertain, it occurred prior to the publication of the work mentioned. *Hosanna to the Son of David* was published in 1956 by Mercury Music Corpora-

tion, a division of Theodore Presser Company, in "The Green Lake Choral Series." George Lynn was the editor of the series.

17. Frank Hruby, "May Festival Impressive," *Musical America* 80 (July 1960): 13.

18. "Composer Lockwood," *The Sunday Star-Bulletin* [Honolulu], 17 July 1960, 7 (Women's Section).

19. R. Russell Porter, as quoted in Randolph P. McDonough, ed., *The University of Denver Pioneer* 11, no. 4 (August 1961): 11.

20. Normand Lockwood, as quoted in Larry Tajiri, "Premiere for New Opera," *The Denver Post*, 4 August 1961, 30.

21. NLA, Box 9.

22. Ibid.

23. Russell Porter, Denver, CO, letter to Normand Lockwood, Honolulu, HI, 20 January 1961. NLA, Box 9.

24. Normand Lockwood, Honolulu, HI, letter to Russell Porter, Denver, CO, 23 January 1961. Emphasis original. NLA, Box 9.

25. Norman D. Rian, Honolulu, HI, letter to Normand Lockwood, Denver, CO, 29 April 1971. Normand Lockwood Commemorative Album, Normand Lockwood Private Papers.

26. Broadcast Music, Incorporated, promotional pamphlet on Normand Lockwood's music, n.d. Normand Lockwood Private Papers. In this case, "published" refers not only to works published by commercial houses, but works available in facsimile edition from the American Composers Alliance.

27. Suzanne L. Moulton-Gertig, Assistant Professor of Music, Lamont School of Music, Denver, CO, letter to Kay Norton, Kansas City, MO, 23 August 1991.

28. *Cervi's Rocky Mountain Journal* (8 August 1962), as quoted in "Normand Lockwood," *American Composers Alliance Bulletin* 11, nos. 2-4 (December 1963): 36-37.

29. Russell Porter, Denver, CO, letter to Normand Lockwood, Denver, CO, 21 April 1971. Normand Lockwood Commemorative Album, Normand Lockwood Private Papers.

30. Normand Lockwood, interview by Kay Norton in Denver, 7 June 1989.

31. Programs, NLA, Box OV 5.

32. Anne Warriner, *Cervi's Rocky Mountain Journal*, as quoted in *Broadcast Music, Incorporated*, 1965.

33. Richard S. Parks, Detroit, MI, letter to Professor Curnow (chair of the Lockwood honorary committee), Denver, CO, 10 January 1977. Normand Lockwood Commemorative Album, Normand Lockwood Private Papers.

34. Kevin Kennedy, Denver, CO, letter to Kay Norton, Kansas City, MO, 18 July 1991.

35. Sharon Lohse Kunitz, Albuquerque, NM, letter to Kay Norton, Kansas City, MO, 20 July 1991.

Chapter Five--RETIREMENT AND REFLECTION

1. Normand Lockwood Commemorative Album, Normand Lockwood Private Papers.

2. Normand Lockwood, as quoted in Barbara Haddad Ryan, "World Premieres Top Concert List," *The Rocky Mountain News*, 4 March 1979, 36.

3. William Hoskins, Jacksonville, FL, letter to Kay Norton, Kansas City, MO, 8 August 1991.

4. Normand Lockwood, Denver, CO, letter to Kay Norton, Kansas City, MO, 4 June 1991.

5. Normand Lockwood, interview by Kay Norton in Kansas City, MO, 16 September 1991.

6. Carl Engel, *Modern Music* 12 (May-June 1935): 200-201.

7. John Briggs, "Records: Works by Scriabin and Ives," *The New York Times*, 23 May 1954, 6 (X).

8. Normand Lockwood, interview by Kay Norton in Denver, CO, 22 September 1989.

9. Normand Lockwood, "On Reading and Setting Whitman," *Pan Pipes* 54 (January 1962): 27. Uppercase in original.

10. Normand Lockwood, as quoted in Oliver Daniel, "Lockwood," *American Composers Alliance Bulletin* 5, no. 1 (1955): 17.

11. Normand Lockwood, interview by Kay Norton in Denver, CO, 2 June 1991.

12. Normand Lockwood, interview by Kay Norton in Denver, CO, 18 February 1988.

13. Normand Lockwood, interview by Kay Norton in Denver, CO, 3 March 1988.

14. Normand Lockwood, Music Review, *Music Library Association Notes* 4, no. 3 (June 1947): 362.

15. Kevin Kennedy, Denver, CO, letter to Kay Norton, Kansas City, MO, 18 July 1991.

16. Normand Lockwood, as quoted in Thomas MacCluskey, "Musical Musings: Concert for Lockwood," *The Rocky Mountain News*, 16 May 1971.

17. Normand Lockwood, interview by Kay Norton in Denver, CO, 24 March 1988.

18. Normand Lockwood, Denver, CO, letter to Kay Norton, Boulder, CO, 1 October 1989.

Chapter Six--CHORAL MUSIC

1. The following studies have addressed these and many of the other choral works to be discussed in this chapter:
T. M. Davis. *A Study of Stylistic Characteristics in Selected Major Choral Works of Normand Lockwood.* DMA Diss., The University of Missouri, Kansas City, 1980.
George Lynn. "Normand Lockwood and Choral Music," *American Composers Alliance Bulletin* 6, no. 4 (1957): 3-6.
James McCray. "Normand Lockwood's Choral Music with

Keyboard Accompaniment," *The Diapason* 73, no. 3 (July 1982): 3-14.

Curtis Sprenger. *A Study of the Text Music Relationships in the Choral Works of Jean Berger, Cecil Effinger, and Normand Lockwood.* EdD Diss., Colorado State College, Greeley, 1969.

2. Robert Stevenson, "Diverging Currents," chap. in *Protestant Church Music in America* (New York: W. W. Norton, 1966), 122.

3. Part III of this book, Catalog of Music, includes a publisher list.

4. Jacob Evanson, "Foreword" to Normand Lockwood, *Dirge for Two Veterans* (New York: M. Witmark and Sons, 1937), 6-7.

5. Evanson, 7.

6. Normand Lockwood, interview by Kay Norton in Denver, 24 March 1988.

7. Normand Lockwood, interview by Kay Norton in Denver, 19 February 1988, emphases original.

8. H. Wiley Hitchcock and Stanley Sadie, eds. *The New Grove Dictionary of American Music.* (London: Macmillan, 1986), s.v. "Randall Thompson," by Elliott Forbes.

9. Normand Lockwood, interview by Kay Norton in Denver, 5 May 1988.

10. Ibid.

11. The "Paumanok" pattern is so named by the author because it appears first in Lockwood's short, secular piece of 1939, *Out of the*

Cradle Endlessly Rocking. This setting of a Walt Whitman text, to be addressed in detail in the following section, opens with the text, "Once Paumanok, When lilac scent was in the air." Paumanok is an American Indian word meaning "fish-shaped," and was once used as a name for Long Island, New York. The Paumanok pattern, often occurring at the outset of a movement or piece, consists of a close-position alternation between a second-inversion tonic chord and a second-inversion seventh chord on the supertonic scale degree. The rhythmic content of the pattern is variable.

12. Louise Cuyler, "May Festival Season Closes Brilliantly; Lockwood Work Given World Premiere," *The Ann Arbor News*, 4 May 1953, 6.

13. Russell MacLaughlin, "May Festival Concludes with Melodious Week," *The Detroit News*, 4 May 1953, 30.

14. Normand Lockwood, interview by Kay Norton in Denver, 24 March 1988.

15. Lockwood's particular brand of serialism usually relies on specific octave position, unlike strict Schoenbergian serialism. The terms "pitch class" and "interval class" are avoided in this discussion to reflect Lockwood's distinctive use of these procedures.

16. Mary Leighton, "National Report," *Musical America* 77 (April 1957): 10.

17. Davis, 39.

18. Lynn, 3.

19. The octatonic scale is a pattern consisting of alternating half- and whole-steps.

20. Augmented fourth intervals and diminished harmonies are natural derivatives of the octatonic scale.

21. Archibald T. Davison, *The Technique of Choral Composition* (Cambridge: Harvard University Press, 1945), 42-3.

22. Recording of *Light Out of Darkness* by Normand Lockwood. Recorded in performance by Buffalo Schola Cantorum and Buffalo Philharmonic Orchestra, under the direction of Josef Krips. Buffalo: Howell Recording Studio, J8-OP-5663. NLA, Box OV 3. For Krips's remarks, see Chapter Four.

23. Berna Bergholtz, "Buffalo Philharmonic Plays First Commissioned Works," *Musical America* 78 (July 1958): 5.

24. Normand Lockwood, interview by Kay Norton in Denver, 5 May 1988.

25. *Life Triumphant* was commissioned by the University Musical Society of the University of Michigan, in memory of Thor Johnson, who for thirty years was guest conductor of the University Choral Union at the Society's May Festivals. Johnson premiered Lockwood's *Prairie* at a University Musical Society May Festival in 1953. (May Festival Program, 26 June 1976, NLA, Box OV 4).

26. Normand Lockwood, "Suggestions for the Choreographer," *Choreographic Cantata*. (Minneapolis: Augsburg Publishing House, 1970), vi.

27. Normand Lockwood, "On Reading and Setting Whitman," *Pan Pipes* 54, no. 2 (January 1962): 27.

28. Review of "Elegy for a Hero" by Normand Lockwood. *American Composers Alliance Bulletin* 2, no. 4 (Winter 1952-53): 22.

29. Normand Lockwood, interview by Kay Norton in Denver, 3 March 1988.

30. Ibid.

31. Ibid.

32. Ibid.

33. Ibid.

34. Ibid.

35. Normand Lockwood, "In the Midst of Life," *Choreographic Cantata*, tr. by Harold Heiberg. (Minneapolis: Augsburg Publishing House, 1970), 13-16.

36. Normand Lockwood, Denver, CO, letter to Kay Norton, Boulder, CO, 19 February 1988, KN Private Collection.

37. Evanson, 6.

38. Lockwood, "On Reading and Setting Whitman," 27.

39. Normand Lockwood, interview by Kay Norton in Denver, 19 February 1988.

40. Ibid.

41. Numbers in parentheses indicate line numbers in Whitman's poem. Lines appear consecutively in the poem unless otherwise noted. Bracketed text was not used by Lockwood.

42. Normand Lockwood, interview by Kay Norton in Denver, 19 February 1988.

43. Lockwood, "On Reading and Setting Whitman," 29.

44. Normand Lockwood, interview by Kay Norton in Denver, 18 February 1988.

45. Ibid.

46. Ibid.

47. Programs, NLA, Box 6.

48. Lynn, 3, emphases original.

Chapter Seven--KEYBOARD WORKS

1. These works are housed in NLA, Box NB 1.

2. See Chapter Six.

3. Normand Lockwood, interview by Kay Norton in Denver, 1 August 1988.

4. Ibid.

5. Vincent Persichetti, *Harmony: Creative Aspects and Practice*, (New York: W. W. Norton, 1961), 268.

6. NLA, Box 21.

7. Normand Lockwood, interview by Kay Norton in Denver, 1 August 1988.

8. Charles Mills, "Over the Air," *Modern Music* 21, no. 3 (Mar-April 1944): 191.

9. NLA, Box 21.

10. Normand Lockwood, Cover Sheet (1987), *Six Piano Pieces*, NLA, Box 21.

11. John Kirkpatrick, Ithaca, NY, letter to Normand Lockwood, New York, 2 February 1947, NLA, Box 21.

12. Ibid.

13. Ibid.

14. Lockwood may still have been influenced by Stravinsky's music, since the latter's *Sonata for Two Pianos* (1943-44) exploits similar serial techniques.

15. Normand Lockwood, interview by Kay Norton in Denver, August 1, 1988. "Turns" may be interpreted as changes in linear direction.

16. Programs, NLA, Box OV 9.

17. E. Power Biggs, as quoted in Barbara Owen, *E. Power Biggs, Concert Organist.* (Bloomington: Indiana University Press, 1987): 55.

18. Ibid.

19. Normand Lockwood, as quoted in Glenn Giffin, "Organ Premiere Has No Choir," *The Denver Post*, 19 November 1976, 29.

20. Ibid.

21. This hymn tune also inspired a memorable movement in his *Choreographic Suite for String Orchestra* (1986).

22. Normand Lockwood, interview by Kay Norton in Denver, 4 February 1988.

23. Ibid.

24. Ibid.

25. Unsigned jacket notes to *Concerto for Organ and Brasses*, Remington Records, R-199-173, 1953.

26. The second phrase of "Langdon" bears a marked similarity to another of Lockwood's favorite hymn tunes, "Old Hundredth."

27. Normand Lockwood, interview by Kay Norton in Denver, 4 February 1988.

28. Normand Lockwood, as quoted in Giffin, "Organ Premiere Has No Choir," 29.

Chapter Eight--CHAMBER WORKS

1. The works for string quartet are discussed later in this chapter. Works for string groups other than string quartets are included in the present discussion.

2. Several of Lockwood's works with chamber instrumentation are discussed and/or catalogued with other chapters for various reasons. *Le Chateau Overture* (1948) and *The Church at Ripton* (1949) are discussed in the chapter on instrumental ensemble music. *Funeral Service* (1988) for soli S, A, T, B and instruments, appears with the choral chapter. Finally, seven pieces were written for solo voice and instruments and were catalogued with the solo songs: *I Have Painted Elijah* (1943), *I Know Starlight* (1952), *Irish Songs*

(1950), *Love's Secret* (1943), *Memories of President Lincoln: When Lilacs Last in the Dooryard Bloom'd* (1920s), *O Lord, Our Lord* (1960), and *(sitting in a tree--)* (1943).

3. The "Paumanok" pattern consists of a homophonic, close-position set of harmonies, beginning with and unified by a recurring second-inversion tonic triad. For a discussion of *Out of the Cradle Endlessly Rocking* and its importance in Lockwood's pool of musical materials, refer to Chapter Six.

4. Persichetti, 264.

5. As mentioned in previous chapters, Lockwood normally departs from strict, Schoenbergian serialism, which presupposes non-specific octave registers.

6. Elsie Bennett, "Normand Lockwood--A Composer Who Listens," *Accordion Times and Modern Musician* (April-May 1969): 8.

7. Frank Hruby, "National Report," *Musical America* 80 (July 1960): 13.

8. Score, *Trio for Violin Cello, and Piano*, NLA, Box 25.

9. *String Quartet 1992* was in progress at the time of this writing, and is therefore not analyzed.

10. The *Third String Quartet* is also frequently called the *String Quartet in D Minor, Number Two*.

11. Review of *D Minor Quartet Number Two* [sic] by Normand Lockwood. *The Cleveland News*, 9 March 1940. Clipping, NLA, Box 26.

12. Herbert Elwell, "Walden Quartet Scores in 'Birthday' Concert," *The Cleveland Plain Dealer*, 5 December 1944. Clipping, NLA Box 26.

13. A. J. Warner, "[Gordon] Quartet Applauded at Festival," *Rochester Times Union*, 13 April 1946, 5.

14. The date assigned *String Quartet Number Six* comes from the records of the American Composers Alliance, Lockwood's primary repository of music. Providing conflicting information about its compositional date is an April, 1947 program for the Seventeenth Annual Festival of American Music at The Eastman School of Music that states: "Mr. Lockwood finished work on this quartet in 1944. [Eastman's] Gordon Quartet gave the first performance in March, 1947 at the Fourth Festival of American Music at the National Gallery in Washington." The National Gallery performance was on March 2, 1947, at which *Number Six* appeared alongside *Quartet Number One* by John Verrall and *Quartet Number One* by Randall Thompson. NLA, Box 27.

15. Ross Parmenter, "Music Fete Opens at Falls Village," *The New York Times*, 23 June 1952, 16.

16. Manuscript, NLA, Box 27.

17. Lou Harrison, "Modernism 'Sacred and Profane,'" *Modern Music* 23 (Summer 1946): 205. Emphases original.

18. Lejaren Hiller, Jacket Notes to "American String Quartets," III (1950-1970), Vox Productions, Inc., SVBX 5306.

19. Charles Cushing, "The International Society for Contemporary Music in California," *Modern Music* 20 (November-December 1942): 45.

20. The highest note of this passage is the second F-flat above middle C.

21. Review of *Six Serenades for String Quartet* by Normand Lockwood, *New York Herald Tribune*, 14 January 1953, 23. The work appeared at the Lexington Avenue (New York) Young Men's and Young Women's Hebrew Association, and was played by instrumentalists from the Bennington, Vermont, Composers Conference.

Chapter Nine--SOLO SONGS

1. The precise dates of these arrangements and recordings are unknown, although they were composed during Lockwood's New York period, 1943-1953. NLA, Box IRREG 2.

2. See Catalog of Music for dedications of the vocal works.

3. Works with no designation, but in which the solo line is notated in treble clef, are presumed to be written for soprano and piano.

4. Normand Lockwood, interview by Kay Norton in Denver, 24 February 1989.

5. Composer John Duke also found inspiration in Crapsey's poetry, setting her "Rapunzel" to music in 1935.

6. Crapsey derived her original poetic form, the cinquain, from concise Japanese verse.

7. Normand Lockwood, "Arbutus," *Five Cinquains of Adelaide Crapsey*, NLA, Box 16.

8. Lockwood's title for the Teasdale text is *I Asked the Heaven of Stars.* NLA, Box 17.

9. Ruth Friedberg, *American Art Song and American Poetry: Volume II, Voices of Maturity* (Metuchen, NJ: The Scarecrow Press, 1984), 109.

10. H. Wiley Hitchcock and Stanley Sadie, eds. *The New Grove Dictionary of American Music.* (London: Macmillan, 1986), s.v. "Normand Lockwood," by Susan L. Porter.

11. Rubén Darío is the pen name of Félix Rubén García (1867-1916), a key contributor to the foundation of literary modernism.

12. Normand Lockwood, "The Grand Canyon," *Five Cinquains of Adelaide Crapsey.* NLA, Box 16.

13. See Chapter Six.

14. Normand Lockwood, *The Dialogue of Abraham and Isaac.* NLA, Box 16.

15. Normand Lockwood, interview by Kay Norton in Denver, 24 February 1989.

16. June R. Boyd, Cassette Tape of "Lecture Recital of Normand Lockwood's Music," 1 June 1988, Greeley, Colorado. NLA, Box IRREG 2.

17. Normand Lockwood, interview by Kay Norton in Denver, 24 February 1989.

18. Peggy Glanville-Hicks, "Parker Recital," *The New York Herald Tribune,* 29 March 1948. Clipping, NLA, Box 19.

19. Normand Lockwood, *Fallen Is Babylon the Great, Hallelujah!* NLA, Box 16.

20. Ibid.

21. The Paumanok pattern consists of a close-position alternation between a second-inversion tonic chord and a second-inversion seventh chord on the supertonic scale degree. The rhythmic content of the pattern is variable.

22. *Apple Orchards* is a choral piece for mixed or treble voices, published by Shawnee Press in 1952.

23. Normand Lockwood, Memo regarding *Four Songs--A Cycle.* NLA, Box 16.

24. Normand Lockwood, "The Texts," *Four Songs--A Cycle.* NLA, Box 17.

25. Normand Lockwood, interview by Kay Norton in Denver, 24 February 1989.

26. Boyd, NLA, Box IRREG 2.

27. Normand Lockwood, "On Parting ...," *Four Poems of Liu Chang-Ch'ing,* Title page. NLA, Box 16.

28. Normand Lockwood, "A Farewell to a Buddhist Monk," *Four Poems of Liu Chang-Ch'ing,* title page. NLA, Box 16.

29. Score, "The Stranger," NLA Box 17.

30. Score, *To Margarita Debayle,* NLA Box 19.

31. Boyd. NLA Box IRREG 2.

32. Score, *To Margarita Debayle*, NLA Box 19.

33. Normand Lockwood, interview by Kay Norton in Denver, 24 February 1989.

34. Friedberg, 5.

35. Ibid.

Chapter Ten--INSTRUMENTAL MUSIC

1. Normand Lockwood, interview by Kay Norton in Denver, 9 November 1989.

2. "Without a shirt" is a vernacular "tag" added to tunes of the day much in the same way as the "shave, hair-cut" tag might have been used.

3. Normand Lockwood, *Symphony* (1941), NLA, Boxes 29-30.

4. Willcox had been head of the Architecture Department at the University of Oregon prior to Lockwood's short tenure there.

5. Deborah Long, American Composers Alliance, New York, letter to Kay Norton, Boulder, 14 November 1989. Kay Norton Private Papers.

6. *Normand Lockwood* (promotional pamphlet), Broadcast Music, Incorporated. Normand Lockwood Private Collection.

7. Ibid.

8. In conversing about this work, Lockwood frequently described his intended timbres in colorful terms; "oily" described the appropriate sound for the B-flat clarinet. Interview by Kay Norton in Denver, 9 November 1989.

9. Lockwood stated, "There is a lot of David Karp in the piece." Interview by Kay Norton in Denver, 9 November 1989.

10. Because Lockwood was offered an unexpected opportunity to have the *Piano Concerto* performed at a composer's conference in Johnson, Vermont, David Karp did not play the premiere performance. Pianist Zita Carno premiered the work during the conference in the summer of 1973; Karp's first performance followed shortly thereafter.

11. David Karp, Dallas, letter to Normand Lockwood, Denver, 8 December 1975. NLA, Box OV 7.

12. David Karp, interview by Teresa Chivoni on KVOD radio, Boulder, Colorado, 15 November 1988.

13. Normand Lockwood, *Piano Concerto*. NLA, Box OV 7.

14. Glenn Giffin, "Music Leader Lockwood Finally Gets Denver Premiere," *The Denver Post*, 16 November 1988, 2(C).

15. Normand Lockwood, Program Notes, *Symphony for Large Orchestra*, The (Denver, CO) Community Arts Symphony, 21 November 1980. NLA, Box OV 10.

16. Allen Young, "Young and Old Bring Zest to Community Arts Concert," *Rocky Mountain News*, 2 February 1986, 6(E).

17. Normand Lockwood, as quoted by Thomas MacCluskey, Program Notes, *Panegyric for String Orchestra*, Arapahoe Chamber Orchestra, 1 February 1981, 1-2. NLA OV 10.

18. Score, NLA, Box OV 6.

19. Ibid.

20. Lockwood's original title for the work is *Coming of the Spirits.*

21. Normand Lockwood, Cover Sheet, *Return of the Spirits.* NLA, Box 31.

22. W. Terry, Jacket Notes to William Schuman, *Undertow.* New World Records, Recorded Anthology of American Music, Inc., 1978, 2.

23. Harvey E. Phillips, Jacket Notes to Peter Mennin, *Symphony Number 7: Variations Symphony*, New World Records, Recorded Anthology of American Music, Inc., 1976, 4.

Chapter Eleven--OPERA AND NON-OPERATIC THEATER MUSIC

1. Orchestral scores for the operas are held in the Special Collections section of the Penrose Library, University of Denver, Denver, Colorado. Any references to instrumentation presume this location, except in the cases of *The Scarecrow* and *Requiem for a Rich Young Man.* Full scores for these operas are included in the Normand Lockwood Archive.

2. Gilbert Chase, *America's Music: From the Pilgrims to the Present*, 3rd. ed., rev. (Urbana: University of Illinois Press, 1987), 545.

3. Hawthorne's subtitle for "Feathertop."

4. Percy MacKaye, *The Scarecrow: Or The Glass of Truth, A Tragedy of the Ludicrous.* (New York: Macmillan Company, 1908), xi-xii. Emphases original.

5. MacKaye, xii. Emphases original.

6. Ibid.

7. MacKaye, xv.

8. S. L. M. Barlow, "In the Theatre," *Modern Music* 22 (May-June 1945): 277.

9. Normand Lockwood, interview by Kay Norton in Denver, 7 June 1989.

10. Mark A. Schubart, "Lockwood Opera Given at Columbia," *The New York Times*, 10 May 1945, 19.

11. Ibid.

12. Normand Lockwood, phone interview, Denver, March 14, 1989.

13. NLA, Box 9.

14. Thomas Scherman, as quoted in Larry Tajiri, "Premiere for New Opera," *The Denver Post*, 4 August 1961, 30.

15. Robert W. Dumm, "*Early Dawn* in Denver," *Christian Science Monitor* (September 11, 1961): 6.

16. NLA, Box 9.

17. Normand Lockwood/Russell Porter, *Early Dawn*, piano-vocal score, I, 6; II, 5; III, 4-6. NLA, Box 9.

18. Ibid.

19. Ibid.

20. Ibid.

21. Marc Blitzstein, "Comments," *Distinguished Composer Series* Number 717, Westminster Spoken Arts, Inc, 1956.

22. Ibid.

23. Normand Lockwood, *Early Dawn*, I, 119. NLA, Box 9.

24. Max Price, "Impressive Premiere Given Opera," *The Denver Post*, 8 August 1961, 51.

25. Tevye is the central character in *Fiddler on the Roof* by Joseph Stein, Sheldon Harnick, and Jerry Bock.

26. Normand Lockwood as quoted in Larry Tajiri, "DU Readies Musical Play," *The Denver Post*, 20 November 1962, 44.

27. R. Russell Porter, *No More From Thrones*, c. 1962. NLA, Box 15.

28. Ibid., handwritten note on libretto.

29. Lockwood prefers the original title, *The Inevitable Hour.* NLA, Box 10.

30. Normand Lockwood, interview by Kay Norton in Denver, June 7, 1989.

31. Normand Lockwood and Russell Porter, "About the Opera," premiere program of *The Hanging Judge*, The University of Denver, 6-7 March 1964. NLA, Box 10. Lockwood stated in an interview on June 7, 1989 that the disclaimer was principally a concern of Porter's.

32. Dennis Riley, "Hanging Judge Premiered Here," *Rocky Mountain News*, 8 March 1964, 3(A).

33. Unsigned review of *The Hanging Judge*, by Normand Lockwood. *Opera News*, 2 May 1964, 26.

34. Opening night program, *Requiem for a Rich Young Man*, by Normand Lockwood. NLA, Box 11.

35. Normand Lockwood, *Requiem*, Piano-vocal score, 6. NLA, Boxes 11 and 12.

36. Lockwood, *Requiem*, piano-vocal score, 67. NLA, Boxes 11 and 12.

37. Genevieve McGiffert, Denver, CO, letter to Normand Lockwood, 15 April 1964. NLA, Box 11.

38. Normand Lockwood, interview by Kay Norton in Denver, June 7, 1989.

39. Allen Young, *Opera News* 29, no. 11 (23 January 1965): 32.

40. Wayne Johnson, "Sardonic *Requiem* in First Performance," *The Denver Post*, 25 November 1964, 7.

41. NLA, Box 11.

42. Allen Young, "The Critics," *The Sentinel*, [Denver], 30 May 1974, 22.

43. Normand Lockwood, *My Sister, My Spouse*, #4, 2. NLA, Box 15.

44. Frances Melrose, "*My Sister, My Spouse* Overwritten," *Rocky Mountain News*, 28 October 1972, 177.

45. Ibid. and Allen Young, *Cherry Creek News*, 26 October 1972, 19, respectively.

46. Normand Lockwood, as quoted in Marjorie Barrett, "Normand Lockwood to have [Organ] Work Premiered at Colorado Women's College," *The Rocky Mountain News*, 15 November 1976, 28.

Bibliography

Articles

Barlow, S. L. M. "In the Theatre." *Modern Music* 22 (May-June 1945): 277.

Barrett, Marjorie. "Normand Lockwood to Have Work Premiered at Colorado Women's College." *Rocky Mountain News*, 15 November 1976. Clipping, NLA Box 28.

Bennett, Elsie. "Normand Lockwood--A Composer Who Listens." *Accordion Times and Modern Musician* (April-May 1969): 5-8.

Bergholtz, Berna. "Buffalo Philharmonic Plays First Commissioned Works." *Musical America* 78 (July 1958): 5.

Blomster, Wes. "A Tribute to Lockwood, Who Earned It." *The Sunday Camera* [Boulder, CO], 24 November 1985, 1(D) and 4(D).

Bookspan, Martin. *The Jewish Advocate* [Boston], 3 June 1954. Reprinted in *American Composers Alliance Bulletin* 4, no. 2 (1954): 15-16.

Briggs, John. "Records: Works by Scriabin and Ives." *The New York Times*, 23 May 1954, 6(X).

Callaghan, J. Dorsey. "Choral Work Enthralls Ann Arbor." *Detroit Free Press*, 4 May 1953, 33.

Cervi's Rocky Mountain Journal (8 August 1962), as quoted in "Normand Lockwood." *American Composers Alliance Bulletin* 11, nos. 2-4 (December 1963): 36-37.

"Composer Lockwood." *The Sunday Star-Bulletin* [Honolulu], 17 July 1960, 7 (Women's Section).

Cushing, Charles. "The International Society for Contemporary Music in California." *Modern Music* 20 (November-December 1942): 45.

Cuyler, Louise. "May Festival Season Closes Brilliantly; Lockwood Work Given World Premiere." *The Ann Arbor News*, 4 May 1953, 6.

Daniel, Oliver. "Lockwood." *American Composers Alliance Bulletin* 5, no. 1 (1955): 17.

_____. "New Recordings." *American Composers Alliance Bulletin* 4, no. 2 (1954): 15-16.

Dexter, John. "The Organization of a Co-operative Commissioning Program." *American Choral Review* 1, no. 4 (Fall 1958): 1.

Dumm, Robert W. "*Early Dawn* in Denver." *Christian Science Monitor*, 11 September 1961, 6.

Elwell, Herbert. *Modern Music* 13 (May-June 1936): 48.

_____. "Walden Quartet Scores in 'Birthday' Concert." *Cleveland Plain Dealer*, 5 December 1944. Clipping, NLA Box 27.

Engel, Carl. *Modern Music* 12 (May-June 1936): 200-201.

Epstein, Dena J. "Frederick Stock and American Music." *American Music* 10, no. 1 (Spring 1992): 20.

Giffin, Glenn. "Music Leader Lockwood Finally Gets Denver Premiere." *The Denver Post*, 16 November 1988, 2(C).

____. "Organ Premiere Has No Choir." *The Denver Post*, 19 November 1976, 29.

Glanville-Hicks, Peggy. "DePaur Chorus." *The New York Herald Tribune*, 18 October 1954, 12.

____. "Parker Recital." *The New York Herald Tribune*, 29 March 1948, 10.

Harrison, Lou. "Modernism 'Sacred and Profane.'" *Modern Music* 23 (Summer 1946): 205.

Hitchcock, H. Wiley and Stanley Sadie, eds. *The New Grove Dictionary of American Music.* London: Macmillan, 1986. S.v. "Awards," by Jane Gottlieb.

____. S.v. "Chamber Music After 1920," by Leonard Burkat and Gilbert Ross.

____. S.v. "Randall Thompson," by Elliott Forbes.

____. S.v. "Normand Lockwood," by Susan L. Porter.

Hruby, Frank. "May Festival Impressive." *Musical America* 80 (July 1960): 13.

Johnson, Wayne. "Sardonic *Requiem* in First Performance." *The Denver Post*, 25 November 1964, 7.

Kolodin, Irving. "Music to My Ears: Nadia Boulanger and Her Dynasty." *Saturday Review* (December 1979): 47.

Leighton, Mary. "National Report." *Musical America* 77 (April 1957): 10.

Lockwood, Normand. "Music Review." *Music Library Association Notes* 4, no. 3 (June 1947): 362.

Lockwood, Normand. "On Reading and Setting Whitman." *Pan Pipes* 54 (January 1962): 27-29.

Lynn, George. "Normand Lockwood and Choral Music." *American Composers Alliance Bulletin* 6, no. 4 (1957): 3-5.

MacCluskey, Thomas. "Musical Musings: Concert for Lockwood." *Rocky Mountain News*, 16 May 1971.

MacLaughlin, Russell. "May Festival Concludes with Melodious Week." *The Detroit News*, 4 May 1953, 30.

Matthews, W. S. B. *The Ann Arbor News*, 9 November 1933, 1 and 13.

McCray, James. "Normand Lockwood's Choral Music with Keyboard Accompaniment." *The Diapason* 73, no. 3 (July 1982): 3-14.

McDonough, Randolph P., ed. *The University of Denver Pioneer* 11 (August 1961): 11. Clipping, NLA Box 9.

McDowell, John. "A Note on Some Facets of Normand Lockwood's Music." *American Composers Alliance Bulletin* 4 (1957): 7-11.

Melrose, Frances. "*My Sister, My Spouse* Overwritten." *Rocky Mountain News*, 28 October 1972, 177.

Mills, Charles. "Over the Air." *Modern Music* 21 (Mar-April 1944): 191.

"Music Arrangers Present Concert." *New York Sun*, 29 September 1946, 14. Clipping, NLA Box 17.

Musical America 14 (January 1954): 23.

"Normand Lockwood: Principal Works and Biographical Note." *American Composers Alliance Bulletin* 6, no. 4 (1957): 5.

"Oberlin's Prize-Winning Composer Highly Rated." *The Cleveland Plain Dealer*, 2 March 1935. Clipping, NLA Box 40.

Parmenter, Ross. "Music Fete Opens at Falls Village." *The New York Times*, 23 June 1952, 16.

Price, Max. "Impressive Premiere Given Opera." *The Denver Post*, 8 August 1961, 51.

Review of *D Minor Quartet Number Two*, by Normand Lockwood. *The Cleveland News*, 9 March 1940. Clipping, NLA Box 27.

Review of *The Hanging Judge*, by Normand Lockwood. *Opera News* (2 May 1964): 26.

Review of *Six Serenades for String Quartet,* by Normand Lockwood. *New York Herald Tribune,* 14 January 1953, 23.

Riley, Dennis. "Hanging Judge Premiered Here." *Rocky Mountain
News,* 8 March 1964, 3(A).

Ryan, Barbara Haddad. "World Premieres Top Concert List."
Rocky Mountain News, 4 March 1979, 36.

Schubart, Mark A. "Lockwood Opera Given at Columbia." *The
New York Times,* 10 May 1945, 19.

Scott, Peggy. "Composer-in-Residence Helps Unlock Student
Musical Ability." *Southeast Missourian* [Cape Girardeau, MO],
19 March 1989, 7(A).

Tajiri, Larry. "Premiere for New Opera." *The Denver Post,* 4
August 1961, 30.

Tajiri, Larry. "DU Readies Musical Play." *The Denver Post,* 20
November 1962, 44.

Tapping, T. Hawley, ed. *The Michigan Alumnus,* 25 November
1933, 143.

Taubman, Harold. "Sixth Music Period is Ended at Yaddo: Thirty-
Eight Works by Thirty-Six Contemporary Composers are Played
at Festival in Saratoga: Merit is Seen in Compositions by
Normand Lockwood and David Diamond." *The New York
Times,* 9 September 1940, 18(L).

Taylor, Harvey. "Acclaim Soprano at May Festival." *The Detroit
Times,* 4 May 1953, 8.

Unsigned review of *Elegy for a Hero* by Normand Lockwood.
American Composers Alliance Bulletin 2, no. 4 (Winter 1952-53): 22.

Warner, A. J. "Quartet Applauded at Festival." *Rochester Times Union*, 13 April 1946, 5.

Warriner, Anne. *Cervi's Rocky Mountain Journal*, as quoted in *Broadcast Music, Inc.*, 1965.

Young, Allen. *Opera News* 29 (23 January 1965): 32.

_____. *Cherry Creek News* (26 October 1972): 19.

_____. "Children's Choir to Perform *A Child's Christmas in Wales.*" *City Edition* [Denver] (12-19 December 1984), 31.

_____. "The Critics." *The Sentinel* [Denver], 30 May 1974. 22.

_____. "Young and Old Bring Zest to Community Arts Concert." *Rocky Mountain News*, 2 February 1986, 6(E).

Books

Chase, Gilbert. *America's Music: From the Pilgrims to the Present*, 3rd. ed., rev. Urbana: University of Illinois Press, 1987.

Cowell, Henry and Sidney Cowell. *Charles Ives and His Music.* New York: Oxford University Press, 1955.

Crawford, Richard. "Music at Michigan: A Historical Perspective." Chap. in *100 Years of Music at Michigan: 1880-1980.* Ann Arbor, MI: University of Michigan and Edwards Brothers, 1979.

Davison, Archibald T. *The Technique of Choral Composition.*
Cambridge: Harvard University Press, 1945.

Dox, Thurston. *American Oratorios and Cantatas.* Metuchen, NJ:
Scarecrow Press, 1982.

Friedberg, Ruth. *American Art Song and American Poetry:*
Volume II, Voices of Maturity. Metuchen, NJ: Scarecrow
Press, 1984.

Hitchcock, H. Wiley. *Music in the United States: A Historical*
Introduction, 3rd ed. Englewood Cliffs, NJ: Prentice-Hall, 1988.

Kirkpatrick, John, ed. *Charles E. Ives: Memos.* New York: W. W.
Norton & Co., 1972.

Lichtenwanger, Bill. "Thor Johnson: A Personal Memoir." Essay in
A Celebration of American Music: Words and Music in Honor
of H. Wiley Hitchcock, ed. by Richard Crawford, R. Allen Lott,
and Carol J. Oja. Ann Arbor: University of Michigan Press,
1989.

Lockwood, Samuel Pierson. *Elementary Orchestration.* Ann Arbor,
MI: George Wahr, 1926.

Luening, Otto. *The Odyssey of an American Composer: The*
Autobiography of Otto Luening. New York: Charles Scribner's
Sons, 1980.

MacKaye, Percy. *The Scarecrow: Or The Glass of Truth (A*
Tragedy of the Ludicrous). New York: Macmillan Company,
1908.

Monsaingeon, Bruno. *Mademoiselle: Conversations with Nadia*
Boulanger, trans. by Robyn Marsack. Manchester, Eng.:

Carcanet Press, 1985, first published as *Mademoiselle: entretiens avec Nadia Boulanger,* Editions Van de Velde, 1981.

Oja, Carol J., ed. *American Music Recordings: A Discography of Twentieth-Century United States Composers.* Brooklyn: Institute for Studies in American Music, 1982.

Owen, Barbara. *E. Power Biggs, Concert Organist.* Bloomington: Indiana University Press, 1987.

Persichetti, Vincent. *Twentieth-Century Harmony: Creative Aspects and Practice.* New York: W. W. Norton & Co., 1961.

Respighi, Elsa. *Ottorino Respighi: His Life Story Arranged by Elsa Respighi,* trans. by Gwyn Morris. London: G. Ricordi & Co., 1962.

Rosenstiel, Leonie. *Nadia Boulanger: A Life in Music.* New York: W. W. Norton, 1982.

Stevenson, Robert. *Protestant Church Music in America.* New York: W. W. Norton, 1966.

Stravinsky, Igor. *Stravinsky: Selected Correspondence, Vol I,* ed. with commentary by Robert Craft. New York: Knopf, 1982.

Warch, Willard. *Our First 100 Years: A Brief History of the Oberlin College Conservatory of Music.* Oberlin, OH: Oberlin College Conservatory of Music, 1967.

Watkins, Glenn. *Soundings: Music in the Twentieth Century.* New York: Schirmer Books, a Division of Macmillan, 1988.

Dissertations

Davis, T. M. *A Study of Stylistic Characteristics in Selected Major Choral Works of Normand Lockwood.* DMA diss., The University of Missouri, Kansas City, 1980.

Norton, Kay. *Normand Lockwood, 1930-1980: Fifty Years in American Composition.* Ph.D. diss., University of Colorado, Boulder, 1990.

Schisler, Charles Harvey. *A History of Westminster Choir College, 1926-1973.* Ph.D. diss., Indiana University, 1976.

Sprenger, Curtis. *A Study of the Text Music Relationships in the Choral Works of Jean Berger, Cecil Effinger, and Normand Lockwood.* Ed.D. diss., Colorado State College, Greeley, 1969.

Interviews

All interviews exist in taped and/or transcribed forms. Those conducted by Susan L. Porter are part of the Normand Lockwood Archive. All others are included in the author's private papers.

Karp, David. Interview by Teresa Chivoni on KVOD radio, Boulder, CO, 15 November 1988.

Lockwood, Heidi. Interview by Kay Norton in Long Beach, CA, 5 August 1991.

Lockwood, Normand. Interview by Susan L. Porter in Denver, 14 July 1980. NLA Box 40.

Lockwood, Normand. Interview by Kay Norton in Denver, 4 February 1988.

Ibid., 18 February 1988.

Ibid., 19 February 1988.

Ibid., 3 March 1988.

Ibid., 24 March 1988.

Ibid., 5 May 1988.

Ibid., 1 August 1988.

Ibid., 24 February 1989.

Ibid., 14 March 1989.

Ibid., 7 June 1989.

Ibid., 4 September 1989.

Ibid., 22 September 1989.

Ibid., 9 November 1989.

Lockwood, Normand. Rehearsal with Mary Louise Burke and Kay Norton, 4 March 1990.

Lockwood, Normand. Interview by Kay Norton in Denver, 2 June 1991.

Lockwood, Normand. Phone interview by Kay Norton, 15 July 1991.

____. Phone interview by Kay Norton, 19 July 1991.

Lockwood, Normand. Interview by Kay Norton in Denver, 9 August 1991.

Lockwood, Normand. Interview by Kay Norton in Kansas City, MO, 16 September 1991.

Lockwood, Vona. Interview by Kay Norton in Denver, 4 September 1989.

Moe, Daniel, Oberlin, OH, phone interview by Kay Norton, 12 September 1991.

Letters

Letters to the author remain in her private papers.

Boatwright, Howard and Helen Boatwright, Syracuse, NY, letter to Normand Lockwood, Denver, 22 April 1971. Normand Lockwood Commemorative Album, NL Private Papers.

Boulanger, Nadia, Garvenville, France, letter to Normand Lockwood, Oberlin, OH, 9 September 1932. NLA Box 39.

Boulanger, Nadia, Paris, letter to Normand Lockwood, Oberlin, OH, 16 October 1938. NLA Box 39.

Christiansen, Olaf C., Northfield, MN, letter to Normand Lockwood, Denver, 23 April 1971. Normand Lockwood Commemorative Album, NL Private Papers.

Christiansen, Paul, Moorhead, MN, letter to Normand Lockwood, Denver, April 1971. Normand Lockwood Commemorative Album, NL Private Papers.

Cooper, Clara Chassell, Berea, KY, letter to Normand Lockwood, Denver, 26 April 1971. Normand Lockwood Commemorative Album, NL Private Papers.

Daniel, Oliver, Scarsdale, NY, letter to Normand Lockwood, Denver, 24 March 1979. Normand Lockwood Commemorative Album, NL Private Papers.

Daniels, Mabel, Boston, MA, letter to Normand Lockwood, Oberlin, OH, 15 March 1942. NLA Box 6.

Dexter, John, Rochester, NY, letter to Normand Lockwood, Denver, 26 April 1971.

Hoskins, William, Jacksonville, FL, letter to Kay Norton, Kansas City, MO, 8 August 1991.

Karp, David, Dallas, letter to Normand Lockwood, Denver, 8 December 1975. NLA Box OV 7.

Kasten, Seth, Reference Librarian, Burke Library, Columbia University, New York, letter to Kay Norton, Kansas City, MO, 16 July 1991.

Kennedy, Kevin, Denver, letter to Kay Norton, Kansas City, MO, 18 July 1991.

Kirkpatrick, John, Ithaca, NY, letter to Normand Lockwood, New York, 2 February 1947. NLA Box 21.

Krips, Josef, Buffalo, letter to Normand Lockwood, Laramie, 26 November 1958. NLA Box OV 3.

Kunitz, Sharon Lohse, Albuquerque, NM, letter to Kay Norton, Kansas City, MO, 20 July 1991.

Lenel, Ludwig, Orefield, PA, letter to Kay Norton, Kansas City, MO, 12 July 1991.

Lockwood, Normand, Honolulu, letter to Russell Porter, Denver, 23 January 1961. NLA Box 9.

Lockwood, Normand, Denver, letter to Karl Kroeger, Boulder, CO, 30 May 1991. NLA Box NB3.

Lockwood, Normand, Denver, letter to Kay Norton, Boulder, CO, 19 February 1988.

Lockwood, Normand, Denver, letter to Kay Norton, Boulder, CO, 7 September 1989.

Lockwood, Normand, Denver, letter to Kay Norton, Boulder, CO, 1 October 1989.

Lockwood, Normand, Denver, letter to Kay Norton, Kansas City, MO, 4 June 1991.

Lockwood, Normand, Denver, letter to Kay Norton, Kansas City, MO, 16 August 1991.

Lockwood, Normand, Denver, letter to Kay Norton, Kansas City, MO, 3-5 October 1991.

Long, Deborah, New York, letter to Kay Norton, Boulder, CO, 14 November 1989.

Lovelace, Austin, Denver, letter to Kay Norton, Kansas City, MO, 17 July 1991.

MacKinnon, Robert, Stanford, CA, letter to Normand Lockwood, Denver, 20 April 1971. Normand Lockwood Commemorative Album, NL Private Papers.

McGiffert, Genevieve, Denver, letter to Normand Lockwood, Denver, 15 April 1964. NLA Box 11.

Mennin, Peter, New York, letter to Normand Lockwood, Denver, 23 April 1971. Normand Lockwood Commemorative Album, NL Private Papers.

Moore, Emily, New York, undated letter to Normand Lockwood, Denver. Normand Lockwood Commemorative Album, NL Private Papers.

Moulton-Gertig, Suzanne L., Denver, letter to Kay Norton, Kansas City, MO, 23 August 1991.

Parks, Richard S., Detroit, MI, letter to Professor Curnow (Chair of the Lockwood Honorary Committee), Denver, 10 January 1977. Normand Lockwood Commemorative Album, NL Private Papers.

Porter, R. Russell, Denver, letter to Normand Lockwood, Honolulu, 20 January 1961. NLA Box 9.

Porter, R. Russell, Denver, letter to Normand Lockwood, Honolulu, 17 April 1961. NLA Box 9.

Porter, R. Russell, Denver, letter to Normand Lockwood, 21 April 1971. Normand Lockwood Commemorative Album, NL Private Papers.

Reynolds, Albertine Lockwood, Keene Valley, NY, letter to Kay
    Norton, Kansas City, MO, 14 July 1991.

Rian, Norman D., Honolulu, letter to Normand Lockwood, Denver,
    29 Denver 1971. Normand Lockwood Commemorative Album,
    NL Private Papers.

Riegger, Jean, New York, letter to Normand Lockwood, Oberlin,
    OH, undated except for year, 1940. NLA Box 6.

Sink, Charles A., Ann Arbor, letter to Normand Lockwood, Denver,
    26 April 1971. Normand Lockwood Commemorative Album, NL
    Private Papers.

Smith, Martha, Cambridge, MA, letter to Normand Lockwood,
    Denver, 24 April 1971. Normand Lockwood Commemorative
    Album, NL Private Papers.

Steiner, Fred, New York, letter to Normand Lockwood, Oberlin,
    OH, 6 July 1943. Normand Lockwood Private Papers.

Washburn, Robert, Potsdam, NY, letter to Kay Norton, Kansas
    City, MO, 15 July 1991.

Webster, Beveridge, New York, letter to Normand Lockwood,
    Denver, 20 May 1979. Normand Lockwood Commemorative
    Album, NL Private Papers.

Wood, William, Albuquerque, NM, letter to Kay Norton, Kansas
    City, MO, 5 July 1991.

Normand Lockwood Archive (NLA), Music Library, University of Colorado, Boulder

Envelope labeled "Normand's Programs." Box NB1.

Evanson, Jacob, foreword. Normand Lockwood, *Dirge for Two Veterans.* New York: M. Witmark and Sons, 1937. Box 2.

Lockwood, Normand. *Children of God* score with Thor Johnson's performance markings in pencil. Box OV 11.

____. *Choreographic Cantata*, "Suggestions for Choreographer." Minneapolis: Augsburg Publishing House, 1970. Box 2.

____. Cover sheet, *Six Piano Pieces.* 1987. Box 21.

____. Memo regarding *Four Songs--A Cycle.* Box 16.

____. Memo regarding *Second String Quartet.* 24 August 1987. Box 26.

____. Memo regarding *String Quartet Number 6.* Box 27.

____. Program Notes, *Symphony for Large Orchestra*, The Community Arts Symphony (Denver, CO) 21 November 1980. Box OV 10.

Lockwood, Normand and Russell Porter. Program Notes, "About the Opera." *The Hanging Judge.* The University of Denver, 6-7 March 1964. Box 10.

Lockwood, Normand. *Three-Voice Invention.* Box NB1.

____. *When Lilacs Last in the Dooryard Bloom'd.* Box 17.

MacCluskey, Thomas. Program Notes, "American Composers." *Panegyric for String Orchestra.* Arapahoe Chamber Orchestra. 1 February 1981.

May Festival Program, University of Michigan, 26 June 1976. Box OV 4.

Opening Program Notes, *Requiem for a Rich Young Man*, by Normand Lockwood and Donald Sutherland. Box 11.

Porter, R. Russell. Libretto, *No More From Thrones* (1962). Box 15.

Programs, Albert Lockwood recitals, 1894. Box NB1.

Program Notes, Seventeenth Annual Festival of American Music (Rochester, NY) April 1947. Box 27.

Tour program, Fred Waring Glee Club, 1962. Box 3.

Normand Lockwood Private Papers

Lockwood, Normand. "Report of Committee on Programs," American Composers Alliance.

Lockwood, Normand, Publicity Release for *Land of Promise*, KVOD radio, Denver.

Normand Lockwood. Promotional pamphlet. Broadcast Music, Incorporated, n.d.

Normand Lockwood Commemorative Album.

Pamphlet, Ditson Fund Award Winners, n.d.

Program, Concert of Award Recipients' Music, National Institute of Arts and Letters, 1947.

U. S. Department of Commerce, Bureau of the Census, George H. Brown, Director, order 1K 5-202-764. Document verifying age of Normand Lockwood (age 4) in 1910. Family of Samuel P. and Angelina Lockwood.

Normand Lockwood Special Collection, Penrose Library, University of Denver

Orchestral scores for the operas, excepting *The Scarecrow* and *Requiem for a Rich Young Man.*

Recordings Consulted

Blitzstein, Marc. "Comments," *Distinguished Composer Series,* Number 717, Westminster Spoken Arts, Inc., 1956.

Boyd, June R. Lecture Recital, 1 June 1988, Greeley, CO. NLA Box IRREG 2.

Hiller, Lejaren. Jacket notes to *American String Quartets,* III (1950-1970), Vox Productions, Inc., SVBX 5306.

Lockwood, Normand. *Children of God.* Reel, Berea, KY, January 1957, NL Private Collection.

_____. *Light Out of Darkness.* Recorded in performance by Buffalo Schola Cantorum and Buffalo Philharmonic Orchestra, Josef Krips, conductor. Buffalo: Howell Recording Studio, J8-OP-5663. NLA Box OV 3.

Phillips, Harvey E. Jacket notes to Peter Mennin *Symphony Number 7: Variations Symphony*. New World Records, Recorded Anthology of American Music, Inc., 1976.

Terry, W. Jacket notes to William Schuman, *Undertow*. New World Records, Recorded Anthology of American Music, Inc., 1978.

Unsigned jacket notes to *Concerto for Organ and Brasses*. Remington Records, R-199-173, 1953.

Miscellaneous Sources Consulted

Bulletin of the University [of Michigan] School of Music 17, no. 1 (June 1923): 90.

Bulletin of Yale University: School of Music for the Academic Year 1952-1953. New Haven, CT: Yale University, 1952.

"Catalogue of the University School of Music: 1917-1918." *Bulletin of the University [of Michigan] School of Music* 12, no. 1 (June 1918): 81, 83.

Catalogue of the Officers and Graduates of Yale University in New Haven, CT: 1701-1924. Information supplied by telephone, 8 September 1989, by Judith Ann Schiff, Chief Researcher and Archivist, Manuscripts and Archives Section, Yale University Library.

Columbia University Alumni Register: 1754-1931. New York: Columbia University Press, 1932.

Columbia University, City of New York: Master's Essays, 1891-1917. New York: Columbia University Press, n.d.

Columbiana Collection, Columbia University, New York. Holly Haswell, Archivist.

Personnel File, Normand Lockwood. Oberlin College Archives. Photocopy from Roland Baumann, Archivist, Oberlin, OH, to Kay Norton, Kansas City, MO, 15 July 1991.

INDEX

Dedications of Compositions
(see Catalog of Music)

Features of Compositions

About the Author

KAY NORTON (B. Mus. Ed., University of Georgia; M.F.A., University of Georgia; Ph.D., University of Colorado, Boulder) is Assistant Professor of Music History at the Conservatory of Music, University of Missouri-Kansas City. She has also served on the faculty of Brenau Women's College in Gainesville, Georgia, where she was Assistant Professor of Music.

Norton is primarily an Americanist, although her research areas also include interdisciplinary studies, aesthetics, and French music of the nineteenth and twentieth centuries. She has contributed to a festschrift forthcoming from the Sonneck Society for American Music, and has published in the *International Federation for Choral Music Bulletin* and *Music Research Forum*. Additionally, she has presented papers at meetings of the American Musicological Society, College Music Society, Music Teachers' National Association, and Music Theory Midwest.